BASIC COMPOUNDING AND PROCESSING OF RUBBER

Harry Long, *Editor*

Technical Manager
Goodall Rubber Company
Trenton, New Jersey

RUBBER DIVISION

Printed in the United States of America by Lancaster Press at Prince and Lemon Streets, Lancaster, Pennsylvania.

ISBN 0-912415-02-9

LIST OF CONTRIBUTORS

William A. Allee, Consultant, Intercole Bolling Corporation

Ronald J. Dill, Manager, Passenger Tire Materials, Goodyear
Tire & Rubber Company

Robert A. Gardiner, President, Hi-Tech Extrusion Systems, Inc.

Peter S. Johnson, Processing Technology Advisor, Technical
Development Division of Polysar Limited, Canada

A. James Lambright, Senior Research Specialist, Monsanto Company

Thomas J. Leo, Vice-President, Technical, Wyrough and Loser, Inc.

Harry Long, Technical Manager, Goodall Rubber Company

John G. Sommer, Section Head, Industrial Materials, Research
Division, GenCorp Inc.

Robert D. Stiehler, Consultant, National Bureau of Standards,
U. S. Department of Commerce

PREFACE

The results of a survey conducted in 1979 by the Education Committee of the Rubber Division, American Chemical Society, disclosed a need for a rubber technology course specially designed for Rubber Group use. In their response to the survey, many Rubber Groups expressed a desire to offer an educational course to the people entering or relatively new in their local rubber industry. It was obvious they wanted a course different from the existing Rubber Division Correspondence Courses, but how?

Upon accepting the overall responsibility for planning the new course and developing a textbook specifically for it, the Editor consulted with many Rubber Group officers as well as members at-large in an effort to establish an appropriate scope and depth for the new course. Subsequently, he learned participants and prospective participants of locally presented technical programs can be roughly divided into two groups in approximately equal numbers. One group consists of chemists and engineers. Another group is composed of people with little or no technical background. The latter group includes some salespersons, customer service personnel, inventory clerks, purchasing assistants, laboratory technicians, technical secretaries, production supervisors, production planners, and quality inspectors.

The first group favors a new course with emphasis on processing, as well as compounding. Many chemists and engineers believe the subject of elastomers is overly dominant in nearly all of the rubber technology courses and textbooks available. They express a strong desire for a course with more coverage on compounding and processing.

A majority of the people in the second group believe they need only a general knowledge in rubber to succeed in their jobs. Hence, they favor a course offering a broad overview instead of an in-depth study in rubber technology.

The new standard rubber technology course for Rubber Group use is designed with the need and desire of the prospective students in mind. This is its basic textbook. Its overall objective is to provide each student with a basic understanding of (1) the materials, equipment, and processes utilized in manufacturing rubber products, and (2) the language used in the rubber industry.

This textbook emphasized practical rather than theoretical aspects of rubber technology. Properties of common elastomers are highlighted to show their advantages as well as their limitations. The function of each major category of compounding ingredients is discussed and a general guide to material selection is provided. Attention is also focused on the basic manufacturing processes, such as mixing, extrusion, calendering, molding and vulcanization, through which raw materials are converted into various end products for industrial or commercial applications. Many common processing problems encountered in a rubber factory are identified together with suggested solutions. However, this is neither a book on polymer chemistry nor a book on product design. It is essentially a broad review of rubber technology written for everyone in the rubber industry regardless of his or her position and background.

The tradenames mentioned in this textbook are solely for identification purposes. They are not specifically recommended over similar products made by other manufacturers. Nothing in this textbook is to be construed as recommending any practice or any product in violation of any patent or any trademark.

The Editor wishes to express his sincere appreciation to all the contributors for their effort and cooperation without which his task would be impossible to complete. He would also like to thank all the organizations who granted contributors permission to publish. Finally, he wants to acknowledge the assistance of Mrs. Mildred Josephson and Miss Sandra Kuprevich for their dedicated secretarial work.

Harry Long

CONTENTS

CHAPTER 1

ENGINEERING PROPERTIES OF ELASTOMERS*

Harry Long

Goodall Rubber Company
Trenton, N. J. 08650

Successful utilization of the engineering properties of elastomers requires an understanding of what an elastomer is, how it behaves as a material of construction, and what limitations are imposed on it by environmental conditions. Although the term rubber is often used for all types of elastomers, the general classification of elastomers has a considerably greater total spectrum when the engineering properties of synthetic materials are carefully considered. Synthetic elastomers are not rubber in a true sense, but are like rubber in the degree of elasticity.

An elastomer is a macromolecular material that at room temperature can be stretched under low stress to at least twice its original length and, after release of the stress, will return to its approximate original dimensions and shape. Rubber is a natural elastomer that can be, or is already, vulcanized. Vulcanization, or cure, is an irreversible process during which an elastomeric compound is, through chemical crosslinking, converted from a soft, tacky, thermoplastic to a strong, temperature-stable thermoset having improved elastic properties. Vulcanization is usually done by heating the elastomeric compound with sulfur or other crosslinking agents.

The first recorded use of rubber dates back to ancient Egypt. Later, Columbus, on his voyages to the New World, recorded in his log the existence of this "bouncy and sticky" material that was used by the Indians.

Early in the nineteenth century several individuals, including Charles MacIntosh and Thomas Hancock of England and Charles Goodyear of the United States, attempted to make practical use of rubber. Their efforts were unsuccessful because of two major problems - rubber became soft and sticky in hot weather, and it became stiff and hard in cold weather. These problems were finally overcome in 1839, when Charles Goodyear and Thomas Hancock independently developed vulcanization. They discovered that when rubber is heated with sulfur it becomes a thermoset material with high strength and good elasticity. The rubber industry was founded on this discovery.

Until the beginning of World War II, natural rubber was the only widely used elastomer. When Singapore fell under the control of the Japanese in 1942, the U.S. and its allies were isolated from the Far East rubber plantations that produced 95 percent of all natural rubber.

Because an immense amount of rubber was needed for the war, the U. S. government sponsored a huge program to accelerate research, development, and mass production of synthetic rubber. Within 2 years, a multi-million dollar synthetic rubber industry was developed - a project that ordinarily would have taken 20 years.

---

* Extracted from the Article Engineering Properties of Elastomers appearing in the May 28, 1981 issue of PLANT ENGINEERING Magazine by permission

Most of the synthetic elastomers that are used extensively today, including neoprene, SBR, nitrile, and butyl were mass produced and became commercially successful between 1942 and 1945. After World War II, many more synthetic elastomers were developed to meet the demands of modern technology. Today, much more synthetic than natural rubber is used. The total consumption of elastomers in 1980 was estimated at 16,000,000 tons. Only an estimated 37 percent (5,920,000 tons) of the total was natural rubber.

PROPERTIES OF ELASTOMERS

Elastomers as a class possess some common basic characteristics. They are elastic, flexible, tough, and relatively impermeable to both water and air. Beyond these common characteristics, each elastomer has its own properties.

A rubber compound consists of many ingredients. Its most important ingredient, the base elastomer, has certain inherent advantages and limitations, but vulcanizing agents, accelerators, fillers, plasticizers, antidegradants, and other special-purpose additives also affect a compound's final properties.

At present more than 20 commercial elastomers are available. Their properties and characteristics differ widely, as do their prices. Like other engineering materials, elastomers must be understood and used correctly. Knowledge of advantages and limitations of each elastomer is essential to selection of the lowest-cost suitable material for a specific application.

Until World War II, there was no need to select elastomers because only natural rubber was commercially available in large quantities. The use of elastomers in solving engineering problems was then restricted by the limitations inherent in properties of natural rubber. Development and application of of elastomers has been greatly expanded since then, and now selection has become more complex.

Developing the lowest-cost compound for a specific application requires selection of the proper base elastomer. General knowledge of engineering properties of all common elastomers is essential to the success of such a task. The properties of 20 commercially available elastomers are compared in Table I, II, and III. These tables summarize data on three basic groups of properties: physical, environmental resistance, and chemical resistance.

This information is the best available from the author's experience and reputable sources. However, it should be recognized that the data are general and these ratings should be used as general guides only, not as specific recommendations.

Literally thousands of compounds can be developed from elastomers currently available. Through wise selection of base elastomers, proper application of compounding skills, and effective use of modern processing equipment, today's chemists can provide suitable material for almost every application. Technology is still expanding. New elastomers may well be developed and become available tomorrow for use where no elastomeric material can function satisfactorily today.

Symbols, chemical compositions, trade names, and advantages and limitations of 20 elastomers are presented here as a general guide to material selection.

<u>NATURAL RUBBER (NR)</u> - Natural Polyisoprene

Advantages: Outstanding resilience; <u>high tensile strength</u>; superior resistance to tear and abrasion; excellent rebound elasticity (snap); good flexibility at low temperatures; excellent adhesion to fabric and metals.

Limitations: Poor resistance to heat, ozone, and sunlight; very little resistance to oil, gasoline, and hydrocarbon solvents.

Remarks: Natural rubber is a low-cost material with excellent physical properties. Generally speaking, it is ideal for applications that require good resistance to abrasion, gouging, and cut growth. It is tough and long wearing and can be compounded for service at temperatures as low as -65°F.

<u>ISOPRENE (IR)</u> - Synthetic polyisoprene
Trade names: Ameripol SN, Natsyn, Trans-PIP

Advantages: Outstanding resilience; superior resistance to tear and abrasion; very good tensile strength; excellent rebound elasticity (snap); good flexibility at low temperatures; lack of odor.

Limitations: Poor resistance to heat, ozone, and sunlight; very little resistance to oil, gasoline, and hydrocarbon solvents.

Remarks: The chemical composition of isoprene is nearly identical to that of natural rubber. Therefore, the properties of these two elastomers are similiar. Isoprene has slightly better resistance to weather, and its properties are more consistent because of its purity and uniformity. It is somewhat inferior to natural rubber in tensile strength, tear resistance and compression set.

<u>SBR (SBR, GR-S, Buna-S)</u> - Styrene-Butadiene
Trade names: ASRC, Ameripol, Baytown, Carbomix, Copo, FR-S, Gentro, Krylene, Krymix, Krynol, Philprene, Plioflex, Synpol.

Advantages: Excellent impact strength; very good resilience, tensile strength, abrasion resistance, and flexibility at low temperatures.

Limitations: Poor resistance to ozone and sunlight; very little resistance to oil, gasoline, and hydrocarbon solvents.

Remarks: SBR is much like natural rubber in most of its properties and is the lowest-cost and highest-volume elastomer available. Although the physical properties are slightly poorer than those of natural rubber, SBR is tougher and slightly more resistant to heat and flex cracking and can be readily substituted for natural rubber in many applications with significant cost savings.

<u>BUTYL (IIR)</u> - Isobutylene-isoprene
Trade name: Bucar

Advantages: <u>Outstanding impermeability to gases and vapor</u>; very good resistance to heat, oxygen, ozone, and sunlight; high energy absorption (damping); excellent resistance to alkalis and oxygenated solvents; good hot tear strength; superior resistance to water and steam.

Limitations: High compression set; poor resistance to oil, gasoline, and hydrocarbon solvents; low rebound elasticity (snap); fair processability, poor resilience.

TABLE I

PHYSICAL PROPERTIES*

Property	Natural Rubber	Isoprene	SBR	Butyl	Butadiene	EPDM	Neoprene	Nitrile	Thiokol	Urethane	Silicone	Hypalon	Acrylic	Fluorocarbon	Epichlorohydrin	Chlorinated Polyethylene	Crosslinked Polyethylene	Vamac	Vynathene	Norsorex
SPECIFIC GRAVITY	0.93	0.92	0.94	0.92	0.91	0.86	1.23	1.00	1.25-1.35	1.02-1.25	0.98-1.60	1.12-1.28	1.09	1.85	1.27-1.36	1.16-1.25	0.92	1.04	0.95-1.02	0.96
HARDNESS RANGE (Shore A)	30-100	30-100	35-100	30-90	45-80	30-90	35-95	30-100	20-80	55-100	25-90	40-95	40-90	55-95	40-90	45-95	90+	40-90	45-95	15-100
TENSILE STRENGTH Max (psi @ Rm. Temp.)	4000	3500	3500	3000	2500	2500	3000	3000	1500	8000	1500	3000	2000	3000	2500	3500	3000	2500	4000	3500
ELONGATION Max (% @ Rm. Temp.)	750	750	600	600	700	500	600	600	450	750	800	600	600	400	400	600	500	700	400	600
RESILIENCE	E	E	G	E	P-F	E	G-E	F-G	P-F	F-E	F-G	F-G	F-G	F	F-G	F-G	P	F	F	G-E
COMPRESSION SET	G	F	G	F	P-F	F	G	F-G	P-F	G-E	G-E	F	G	G	F	F-G	F	G	G-E	G
IMPERMEABILITY TO GASES	F	F	F	E	E	F	F	F-G	G	E	P-F	G	G	G-E	E	G	G	F	G	G-E

E = Excellent   G = Good   F = Fair   P = Poor

*Extracted from the article Engineering Properties of Elastomers appearing in the May 28, 1981 issue of PLANT ENGINEERING magazine.

TABLE I

PHYSICAL PROPERTIES (Cont'd)*

	Natural Rubber	Isoprene	SBR	Butyl	Butadiene	EPDM	Neoprene	Nitrile	Thiokol	Urethane	Silicone	Hypalon	Acrylic	Fluorocarbon	Epichlorohydrin	Chlorinated Polyethylene	Crosslinked Polyethylene	Vamac	Vynathene	Norsorex
FLEX CRACKING RESISTANCE	F	F	G	E	G	G	F	P-F	E	F-E	G	F	G	G	G-E	G-E	G	G	G	
TEAR STRENGTH	G	G	G	G	F-G	F-G	F-G	P-F	E	P-F	F-G	P-F	F	F-G	G	G-E	G-E	F-G	G	
ABRASION RESISTANCE	E	G-E	G	G	G-E	G-E	G-E	P	E	E	G-E	E-G	F-G	F-G	G-E	G	G	G	G-E	
IMPACT STRENGTH	E	E	G	E	G	G	G	P-F	E	P-G	G	P	P	E	E	F-G	G	F-G	E	
CUT GROWTH RESISTANCE	E	G	E	F-G	G	G	G	P	G-E	P-F	G	F-G	P	G	F	P	G-E	F	G	

E = Excellent   G = Good   F = Fair   P = Poor

* Extracted from the article Engineering Properties of Elastomers appearing in the May 28, 1981 issue of PLANT ENGINEERING magazine.

TABLE II

ENVIRONMENTAL RESISTANCE PROPERTIES*

	Natural Rubber	Isoprene	SBR	Butyl	Butadiene	EPDM	Neoprene	Nitrile	Thiokol	Urethane	Silicone	Hypalon	Acrylic	Fluorocarbon	Epichlorohydrin	Chlorinated polyethylene	Crosslinked polyethylene	Vamac	Vynathene	Norsorex
OXIDATION RESISTANCE	F-G	F-G	E	F-G	F-G	G-E	F-G	G-E	G-E	E	E	E	E	G-E	E	E	E	E	F-G	
OZONE RESISTANCE	P	P	P	G-E	P	E	G	P	E	E	E	E	G-E	E	E	E	E	E	P	
WEATHERING RESISTANCE	F	F	E	F	F	G	F-G	G-E	E	E	G-E	G-E	E	G-E	G	G-E	E	E	F	
SUNLIGHT RESISTANCE	P-F	P-F	F	E	E	E	G-E	P-F	G-E	E	E	E	E	G-E	G	G	E	E	F	
WATER RESISTANCE	E	E	E	E	E	G	G-E	G	G	G	G	P-F	P-F-G	G	G	G	G	G-E	E	
FLAME RETARDANCE	P	P	P	P	P	P	G	P	P-G	F-G	G	G	P	E	F-G	F	F-G	P	F	
HEAT RESISTANCE	F	P-F	G	P-F	G-E	F	G	F	F-G	E	G	E	E	G-E	G	F	G-E	G-E	F	
LOW TEMPERATURE FLEXIBILITY	G-E	G	F-G	P-F	G-E	F	F-G	F-G	G	E	E	P-F-F-G	P-F-F-G	F-E	F-G	F	P-F	G	G	

E = Excellent   G = Good   F = Fair   P = Poor

* Extracted from the article Engineering Properties of Elastomers appearing in the May 28, 1981 issue of PLANT ENGINEERING magazine.

TABLE III

CHEMICAL RESISTANCE PROPERTIES*

	Natural Rubber / Isoprene	SBR	Butyl	Butadiene / EPDM	Neoprene	Nitrile	Thiokol	Urethane	Silicone	Hypalon	Acrylic	Fluorocarbon	Epichlorohydrin	Crosslinked Polyethylene / Chlorinated Polyethylene	Vamac	Vynathene	Norsorex
OIL AND GASOLINE	P	P	P	P	F-G	G-E	E	G-E	F-G	G	E	G-E	F-G	G-E	F	F	P
ANIMAL & VEGETABLE OILS	F	F	F	G	G-E	G-E	G	G	G-E	G-E	E	G	G	G-E	E-F	F	F
ALCOHOLS	G	G	G	F-G	F-G	G	F-G	G-E	G-E	F-E	G-E	E	E	P-F	E-F	F	G
ALKALIES	F	F	F	E	E	G	P	P	E	P	F-E	E	E	E	G	G	G
ACIDS	F-G	F-G	G-E	G	G-E	G	P-F	F	G-E	F	F-G	G	E	E	E-F	F-G	F-G
ALIPHATIC HYDROCARBON SOLVENTS	P	P	P	P	G	E	G	P-F	F	E	E	E	E	G-E	F	P	P
AROMATIC HYDROCARBON SOLVENTS	P	P	P	P-F	F-G	G-E	P-F	P-F	F	G	E	P-F	G	E	P-F	P	P
OXYGENATED SOLVENTS	G	G	G	G-E	P	G-E	P	F	F	E	P-F	P-F	F	G	P	F	G

E = Excellent   G = Good   F = Fair   P = Poor

* Extracted from the article Engineering Properties of Elastomers appearing in the May 28, 1981 issue of PLANT ENGINEERING magazine.

Remarks: Butyl is chemically unlike natural rubber or other synthetic elastomers in that it is inherently resistant to ozone and corrosive chemicals, including some mineral acids, ketones, and phosphate-ester-type hydraulic fluids. On the negative side, its creep, cold flow, and compression set characteristics leave much to be desired. The processing properties of butyl are only fair. Because of its low level of unsaturation, butyl is difficult to break down during mixing, and it is very susceptible to contamination. Slight contamination causes improper cure and poor physical properties. Chlorinated and brominated versions are less susceptible to contamination and offer lower compression set and improved heat resistance.

BUTADIENE (BR) - Polybutadiene
Trade names: Ameripol CB, Budene, Cis-4, Cisdene, Diene, Duragen, Synpol E-BR, Taktene, Trans-4

Advantages: Outstanding resilience; excellent flexibility at low temperatures; superior resistance to abrasion, cut growth, and flex cracking.

Limitations: Inferior processability; poor resistance to oil, gasoline and hydrocarbon solvents; very little resistance to heat and ozone.

Remarks: Butadiene is basically similar to natural rubber, isoprene, and SBR in its superior resistance to wear and abrasion. With the exception of silicone, butadiene has the lowest glass-transition temperature of all commercial elastomers and offers unusually good performance at temperatures as low as $-80°F$. Because of low elastic recovery in the unvulcanized state, butadiene is difficult to process and is used primarily in blends with other elastomers to attain desirable properties.

EPDM (EPDM, EPM, EPT, EPT) - Ethylene-propylene, ethylene-propylene-diene
Trade names: Epcar, Epsyn, Nordel, Royalene, and Vistalon

Advantages: Excellent resistance to heat, ozone, and sunlight; very good flexibility at low temperatures; good resistance to alkalis, acids, and oxygenated solvents; superior resistance to water and steam; excellent color stability.

Limitations: Poor resistance to oil, gasoline, and hydrocarbon solvents, adhesion to fabrics and metals is poor.

Remarks: Because of its unique combination of physical properties, EPDM can be used in an unusually broad range of products. Aside from applications requiring resistance to oil and hydrocarbon solvents, there is scarcely an application in which EPDM is totally unsuitable. Because of its excellent resistance to ozone, sunlight, and severe weather conditions, EPDM is ideal for outdoor service. In general, EPDM is similar to butyl but has slightly less susceptibility to contamination. Chlorobutyl (chlorinated version of butyl) is much superior to EPDM in attaining good adhesion to fabrics and metals.

NEOPRENE (CR) - Polychloroprene
Trade names: Baypren, Butaclor

Advantages: Good inherent flame resistance; moderate resistance to oil and gasoline; excellent adhesion to fabrics and metals; very good resistance to weather, ozone, and natural aging; good resistance to abrasion and flex cracking; very good resistance to alkalis and acids.

Limitations: Poor to fair resistance to aromatic and oxygenated solvents; limited flexibility at low temperatures.

Remarks: Neoprene is an excellent all-purpose elastomer with a nearly ideal balance of properties and few practical limitations. General purpose neoprenes are classified in two groups; a sulfur-modified type and a mercaptan-modified type. Sulfur-modified neoprene has increased tear strength and resilience and mercaptan-modified neoprene is superior in resistance to heat and compression set.

NITRILE (NBR, Buna-N) - Acrylonitrile-butadiene

Trade names: Breon, Butaprene, Butacril, Chemigum, Chemivic, Elaprim, FR-N, Hycar, Krynac, NYsyn, NYsynblak, Paracril, Paracril OZO, Perbunan N, Tylac, Nipol.

Advantages: Very good resistance to oil and gasoline; superior resistance to petroleum-based hydraulic fluids; wide range of service temperatures (-65 to 300°F); good resistance to hydrocarbon solvents; very good resistance to alkalis and acids.

Limitations: Inferior resistance to ozone, sunlight, and natural aging; poor resistance to oxygenated solvents.

Remarks: Nitrile and neoprene are the highest-volume oil-resistant elastomers. Nitrile is superior to neoprene in resistance to oil, gasoline, and aromatic solvents. However, it does not perform as well as neoprene in applications requiring exposure to weather, ozone, and sunlight. Furthermore, it has no inherent flame resistance.

The properties of nitrile vary considerably with the ratio of acrylonitrile and butadiene. In general, as the acrylonitrile content of the elastomer increases, oil and solvent resistance and abrasion resistance improve. When the acrylonitrile content decreases, these properties deteriorate, and low-temperature flexibility and resilience improve.

When nitrile is modified by polyvinyl chloride (PVC) resins, its resistance to weather, ozone, and sunlight improves considerably without significant sacrifice in oil-resisting properties. PVC/nitrile is similar to neoprene, in general, however, it is much inferior to neoprene in adhesion to fabrics and metals.

Carboxylated nitrile is generally tougher and more resistant to tear and abrasion than conventional nitrile, but it is less resilient and flexible at low temperatures.

THIOKOL (T, PTR) - Polysulfide

Trade name: Thiokol

Advantages: Outstanding resistance to oil, gasoline, and solvents; good resistance to weather, ozone, and sunlight; excellent impermeability to gases and vapor.

Limitations: Poor resistance to abrasion, tear, cut growth, and flex cracking; low tensile strength; inferior compression set, objectionable odor; poor resilience.

Remarks: Thiokol is a specialty elastomer used mainly for handling a wide range of oils, solvents, and petroleum-based fuels and is affected very little by the common alcohols, ketones, and esters used in paints, varnishes, and inks. On the negative side, its pungent odor is objectionable to many people, and its physical properties are very poor. The general acceptance and use of Thiokol has been limited.

URETHANE (AU, EU) - Polyurethane diisocyanate
Trade names: Adiprene, Arcon, Castomer, Cyanaprene, Elastothane, Estane,
Genthane, Multrathane, Rucothane, Solithane, Texin, Vibrathane

Advantages: Outstanding resistance to abrasion and tear; very high tensile
strength with good elongation; excellent resistance to weather, ozone, and sunlight; good resistance to oil and gasoline; excellent adhesion to fabrics and
metals.

Limitations: Poor resistance to alkalis, acids, and oxygenated solvents;
inferior resistance to hot water.

Remarks: Urethane is notable for its combination of hardness with elasticity,
and outstanding abrasion resistance and tear strength. It may be either ether or
ester based. The ester-based polymer is superior in resistance to abrasion and
heat and the ether-based polymer has better flexibility at low temperatures.
Urethanes are sold in liquid or dry form and a casting process is usually used
for viscous liquid form. Conventional rubber equipment is used for processing
urethane in millable-gum form. The dry type has physical properties slightly inferior to those of the liquid type. Urethane is a relatively expensive elastomer
whose use is usually limited to applications that require a combination of its
outstanding properties, such as toughness, tear strength, and abrasion resistance.

SILICONE (Si) - Polysiloxane
Trade names: Gensil, Electrisil, SE, Silastic, SWS

Advantages: Outstanding resistance to high heat; excellent flexibility at
low temperatures; low compression set; very good electrical insulation; excellent
resistance to weather, ozone, sunlight, and oxidation; superior color stability.

Limitations: Poor resistance to abrasion, tear, and cut growth; low tensile strength; inferior resistance to oil, gasoline, and solvents; poor resistance
to alkalis and acids.

Remarks: The most outstanding feature of silicone is its ability to retain
rubbery properties through extremes in temperature. It is the most heat-resist-
ing elastomer in the market today and the most flexible at low temperatures.
Service temperatures range from -150 to 500°F. Silicone generally does not have
high tensile strength, but much of the strength it does have can be retained at
very high temperatures. Because silicone is relatively expensive, it is not
normally used unless extreme temperature resistance is essential.

HYPALON (CSM) - Chlorosulfonated polyethylene
Trade name: Hypalon

Advantages: Good flame retardance; good abrasion resistance; superior resistance to weather, ozone, sunlight, and oxidation; excellent resistance to
alkalies and acids; very good color stability; moderate resistance to oil and
gasoline.

Limitations: Poor to fair resistance to aromatic solvents; limited flexibility at low temperatures; fair resilience and compression set.

Remarks: Hypalon is a close match to neoprene in most properties, but it
is superior in resistance to acids, solvents, ozone, and oxidation and has
decidedly better color stability.

ACRYLIC (ACM) - Polyacrylate
Trade names: Acrylon, Cyanacryl, Thiacril

   Advantages: Outstanding resistance to heat and hot oil; excellent resistance to weather, ozone, sunlight, and oxidation; very good resistance to gasoline and oil, especially those that contain sulfur.

   Limitations: Poor resistance to alcohols, alkalis, solvents, and aromatic
solvents; limited flexibility at low temperatures; inferior resistance to water
and steam; slow vulcanization rate.

   Remarks: Heat resistance of acrylic is superior to that of any other
elastomer except silicone and fluorocarbon. It performs well in both hot air
and hot oil for extended periods without significant loss of physical properties. Acrylic has moderate resistance to cut growth and flex cracking. Use of
acrylic is limited by its inferior flexibility at low temperatures, poor processing properties, and slow vulcanization rate. A post-cure is necessary to obtain
the best characteristics. Low-temperature service of acrylic is possible to only
about -20°F. However, some types of acrylic that have improved low-temperature
flexibility at the expense of tensile strength and oil resistance are available.

FLUOROCARBON (FPM) - Fluorinated hydrocarbon
Trade names: Fluorel, Viton

   Advantages: Outstanding resistance to high heat; excellent resistance to
oil, gasoline, hydraulic fluids and hydrocarbon solvents; good flame retardance;
very good impermeability to gases and vapor; very good resistance to weather,
oxygen, ozone, and sunlight.

   Limitations: Poor resistance to tear and cut growth; very little resistance
to oxygenated solvents; fair adhesion to fabrics and metals.

   Remarks: Fluorocarbon is a very expensive elastomer with outstanding resistance to a wide variety of oils, fuels, acids, and solvents at elevated temperatures, heat resistance that is almost as good as that of silicone, a resistance to hot oil that exceeds that of acrylic, and weathering properties superior
to those of neoprene. Because of its very high price, fluorocarbon is used only
in applications requiring excellent stability under extremely severe operating
conditions. Subjecting fluorocarbon to a two-stage cure cycle produces the best
balance of properties.

EPICHLOROHYDRIN (ECO, CO) - Epichlorohydrin-ethylene oxide or polyepichlorohydrin
Trade names: Herclor, Hydrin

   Advantages: Excellent resistance to oil and gasoline; superior impermeability
to gases and vapor; very good resistance to weather, ozone, sunlight, and oxidation;
wide range of service temperatures; good resistance to petroleum-based fluids and
solvents.

   Limitations: Inferior resistance to oxygenated solvents; poor resistance to
steam and acids.

   Remarks: Epichlorohydrin is a specialty polyether elastomer that appears to
possess a combination of many desirable properties of nitrile and neoprene. On
the negative side, its adhesion to fabrics and metals is much inferior to neoprene's
and its superior impermeability to gases often causes processing problems and product defects because of air entrapment. Epichlorohydrin is available as a homopolymer (CO) and a copolymer (ECO) of epichlorohydrin containing about 50 percent
ethylene oxide. The homopolymer is superior in ozone resistance and gas impermeability and the copolymer is better in resilience and flexibility at low temperatures.

Oil resistance of the homopolymer and the copolymer is about the same. Epichloro-hydrin is now also available as a terpolymer of epichlorohydrin, ethylene oxide, and a third monomer. The new terpolymer has properties similar to those of the copolymer. However, unlike the copolymer, the terpolymer can easily be blended with SBR and nitrile, and sulfur cured: and its adhesion to fabrics and metals is reportedly the best among the three versions of epichlorohydrin elastomer.

CHLORINATED POLYETHYLENE (CPE, CM) - Chlorinated polyethylene
Trade names: Dow CPE, Dow CM

Advantages: Outstanding resistance to alcohols, alkalis, and acids; very good resistance to weather, ozone, sunlight, and oxidation; good impermeability to gases and vapor; excellent resistance to abrasion and flex cracking; superior color stability.

Limitations: Poor to moderate resistance to aromatic and oxygenated solvents; only fair processability.

Remarks: Chlorinated polyethylene, produced by random chlorination of high-density polyethylene, appears to possess a combination of many desirable properties of neoprene, Hypalon, nitrile, and epichlorohydrin, yet is very reasonable in price. In terms of cost effectiveness, chlorinated polyethylene is more attractive than many other elastomers. Thus far, the general acceptance and use of chlorinated polyethylene has been somewhat limited because it requires a peroxide cure system. Many existing autoclave vulcanizers in the rubber industry cannot provide steam heat at temperatures high enough for effective peroxide cure. And, superior im-permeability to gases often cause processing problems and product defects because of air entrapment.

CROSSLINKED POLYETHYLENE (XLPE) - Chemically crosslinked polyethylene
Trade name: Polycure

Advantages: Outstanding resistance to alcohols, alkalis, and acids; excellent resistance to weather, ozone, sunlight, and oxidation; very good resistance to oil, gasoline, and solvents.

Limitations: Poor resilience and tear strength; inferior resistance to abra-sion and cut growth; poor adhesion to fabrics and metals, limited flexibility at low temperatures.

Remarks: Through chemical crosslinking by means of a peroxide, thermoplastic polyethylene is converted to a thermoset material that will not deform and flow at high temperatures. Crosslinked polyethylene has outstanding mechanical toughness and chemical resistance. Like fluorocarbon, it performs very well in applications requiring contact with a wide variety of oils, fuels, acids, and solvents. Cross-linked polyethylene is superior to fluorocarbon in resistance to oxygenated solvent, but does not match fluorocarbon in heat aging properties.

VAMAC (E/A) - Ethylene/acrylic
Trade name: Vamac

Advantages: Excellent resistance to heat, ozone, and sunlight; good resist-ance to tear, flex cracking, and cut growth; moderate resistance to oil, gasoline, and hydraulic fluids; high energy absorption (damping).

Limitations: Poor resistance to aromatic and oxygenated solvents, limited flexibility at low temperatures; inferior resistance to alcohols and acids.

Remarks: Vamac is a relatively new specialty elastomer that is basically a copolymer of ethylene and methyl acrylate with carboxylic crosslinking sites. Vamac combines moderate oil resistance with excellent heat aging properties. Of all commercial elastomers, only silicone and fluorocarbon surpass Vamac in heat resistance. Vamac is similar to acrylic in most properties but has slightly superior flexibility at low temperatures. Low-temperature service is possible to about -30°F. On the negative side, Vamac's processing properties are only fair because it has a strong tendency to stick to the rotor of mixer and mill or calender rolls. It is easily contaminated by metal oxides, and becomes very erratic with severe loss of its heat resistance. Vamac is currently available only in the form of lightly loaded masterbatches, not as a raw polymer. Its gum viscosity is very low and a post-cure is necessary to achieve maximum resistance to compression set.

VYNATHENE (VAE) - Vinyl acetate-ethylene
Trade name: Vynathene

Advantages: Excellent resistance to heat, ozone, and sunlight; wide range of service temperature (-65 to 350°F): moderate resistance to oil and gasoline; low compression set; good energy absorption (damping); excellent color stability.

Limitations: Poor resistance to aromatic and oxygenated solvents; fair processability.

Remarks: Vynathene is a new series of vinyl acetate-ethylene copolymers ranging from 40 to 60 percent by weight in vinyl acetate content. As the vinyl acetate content increases, heat resistance and oil resistance increase at the expense of tear strength. Vynathene is similar to Vamac in many properties, but has a wider range of service temperatures. Like Vamac, it has a strong tendency to stick to the rotor of mixer and mill or calender rolls. Thus far, the general acceptance and use of Vynathene has been somewhat limited by the requirement for a peroxide cure system. Many existing autoclave vulcanizer in the rubber industry cannot provide steam heat at a temperature high enough for effective peroxide cure. Vynathene does not perform well in applications requiring contact with hydrocarbon and oxygenated solvents.

NORSOREX (PNR) - Polynorbornene
Trade name: Norsorex

Advantages: High strength with low hardness; wide range of energy absorption (damping); good resistance to abrasion and tear; very good impermeability to gases and vapor.

Limitations: Poor resistance to weather, ozone, and sunlight; very little resistance to oil, gasoline, and hydrocarbon solvents.

Remarks: Norsorex, one of the newest commercial elastomers, has a glass-transition temperature of approximately 95°F and can actually be classified as a low-melting thermoplastic. However, once compounded with plasticizers, the glass-transition temperature can be lowered to about -76°F and processing characteristics become very similar to conventional elastomers. Norsorex is normally available as a dry powder. Each particle has a porous surface that absorbs an extraordinarily large quantity of plasticizer and filler. The properties of Norsorex compound can be varied widely by selection of the type and amount of plasticizer. The most useful properties of Norsorex are its good strength in soft compounds and its capability to be highly extended. At the present, technical data on Norsorex is still limited and its potential applications are still being discovered and defined.

ENGINEERING PROPERTIES OF ELASTOMERS

Tradenames Mentioned

(in order of appearance in article)

Ameripol SN	B. F. Goodrich Chemical Co.
Natsyn	Goodyear Tire & Rubber Co.
Trans-PIP	Polysar, Inc.
ASRC	American Synthetic Rubber Corp.
Ameripol	B. F. Goodrich Chemical Co.
Baytown	Ashland Chemical Co.
Carbomix	Copolymer Rubber & Chemical Corp.
Copo	Copolymer Rubber & Chemical Corp.
FR-S	Firestone Synthetic Rubber & Latex Co.
Gentro	General Tire & Rubber Co.
Krylene	Polysar, Inc.
Krymix	Polysar, Inc.
Krynol	Polysar, Inc.
Philprene	Phillips Chemical Co.
Plioflex	Goodyear Tire & Rubber Co.
Synpol	Texas-U.S. Chemical Co.
Bucar	Cities Service Co.
Ameripol CB	B. F. Goodrich Chemical Co.
Budene	Goodyear Tire & Rubber Co.
Cis-4	Phillips Chemical Co.
Cisdene	American Synthetic Rubber Co.
Diene	Firestone Synthetic Rubber & Latex Co.
Duragen	General Tire & Rubber Co.
Synpol E-BR	Texas-U.S. Chemical Co.
Taktene	Polysar, Inc.
Trans-4	Phillips Chemical Co.
Epcar	B. F. Goodrich Chemical Co.
Epsyn	Copolymer Rubber & Chemical Corp.
Nordel	E. I. duPont deNemours & Co
Royalene	Uniroyal Chemical Div.
Vistalon	Exxon Chemical Co.
Baypren	Bayer AG
Butaclor	Distugil
Breon	BP Chemicals International, Ltd.
Butaprene	Firestone Synthetic Rubber & Latex Co.
Butacril	Ugine Kuhlmann
Chemigum	Goodyear Tire & Rubber Co.
Chemivic	Goodyear Tire & Rubber Co.
Elaprim	Montedison, S.p.A.
FR-N	Firestone Synthetic Rubber & Latex Co.
Hycar	B. F. Goodrich Chemical Co.
Krynac	Polysar, Inc.
NYsyn	Copolymer Rubber & Chemical Co.
NYsynblak	Copolymer Rubber & Chemical Co.
Paracril	Uniroyal Chemical Div.
Paracril OZO	Uniroyal Chemical Div.
Perbunan N	Bayer AG
Nipol	Nippon Zeon Co., Ltd.

Tradenames Mentioned

(in order of appearance in article)

Tylac	Reichhold Chemicals, Inc.
Thiokol	Thiokol Chemical Co.
Adiprene	E. I. duPont deNemours & Co.
Arcon	Allied Resin Co.
Castomer	Witco Chemical Co.
Cyanaprene	American Cyanamid Co.
Elastothane	Thiokol Chemical Co.
Estane	B. F. Goodrich Chemical Co.
Genthane	General Tire & Rubber Co.
Multrathane	Mobay Chemical Co.
Rucothane	Hooker Chemicals & Plastic Corp.
Solithane	Thiokol Chemical Co.
Texin	Mobay Chemical Co.
Vibrathane	Uniroyal Chemical Div.
Gensil	General Electric Co.
Electrisil	General Electric Co.
SE	General Electric Co.
Silastic	Dow Corning Corp.
SWS	SWS Silicones Corp.
Hypalon	E. I. duPont deNemours & Co.
Acrylon	Borden Chemical Co.
Fluorel	3M Co.
Viton	E. I. duPont deNemours & Co.
Herclor	Hercules, Inc.
Hydrin	B. F. Goodrich Chemical Co.
Polycure	Cooke Div. of Reichhold Chemicals, Inc.
Vamac	E. I. duPont deNemours & Co.
Vynathene	U. S. Industrial Chemicals Co.
Norsorex	CdF Chimie

GENERAL REFERENCES

1. Babbit, R.O., ed., "The Vanderbilt Rubber Handbook", R. T. Vanderbilt Co. Inc., Norwalk, CT (1978)

2. Blow, C.M., ed., "Rubber Technology and Manufacture", Butterworth & Co., London, England (1971)

3. Eirich, F. R. ed., "Science and Technology of Rubber", Academic Press, New York, (1978)

4. Harper, C.A. ed., "Handbook of Plastics and Elastomers", McGraw-Hill Book Co., New York (1975)

5. Kirk, R.E. and Othmer, D.F., eds., "Encyclopedia of Chemical Technology", Wiley-Interscience, New York (second edition, 1968)

6. Mernaugh, L.R., ed., "Rubber", Robert Maxwell and Co., Ltd., Oxford, England (1971)

7. Morton, M., ed., "Rubber Technology", Van Nostrand Reinhold Company, New York (1973)

8. Roff, W.J. and Scott, J.R., "Handbook of Common Polymers", Chemical Rubber Co., Cleveland, Ohio (1971)

9. Stern, H.J., "Rubber: Natural and Synthetic", MacClaren and Sons, Ltd. London, England (1967)

10. Supplier's technical literature on various elastomers

11. Winding, C.C. and Hiatt, G.D., "Polymeric Materials", McGraw-Hill Book Co., Inc., New York (1961)

WORK ASSIGNMENT NO. 1
CHAPTER 1.   ENGINEERING PROPERTIES OF ELASTOMERS

INSTRUCTIONS: Read each question carefully, select one, and only one, appropriate answer to complete each statement.

1. An elastomer is best described as

___(a) an impermeable material which can be stretched at ambient temperature
___(b) a flexible material with high tensile strength and resilience
___(c) any natural or synthetic polyisoprene
___(d) a macromolecular material that at room temperature can be stretched under low stress to at least twice its original length and, after release of the stress, will return to its approximate original dimensions and shape

2. Vulcanization is

___(a) a method for increasing the elongation of a rubber compound
___(b) usually done by heating a rubber compound with sulfur or other crosslinking agents
___(c) a reversible process to change the stiffness of thermoplastic material
___(d) none of above

3. All elastomers are

___(a) resilient and highly resistant to sunlight and weathering
___(b) elastic, flexible, tough, and relatively impermeable to both water and air
___(c) unaffected by oils and solvents
___(d) highly resistant to abrasion and cut

4. The properties of a rubber compound are

___(a) entirely dependent upon its base elastomers
___(b) not affected by vulcanization
___(c) affected by all of its ingredients
___(d) dependent upon how many ingredients are used

5. Natural rubber has

___(a) outstanding resilience and resistance to sunlight and heat
___(b) very good resistance to oil and gasoline
___(c) outstanding resilience, high tensile strength and very good resistance to tear and abrasion
___(d) very high specific gravity

6. Isoprene has properties very similar to

___(a) EPDM
___(b) natural rubber
___(c) Neoprene
___(d) none of above

7. SBR is styrene-butadiene rubber. It is one of the lowest-cost and highest-volume elastomers. Its properties are very similar to

___(a) nitrile
___(b) natural rubber
___(c) butyl
___(d) EPDM

8. Butyl is isobutylene-isoprene rubber. It is often used to take advantage of its

___(a) outstanding impermeability to gases and vapor and its very good resistance to heat and sunlight
___(b) good resistance to hydrocarbon solvents
___(c) excellent resilience and resistance to compression
___(d) outstanding physical properties resulting from its immunity to contamination

9. Because of its relatively poor processability, butadiene rubber is used primarily in blends with other elastomers to improve

___(a) resistance to abrasion, cut growth, and flex-cracking
___(b) resistance to oil and gasoline
___(c) resistance to sunlight and ozone
___(d) none of above

10. EPDM is ethylene-propylene rubber. It is nearly ideal for

___(a) tire tread because of its outstanding resilience, high tack, and very good adhesion
___(b) outdoor service because of its excellent resistance to heat, ozone, sunlight and severe weather conditions
___(c) fuel oil delivery hose because of its excellent resistance to oil and gasoline
___(d) wire and cable jacket because of its excellent flame resistance

11. Neoprene has a good balance of properties. Beside its inherent flame retardance, it has

___(a) good resistance to weather, plus moderate resistance to oil and gasoline
___(b) outstanding flexibility at low temperature
___(c) very good resistance to aromatic hydrocarbon solvents
___(d) none of above

12. Two types of Neoprenes are widely used. The sulfur-modified type (Type G) has increased tear strength and resilience while the mercaptan-modified type (Type W) has

___(a) much better resistance to oil and gasoline
___(b) more tackiness and faster cure rate
___(c) superior resistance to heat and compression
___(d) none of above

13. Nitrile is well known for its superiority over Neoprene in

___(a) flame retardance
___(b) resistance to oil and gasoline
___(c) resistance to sunlight and weathering
___(d) none of above

14. The properties of nitrile vary considerably with the ratio of acrylonitrile and butadiene. As its acrylonitrile content decreases, its low-temperature flexibility improves at the expense of

___(a) resilience
___(b) tensile strength
___(c) oil resistance
___(d) none of above

15. Some nitrile is modified by PVC resins to improve

___(a) oil resistance
___(b) tear strength
___(c) resistance to weather, ozone, and sunlight
___(d) adhesion to fabric and metals

16. Carboxylated nitrile is generally better than conventional nitrile in

___(a) resilience
___(b) flexibility at low temperatures
___(c) resistance to tear and abrasion
___(d) processing safety due to its longer scorch time

17. Although its physical properties are relatively poor, Thiokol is a very desirable elastomer for handling

___(a) oils, solvents, and petroleum-based fuels
___(b) food
___(c) sands and stones
___(d) none of above

18. Urethane is polyurethane diisocyanate. It is well-known for its outstanding resistance to

___(a) acids and solvents
___(b) hot water
___(c) abrasion and tear
___(d) none of above

19. Silicone is polysiloxane. Although its tensile strength is relatively low, it is outstanding in

___(a) resistance to oil and gasoline
___(b) heat resistance and low-temperature flexibility
___(c) resistance to abrasion and cut growth
___(d) none of above

20. The properties of Hypalon are very much similar to Neoprene. However, Hypalon is superior to Neoprene in

___(a) resilience
___(b) resistance to compression set
___(c) resistance to acid, solvents, ozone, and oxidation
___(d) none of above

21. Acrylic has outstanding resistance to heat and hot oil. On the negative side, acrylic is inferior in

___(a) resistance to ozone and sunlight
___(b) resistance to oxidation
___(c) resistance to water and steam
___(d) resistance to gasoline and similar hydrocarbon solvents

22. Fluorocarbon elastomer has excellent resistance to a wide variety of oils, fuels, acids, and chemicals. However, it has very little resistance to

___(a) hydraulic fluids
___(b) oxygen, ozone, and sunlight
___(c) oxygenated solvents, such as methyl ethyl ketone (MEK)
___(d) none of above

23. Epichlorohydrin is a specialty polyester elastomer that appears to possess a combination of many desirable properties of

___(a) natural rubber and SBR
___(b) nitrile and neoprene
___(c) EPDM and butyl
___(d) Hypalon and chlorinated polyethylene (CPE)

24. Chlorinated polyethylene (CPE) is produced by random chlorination of high-density polyethylene. It has outstanding resistance to

___(a) aromatic hydrocarbon solvents, such as toluene
___(b) oxygenated solvents, such as methyl ethyl ketone
___(c) alcohols, alkalis, and acids
___(d) none of above

25. Like fluorocarbon elastomer, crosslinked polyethylene has outstanding chemical resistance. It too has not much resistance to

___(a) high heat
___(b) tear and cut growth
___(c) ozone and sunlight
___(d) none of above

26. Vamac is basically a copolymer of ethylene and methyl acrylate. It combines moderate oil resistance with excellent heat aging properties. Like acrylic, it has

___(a) poor resistance to alkalis
___(b) limited flexibility at low temperatures
___(c) inferior resistance to water
___(d) none of above

27. Vynathene is a copolymer of vinyl acetate and ethylene. Its service temperature covers a wide range. In other properties, it is very similar to

___(a) Nitrile
___(b) Butyl
___(c) EPDM
___(d) Vamac

28. Norsorex is polynorbornene. One of its most unique properties is

___(a) outstanding resistance to weather, ozone, and sunlight
___(b) unaffected by oil and gasoline
___(c) high strength with low hardness
___(d) none of above

29. Elastomers are often separated into two groups, namely non-oil resistance and oil resistance. Of the four widely used elastomers listed below, the only one with oil resistance property is

___(a) SBR
___(b) natural rubber
___(c) Neoprene
___(d) EPDM

30. Many specialty elastomers require a two-stage cure cycle to produce the best balance of properties. Of the four elastomers listed below, the one that usually does not require a post-cure is

___(a) acrylic
___(b) fluorocarbon
___(c) Vamac
___(d) crosslinked polyethylene

CHAPTER 2

INTRODUCTION TO RUBBER COMPOUNDING*

Harry Long

Goodall Rubber Company
Trenton, New Jersey 08650

INTRODUCTION

What is rubber compounding? Why are we doing it? How can we do it successfully? Rubber compounding is the art and science of selecting and combining
elastomers and additives to obtain an intimate mixture that will develop the
necessary physical and chemical properties for a finished product.

The objectives of rubber compounding are threefold: (1) to secure certain
properties in the finished product to satisfy service requirements, (2) to
attain processing characteristics necessary for efficient utilization of available equipment, and (3) to achieve the desirable properties and processability
at the lowest possible cost. In other words, the most important criteria in
compounding is to secure an acceptable balance among demands arising from these
three criteria.

A practical compound formulation is usually one that consists of 10 or more
ingredients (Table I shows a typical formulation). Each ingredient has a specific function and each has an impact on properties, processability, and price.
Literally hundreds of ingredients are available today. In order to develop the
lowest-cost compound suitable for certain applications, knowledge on the function and effectiveness of compounding ingredients is indispensible.

Compounding ingredients can be classified into ten major categories as
shown in Table II. In the following pages, the function and examples of ingredients in each category will be presented as a general guide to material selection.

ELASTOMERS

The most important and usually the first step in compounding is the selection of a base elastomer or elastomers. Elastomers as a class of engineering
materials possess some common basic characteristics. All elastomers are elastic, flexible, tough, and relatively impermeable to both water and air. Beyond
these common characteristics, each elastomer has its own unique properties.
Today there are more than twenty different elastomers commercially available.
Their properties differ widely, so do their prices. The basic properties of
twenty relatively popular elastomers are compared in Chapter 1. Again, selection
of elastomers should be based on properties, processability, and price.

VULCANIZING AGENTS

Vulcanizing agents are ingredients which must be present to cause chemical
reaction, resulting in crosslinking of elastomer molecules. Through chemical
crosslinking, an elastomeric compound is converted from a soft, tacky thermoplastic to a strong temperature-stable thermoset. Sulfur is by far the most

---

* Presented at an educational symposium on rubber compounding sponsored by the
  Rubber Division, American Chemical Society, Chicago, Illinois, October 6, 1982.

TABLE I

TYPICAL COMPOUND FORMULATION

Ingredient	Type of Ingredient	Amount in phr*
#1 - RSS (Natural Rubber)	Elastomer	100.00
Soft Clay	Filler	100.00
Calcium Carbonate	Filler	50.00
Naphthenic Oil	Plasticizer	5.00
Activated Dithio-bisbenzanilide (Pepton 44)	Processing Aid (Peptizer)	0.25
Stearic Acid	Activator	2.00
Zinc Oxide	Activator	5.00
Red Iron Oxide	Color Pigment	15.00
Paraffin Wax	Processing Aid	2.00
Alkylated Bis-phenols	Antidegradant	2.00
DPG	Accelerator (secondary)	0.50
MBTS	Accelerator (primary)	1.00
Sulfur	Vulcanizing Agent	2.75
		285.50

*Parts per hundred of rubber. Ingredients used in a compound formulation are normally given in amounts based on a total of 100 parts of the rubber or combination of rubbers used.

TABLE II

CLASSIFICATION OF COMPOUNDING INGREDIENTS

1. Elastomers

2. Vulcanizing Agents (Curatives)

3. Accelerators

4. Activators and Retarders

5. Antidegradants (Antioxidants, Antiozonants, Protective Waxes)

6. Processing Aids (Peptizers, Lubricants, Release Agents)

7. Fillers (Carbon Blacks, Non-black Materials)

8. Plasticizers, Softeners, and Tackifiers

9. Color Pigments

10. Special Purpose Materials (Blowing Agents, Reodorants, etc.)

widely used vulcanizing agent. Sulfur-bearing materials such as thiuram di-sulfides (TMTD) and dithiodimorpholine (DTDM) are sometimes used as complete or partial replacements of elemental sulfur in a low sulfur or sulfur-less cure system to improve heat resistance of a compound. Table III shows each popular type of vulcanizing agent and its use. Selection of cure systems, vulcanizing agents and accelerators, is the second (to elastomers) most important task in compounding. Unless a suitable vulcanizing agent in the proper concentration is used, a compound will not develop its optimum properties and adequate pro-cessability.

ACCELERATORS

Accelerators are ingredients used to reduce the vulcanization time, or cure time, by increasing the speed of vulcanization. Most accelerators being used today are organic substances containing both nitrogen and sulfur. Of the inorganic accelerators widely used years ago, three remain popular. They are litharge, lime, and magnesia. Table IV shows each major category of organic accelerators, examples of them and their typical use. The thiazoles are by far the most widely used accelerators. Although it usually constitutes a very small part of a compound, an accelerator has a profound influence on the nature of crosslinking, which, in turn, largely determines the physical properties (tensile strength, modulus, resilience, etc.), the resistance to aging, and the processing characteristics (scorchiness and cure rate). The importance of using correct accelerators in accurate concentration cannot be overemphasized.

ACTIVATORS AND RETARDERS

Activators are ingredients used to activate the accelerator and improve its effectiveness. The most widely used activators are zinc oxide, stearic acid, litharge, magnesia, and amines. A cure system consisting of sulfur and organic accelerators usually requires the presence of an adequate amount of zinc oxide and stearic acid to attain good crosslinking efficiency.

The retarders are ingredients used to reduce the scorchiness of a compound. Many popular "retarders", such as phthalic anhydride, salicylic acid, and sodium acetate, are not true retarders because they reduce both scorchiness and cure rate. The most widely used true retarder is cyclohexyl-N-thiophthalimide. It makes a sulfenamide or thiazole accelerated compound much less scorchy and gives it more processing safety without affecting its cure rate or vulcanizate proper-ties.

ANTIDEGRADANTS

Antidegradants are ingredients used to retard the deterioration of rubber compounds initiated by oxygen, ozone, heat, light, metal catalysis, and mechani-cal flexing. An antidegradant is needed to impart good aging properties to a compound and extend its useful life. Table V shows each widely used type of antidegradant, an example of it, and its relative effectiveness in various areas of protection. Waxes are often used with antidegradants to provide a protective coating which shields the rubber compound from the effect of ozone. In the selection of antidegradants, the following factors must be considered; (1) type of protection desired, (2) chemical activity, (3) persistance, (volatility and extractability), (4) discoloration and staining, and (5) cost.

TABLE III

VULCANIZING AGENTS

TYPE	COMMON USE
Sulfur or Sulfur-bearing Materials	Natural Rubber, Isoprene, SBR, Butyl, Butadiene, EPDM, Nitrile, Norsorex
Organic Peroxides	Urethane, Silicone, Chlorinated Polyethylene, Crosslinked Polyethylene, Vamac, Vynathene, PVC/Nitrile
Metallic Oxides	Neoprene, Hypalon, Thiokol
Organic Amines	Acrylic, Fluorocarbon, Epichlorohydrin, Vamac
Phenolic Resins	Butyl

TABLE IV

ORGANIC ACCELERATORS

Type	Example	Typical Use
Aldehyde-amine	Reaction product of butyraldehyde and aniline	Fast curing accelerator for reclaim, hard rubber and self-curing cements
Amines	Hexamethylene tetramine	Delayed action slow accelerator for natural rubber.
Guanidines	Diphenyl guanidine (DPG)	Secondary accelerator to activate thiazole type accelerator
Thioureas	Ethylene thiourea (ETU)	Fast curing accelerator for Neoprene, Hypalon and Epichlorohydrin
Thiazoles	Benzothiazyldisulfide (MBTS)	Safe-processing moderately fast curing accelerator for natural rubber, Isoprene, SBR, Nitrile and EPDM
Thiurams	Tetramethylthiuram disulfide (TMTD)	Fast curing sulfur-bearing accelerator for SBR, Nitrile, Butyl and EPDM
Sulfenamides	N-cyclohexyl-2-benzothiazyl-sulfenamide (CBTS)	Safe-processing, delayed action accelerator for natural rubber, SBR and Nitrile
Dithiocarbamates	Zinc dimethyldithiocarbamate (ZDMC)	Fast curing accelerator for SBR and Butyl
Xanthates	Dibutylxanthogen disulfide	Fast curing, low temperature accelerator for natural rubber and SBR

TABLE V
ANTIDEGRADANTS

TYPE	EXAMPLE (Tradename)	STAINING	Oxygen	Heat	RESISTANCE TO		
					Flexing	Metal Catalysis	Ozone
1. Hindered Phenols	2,6-Di-t-butyl-p-cresol (CAO-1)	None to slight	F	F	F - P	P	P
2. Hindered Bis-phenols	2,2'-Methylene-bis-(4-methyl-6-t-butylphenol)(Antioxidant 2246)	None to Slight	G - F	G - F	F - P	G	P
3. Hindered Thiobisphenols	4,4'-thiobis(6-tert-butyl-m-cresol)(Santowhite Crystals)	Slight	G - F	G - F	F - P	F	P
4. Hydroquinones	2,5-di(tert-amyl)hydroquinone (Santovar A)	None to Slight	G - F	F	F - P	P	P
5. Phosphites	Tri(mixed mono and di-nonyl-phenyl)phosphite (Polygard)	None to Slight	G - F	F	F - P	P	P
6. Diphenylamines	Octylated diphenylamine (Cyanox 8)	Slight to moderate	G - F	G - F	F	P	P
7. Naphthylamines	Phenyl-alpha-naphthylamine (Akrochem PANA)	Moderate	G	G	G - F	F	P
8. Quinolines	Polymerized 2,2,4-trimethyl-1,2-dihydroquinoline (AgeRite Resin D)	Slight to moderate	G	E	F	P	F - P
9. Carbonyl-amines Condensation Prod.	Reaction product of di-phenylamine & acetone (BLE-25)	Considerable	G	E	E - G	P	F - P
10. Para-phenylene-diamines	Mixed Diaryl-p-phenylene-diamines (Wingstay 100)	Considerable to severe	E - G	E - G	E - G	E	E - G

E = Excellent; G = Good; F - Fair; P = Poor

PROCESSING AIDS

Processing aids are the ingredients added to a rubber compound to facilitate processing operations, such as mixing, calendering, extrusion, and molding. TABLE VI is a list of typical processing aids and their function.

FILLERS

Fillers are those ingredients used to reinforce physical properties, to impart certain processing characteristics, or to reduce cost. A reinforcing filler enhances the hardness, tensile strength, modulus, tear strength, and abrasion resistance of a compound. It is usually either a carbon black or a fine-particle mineral pigment.

An extending filler, or diluent, is a loading and non-reinforcing material. It is normally selected to reduce cost or to impart certain desirable processing properties, such as uncured firmness ("green strength"), smooth extrusion, and reduction of die swell and "nerviness". As a general rule, non-black materials are not as good for reinforcement as carbon blacks. TABLE VII is a list of widely used fillers.

Selection of reinforcing filler is the third (next to elastomer and cure system) most important task in compounding. Reinforcing filler has a profound influence on a compound's physical and processing properties. The properties and processability of a carbon black reinforced compound is greatly affected by the particle size and structure of the type of black it contains. Table VIII and IX show the particle size and structure of the five very widely used carbon blacks and their effects. Increasing index values indicate increasing particle size or increasing structure.

The degree of reinforcement increases with a decrease in particle size. The finer fillers require more energy for their disperion into the elastomer and is therefore more difficult to process. The particle size of fillers play a major role in the tensile strength of rubber compounds. Compounds containing small particle size blacks produce the highest tensile strength at optimum loading. Carbon blacks activate cure.

Modulus is primarily a function of carbon black structure and loading. Compounds containing higher structured blacks have the highest modulus. Modulus usually increases with additional loading. Like modulus, elongation is basically a function of carbon black structure with higher structured blacks giving lower elongation. Increased loading reduces elongation dramatically. Compounds containing thermal black (MT) generally have the highest elongation and are less affected by loading increases.

Mooney viscosity in most elastomers is mainly dependent on carbon black structure and loading. High structure blacks contribute the highest Mooney viscosity with particle size having a lesser effect. Mooney viscosity rises rapidly with increased loading for all compounds except those containing thermal black (MT) where loading does not seem to have much effect.

Mooney scorch is greatly affected by particle size. The largest particle size blacks provide the greatest scorch resistance while high structure, small particle-size black usually reduces the scorch resistance.

TABLE VI

PROCESSING AIDS

COMPOSITION	EXAMPLE(tradenames)	FUNCTION
Activated Dithio-bisbenzanilide	Pepton 44	Peptizer for NR
Poly-paradinitrosobenzene	Polyac	Chemical conditioner for IIR
Xylyl mercaptans	RPA 3	Peptizer for NR,IR,SBR and NBR. Stabilizer for cement viscosity
Low-molecular-weight polyethylene	A-C Polyethylene 617A	Release agent, lubricant
Calcium oxide	DesiCal P	Dessiccant
Aliphatic-naphthenic-aromatic resins	Strucktol 60NS	Homogenizing agent for all elastomers
Paraffin Wax	Numerous	Release agent, lubricant
Polyethylene glycol	Carbowax PEG3350	Activator for silica lubricant
Petroleum hydrocarbon	Petrolatum	Release agent, lubricant

TABLE VII

FILLERS

Reinforcing Type

      Carbon Black (listed in order   N220 (ISAF)
      of increasing particle size)   N330 (HAF)
                                        N550 (FEF)
                                        N762 (SRF-LM)
                                        N990 (MT)

      Non-Black - Silica
                     Zinc Oxide
                     Magnesium Carbonate
                     Aluminum Silicate
                     Sodium Aluminosilicate
                     Magnesium Silicate

Extending Type

      Calcium Carbonate
      Barium Sulfate
      Aluminum Trihydrate
      Talc and Soapstone

TABLE VIII

PARTICLE SIZE AND STRUCTURE OF CARBON BLACKS

ASTM DESIGNATION	PARTICLE SIZE INDEX	STRUCTURE INDEX
N220 (ISAF)	22	114
N330 (HAF)	27	102
N550 (FEF)	41	121
N762 (SRF-LM)	75	62
N990 (MT)	250	42

TABLE IX

EFFECT OF PARTICLE SIZE AND STRUCTURE

PROPERTY OF COMPOUND	DECREASING PARTICLE SIZE (Constant Structure)	INCREASING STRUCTURE (Constant Particle Size)
Hardness	Increases	Increases
Tensile Strength	Increases	Variable
Modulus	Not a major factor	Increases
Elongation	Not a major factor	Decreases
Resilience	Decreases	Not a major factor
Dispersibility	Decreases	Increases
Dimensional Stability ("Green Strength")	Not a major factor	Increases
Extrusion Shrinkage and Die Swell	Not a major factor	Decreases

PLASTICIZERS, SOFTENERS, AND TACKIFIERS

Plasticizers, softeners, and tackifiers are ingredients used to either aid mixing, modify viscosity, produce tack, provide flexibility at low temperatures, or replace a portion of the base elastomer without substantial loss in physical properties. Many ingredients in this group may also be considered as processing aids or extending fillers, or diluents. TABLE X is a list of widely used plasticizers, softeners, and tackifiers.

The important criteria in selection of plasticizers are elastomer compatibility, efficiency, stain resistance, and cost. If the plasticizer selected is not compatible with the base elastomers, it will bleed out and cause poor physical properties and surface stickiness. Aromatic type oil is not compatible with Natural Rubber, Isoprene, Butyl, and EPDM. Paraffinic type oil is not compatible with SBR, Butadiene, Nitrile, and Neoprene.

In general, the most effective plasticizers are also good solvents for the elastomer. Solvent plasticizers impart softness to the unvulcanized compound but do not reduce its "nerve". They also impart good resilience and reduction of hardness to the vulcanized compound. Less effective plasticizers are sometimes used to improve processability. They impart smooth, low shrinkage characteristics and reduce stickiness of unvulcanized compounds.

The physical characteristics of the plasticizers have an important effect on the properties of the compound containing it. A low-boiling plasticizer would evaporate during processing and lose its effectiveness. The melting point of the plasticizer affects the low temperature flexibility of the compound containing it. The viscosity of the plasticizer influences the hardness of the vulcanized compound.

COLOR PIGMENTS

Color pigments are ingredients needed to impart specific coloring to a non-black rubber compound. Color pigments may be divided into two groups, namely inorganic and organic. Most widely used inorganic pigments are those of iron oxide, chromium oxide, titanium dioxide, cadmium sulfide, cadmium selenide, antimony sulfide, mercuric sulfide, nickel titanate, lithopone, and ultramarine blue.

In recent years research by the manufacturers of organic pigments has produced a large variety of color dyes for the rubber and plastic industry. Organic dyes are much more expensive than inorganic pigments. Their advantages are high efficiency, brilliancy in color, much lower specific gravity. Moreover, organic dyes can provide many delicate shades which are not possible to obtain with inorganic pigments. However, most organic dyes are not stable to steam, light, and acid or alkali solution. Some of them have a tendency to migrate to the surface. In general, a combination of organic and inorganic pigments usually produces a better overall result in terms of brilliancy and stability.

SPECIAL PURPOSE MATERIALS

Special purpose materials are those used for specific purpose which are not normally required in the majority of rubber compounds. Blowing agents, reodorants, adhesion promoters, flame retardants, fungicide, and UV light absorbers are some of the ingredients belonging to this category.

TABLE X

PLASTICIZERS, SOFTENERS, AND TACKIFIERS

CATEGORY OF MATERIAL	FUNCTION

Petroleum Oils - Aromatic
                 Paraffinic
                 Naphthenic
	Plasticizer, Softener

Ester Plasticizers - Dioctyl phthalate
                      Dioctyl sebacate
                      Tributoxyethyl phosphate
                      Di (butoxyethoxyethyl) formal
                      Triglycol ester of vegetable oil
	Low temperature
	  plasticizers

Vulcanized Vegetable Oils	Extender, Plasticizer
Asphaltic Hydrocarbon	Extender, Plasticizer
Pine Tar	Plasticizer, Tackifier

Resins - Coumarone - indene
         Petroleum
         Phenolic
	Tackifier, Plasticizer

Polymeric esters	Extender, Plasticizer
Rosins - Hydrogenated rosin	Tackifier

PROCEDURE FOR COMPOUND DEVELOPMENT

Nearly all new compounds are modifications of some existing formulations. Nowadays, development of a completely new compound is seldom attempted. Moreover, such an attempt is usually unnecessary. In order to be efficient and effective in rubber compounding, a chemist should take full advantage of technical information readily available inside as well as outside of his organization. He must be analytical, resourceful, and innovative. The following is a useful procedure to guide compound development:

1. Set _specific_ objectives (properties, price, etc.).
2. Select base elastomer(s).
3. Study test data of existing compounds.
4. Survey compound formulations and properties data presented by material suppliers in their literature (see General References).
5. Choose a starting formulation.
6. Develop compounds in laboratory to meet objectives.
7. Estimate cost of compound selected for further evaluation
8. Evaluate processability of compound in factory.
9. Use compound to make a product sample.
10. Test product sample against performance specification.

SUMMARY

Rubber compounding is one of, if not the most difficult and complex subjects to master in the field of rubber technology. Compounding is not really a science. It is part art, part science. In compounding one must cope with literally hundreds of variables in material and equipment. There is no infallible mathematical formulation to help the compounder. That is why compounding is so difficult a task. Based on an article entitled "The Rubber Compounder" written by Mr. R.A. Claussen in the February 1966 issue of Rubber Age, "it usually takes a couple of years of guidance and, after that, an additional ten years of experience to make a good rubber compounder".

To be successful in compounding, one must not only understand the properties and function of hundreds of elastomers and rubber chemicals, he must also have intimate knowledge of the equipment used for mixing, extrusion, calendering, molding and vulcanization. Only with this knowledge can he successfully develop compounds meeting the three basic criteria in compounding, namely properties, processability and price.

Finally, it is not the intention of this chapter to cover compounding for properties required in specific applications. Consequently, no typical compound for any product is provided. A large reservoir of information on compounding for specific properties is readily available from suppliers of elastomers and rubber chemicals to the rubber industry. To this source of information the readers are directed for current data and timely assistance to carry out their compounding assignments.

Although much information has been discussed here, we have merely touched the surface of a very complex subject. This is just an introduction to rubber compounding. Not withstanding its importance, knowledge cannot be substituted for experience. As pointed out by Mr. Claussen in the aforementioned article:

$$SUCCESS = KNOWLEDGE + EXPERIENCE + TIME$$

GENERAL REFERENCES

1. Alliger, G. and Sjothun, I.J., "Vulcanization of Elastomers", Reinhold Publishing Corp., New York, (1964)

2. Babbit, R.O. ed., "The Vanderbilt Rubber Handbook", R. T. Vanderbilt Co., Inc., Norwalk, CT (1978)

3. Blow, C.M., ed., "Rubber Technology and Manufacture", Butterworth & Co., London, England (1971)

4. Eirich, F.R., ed., "Science and Technology of Rubber", Academic Press, New York (1978)

5. Kirk, R.E. and Othmer, D.F., eds., "Encyclopedia of Chemical Technology", Wiley-Interscience, New York (second edition, 1968)

6. Kraus, G., ed., "Reinforcement of Elastomers", Wiley-Interscience, New York. (1965)

7. Morton, M. ed., "Rubber Technology", Van Nostrand Reinhold Co., New York (1973)

8. Proceedings of Educational Symposium No. 4, "Compounding with Non-Black Fillers", ACS Rubber Division Meeting, Oct. 1979

9. Proceedings of Educational Symposium No. 9, "Rubber Compounding", ACS Rubber Division Meeting, Oct. 1982

10. Proceedings of Educational Symposium No. 10, "Practical Plastization and Plasticizer Theory", ACS Rubber Division Meeting, May 1983

11. "Rubber World Blue Book - Materials, Compounding Ingredients & Machinery for Rubber", Bill Communications, Inc., New York (1983)

12. Suppliers' technical literature on various elastomers and rubber chemicals

WORK ASSIGNMENT NO. 2

CHAPTER 2. INTRODUCTION TO RUBBER COMPOUNDING

INSTRUCTIONS: Read each question carefully, select one, and only one, appropriate answer to complete each statement.

1. Rubber compounding is

____(a) the method of combining rubber and rubber chemicals
____(b) the science of mixing and vulcanization of rubber
____(c) the art and science of selecting and combining elastomers and additives to obtain an intimate mixture that will develop the necessary properties for a finished product
____(d) the art and science of selecting the type of rubber most suitable for a specific application

2. To be successful in rubber compounding, a chemist may pay attention to all compounding criteria, of which the most important are

____(a) the type and the percentage of elastomer in a compound
____(b) the properties, processability, and price of a compound
____(c) the mixing time and the cure rate of a compound
____(d) the compatibility of ingredients and the final properties of a compound

3. A practical rubber compound usually contains at least several ingredients. Ingredients used in a compound formulation are usually given in amounts based upon

____(a) percentage of a compound's total weight
____(b) percentage of a compound's total volume
____(c) a total of 100 parts of the rubber or combination of rubbers used (phr)
____(d) ratio of its specific gravity to the specific gravity of the elastomers used

4. Vulcanizing agents are ingredients which must be present in a compound to

____(a) cause chemical reaction, resulting in crosslinking of elastomer molecules
____(b) reduce its viscosity
____(c) increase the speed of mixing
____(d) none of above

5. Accelerators are ingredients used to

____(a) reduce a compound's viscosity
____(b) reduce vulcanization time, or cure time
____(c) reduce deteriorative effects of accelerated aging
____(d) facilitate processing operation such as mixing

6. Activators are ingredients used to

____(a) improve the effectiveness of the accelerators
____(b) cause vulcanization
____(c) improve dispersion of ingredients
____(d) increase softening effect of plasticizers

7. To attain a good cure rate, a cure system consisting of sulfur and organic accelerators usually requires the presence of an adequate amount of

___(a) petroleum oils
___(b) stearic acid and zinc oxide
___(c) carbon blacks
___(d) calcium carbonate

8. Antidegradants are ingredients used to retard the deterioration of rubber compounds initiated by

___(a) oil and gasoline
___(b) oxygen, ozone, heat, light, and mechanical flexing
___(c) acids and solvents
___(d) water

9. In the selection of antidegradants, the one factor seldom being considered is

___(a) type of protection desired
___(b) persistance (volatility and extractability)
___(c) discloration and staining
___(d) specific gravity

10. Processing aids are those ingredients added to a rubber compound to facilitate processing operations, such as mixing, calendering, extrusion and molding. Examples of widely used processing aids are

___(a) petrolatum and paraffin wax
___(b) sulfur and sulfur-bearing materials
___(c) zinc oxide and magensium oxide
___(d) iron oxide and titanium dioxide

11. Fillers are those ingredients used in rubber compounding to

___(a) reinforce physical properties, impart certain processing characteristic or reduce cost
___(b) lower viscosity for more efficient molding operation
___(c) reduce cure rate and cure time
___(d) extend shelf-life of a compound

12. Use of extending filler, or diluent, is often necessary for

___(a) improvement in physical properties, such as tensile strength
___(b) protection against deteriorative effect of mechanical flexing
___(c) smoother extrusion and reduction of die swell
___(d) dilution of liquid plasticizers

13. The properties and processability of a carbon black reinforced compound is greatly affected by

___(a) the specific gravity of the type of black it contains
___(b) the particle size and structure of the type of black it contains
___(c) the cost of the carbon blacks used
___(d) none of above

14. The most important criteria in selection of plasticizers are

___(a) elastomer compatibility, stain resistance, and cost
___(b) viscosity and specific gravity
___(c) odor and taste
___(d) none of above

15. To achieve a better overall result in terms of color brilliancy and stability, a non-black compound usually contains

___(a) organic pigments alone
___(b) inorganic pigments only
___(c) a combination of organic and inorganic pigments
___(d) none of above

CHAPTER 3

MIXING EQUIPMENT AND THE MIXING PROCESS

Peter S. Johnson

Polysar Limited
Sarnia, Ontario, Canada

INTRODUCTION

Rubber mixing has always been regarded as more of an art than a science. Advances in mixing technology have usually been made as a result of empirical cause-and-effect studies, rather than by the application of fundamental scientific understanding.

However, in recent years a number of developments has increased our understanding of the physical processes that take place during the mixing of elastomers. The veil of magic or art has been to some extent drawn aside and some light has been shed on the process by the application of science. There is still a long way to go, but there is no doubt that the increased efficiency in energy and equipment utilization, which is being dictated by rising costs and restriction on the availability of energy, can only be achieved by such application.

The objective of the mixing process is to produce a compound with its ingredients sufficiently thoroughly incorporated and dispersed so that it will process easily in the subsequent forming operations, cure efficiently and develop the necessary properties for end-use; all with the minimum expenditure of machine time and energy. The four properties that are pertinent to subsequent operations are viscosity, dispersion, scorch stability and cure rate. Thus, in order to mix efficiently and profitably, one must direct his attention to raw materials, mixing procedures, mixing equipment and quality control.

This chapter is divided into two sections: Mixing Equipment and The Mixing Process. The first section describes the equipment used to carry out the mixing process described in the second section. Literature references are provided at the end of the chapter for those who desire further reading for more details.

MIXING EQUIPMENT

The equipment will be described in this section in the order in which it appears in the second section. No attempt will be made to give engineering details, sizes or capacities. These can be readily obtained from the equipment manufacturers. Nor will any one manufacturer's equipment be recommended over any others.

Internal Batch Mixers

A number of companies make internal mixers for the rubber industry and whatever their design, they have certain common features. These are (a) the ability to exert a high localized shear stress to the material being mixed (a nip-action) and (b) a lower shear rate stirring (a homogenizing action). The effectiveness of dispersive mixing results from the combination of high shear stress and large shear deformation.

There are two basic designs of rotor in internal mixers; non-intermeshing (e.g. Banbury, Bolling and Werner-Pfleiderer type) and intermeshing (e.g. Intermix and Werner-Pfleiderer type). Representative rotor designs are shown in

Figures 1, 2, and 3. Intermeshing rotors provide better heat-transfer and are therefore better for heat-sensitive compounds with lengthy mixing cycles. However, in general, rotor design is relatively unimportant as a determinant of internal mixer efficiency. This is probably a result of the importance of elongational flow in the mixing process; elongational flow being the result of converging flow lines irrespective of rotor design.

Internal mixer design is a compromise, based on experience to best accommodate the wide range of compounds typical of a manufacturing operation involving mixed product. To some extent mixers can be designed to meet specialized requirements but the theoretical foundations are not very well understood, or at least rarely published.

1. Banbury Mixer - Basically the Banbury mixer consists of a completely enclosed mixing chamber in which two spiral-shaped rotors operate, a hopper at the top to receive compounding ingredients for mixing and a door at the bottom for discharging the mixed batch of compound. The rotors are driven by an electric motor while pressure is applied from the top by a plunger or ram. The two rotors subject the compound to a certain amount of shear by revolving in opposite directions and at a slightly different speed. The bulk of the shearing action, however, occurs between the rotors and the chamber wall. Water or steam is usually circulated through the hollow rotors and the chamber wall to provide cooling or heating. At the specified mixing time or temperature, the compound is discharged onto a two-roll mill where the material is sheeted off to auxiliary equipment, such as a slab cooling system. Figure 4 shows a Model F620 Banbury mixer.

2. Bolling Mixer - In the operation of a Bolling mixer, as the ram pushes down toward the mixing chamber, the ingredients are forced between helically fluted rotors. As in the Banbury mixer, the bulk of shearing action occurs between the rotors and the chamber wall. A so-called spiral flow arrangement inside the shell of the chamber wall is designed for circulation of steam to provide heat around the shell through baffles cast into the shell liner. Separate channels running through the shell liner provide water for cooling.

3. Shaw Intermix - Here the great bulk of shearing action occurs between the rotors rather than between the rotors and the chamber wall. The new Werner & Pfleiderer GK-E mixers have a similar mixing action.

Mixing Mills

The open two-roll mill consists of two parallel, horizontal rolls rotating in opposite directions. The rotation of the rolls pulls the ingredients through the nip (or bite), which is the clearance between the rolls. The remaining surface of the roll is used as a means of transportation for returning the stock to the nip for further mixing. The back roll is usually rotating faster than the front roll by a ratio called the "friction ratio". Most of the work is done on the slow front roll during incorporation of ingredients. Cold or hot water, steam or hot oil may be circulated through the hollow rolls to modify the temperature of material coming into direct contact with roll surfaces during mixing operations. Figure 5 is a picture of a two-roll mill with rubber compound.

The use of open two-roll mills for mixing (as distinct from finishing) is declining, at least in part because of environmental regulations.

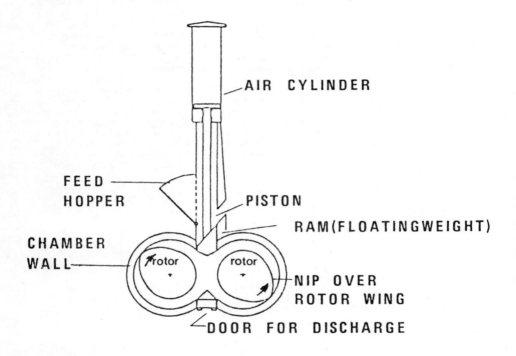

Fig. 1

Principal components of an internal rubber mixer

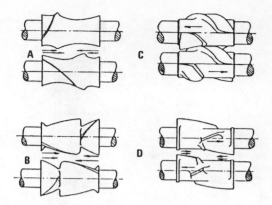

Fig. 2   Examples of rotor designs (Courtesy of H. Palmgren)

A. Banbury two-wing   C. Shaw Intermix three-wing

B. Banbury four-wing   D. Werner & Pfleiderer four-wing

The pumping action of the wings is indicated by arrows

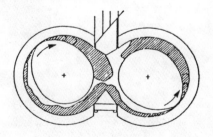

Fig. 3   Probable flow lines and filling configuration of an
internal rubber mixer (courtesy of H. Palmgren)

Fig. 4

Model F620 Banbury internal rubber mixer (Courtesy of Farrel Co.)

Fig. 5   Two-roll mill with rubber compound.   (Courtesy of Farrel Company)

Continuous Internal Mixers and Mixing Extruders

A masterbatch line for tire compounds that consists of an internal mixer dumping the compound into the hopper of a continuous mixer, or mixing extruder, can be considered continuous. The hopper holds 2-3 batches at a time and the output from the pelletizer or roller die is essentially continuous. The continuous mixer or mixing extruder refines or homogenizes the product from the batch mixer and therefore allows shorter mixing cycles.

The Farrel Continuous Mixer (FCM) is a true internal mixer, with rotors and mixing action similar to the Banbury mixer. The machine does not work on the extruder principle. In operation, raw materials are fed automatically from feed hoppers into the FCM, where the first section of the rotor acts as a screw conveyor, propelling the ingredients to the mixing section. The action within this mixing section is similar to that within a Banbury mixer, incorporating intensive shear of material between rotor and chamber wall and a rolling action of the material itself. Interchange of material between the two bores of the mixing section is an inherent feature of the design of the rotors. The amount and quality of mixing is flexible and can be controlled by adjustment of speed, feed rates and orifice opening. As the feed screw is constantly starved and the mixing action is rotary, there is little thrust or extruding action involved. Production rates and temperature are controlled by the rotor speed and the discharge orifice.

The Adamson Transfermix is a single screw continuous mixer which is force fed and is more of a mixing extruder than a true internal mixer.

The Stewart-Bolling Mixtrumat is a high intensity continuous mixer-extruder which consists of a combined twin rotor mixing station and extruder. The mixing section provides a working action of the type described earlier for internal batch mixers. The extruder section provides the coordinated means of handling the discharge from the mixing section and converting it to usable form, such as strip, pellet or, in some cases, finished shape. Both sections of the Mixtrumat are integral, permitting direct transfer from mixer to extruder without heat loss. At the transfer section there is a reduction in pressure and a vacuum port can be installed to remove moisture and volatiles. Although the mixer could be operated at a constant speed, normal operation to obtain maximum quality dictates a variable speed drive be used for both the mixer and extruder sections.

Equipment for Processing Particulate Rubber

Powdered or particulate rubber can be processed in internal batch mixers as described later in the section under Continuous Mixing. The two systems mentioned there, the Bayer Sikoplast Screw/Hopper and the Farrel M.V.X. are shown schematically in Figures 6 and 7.

THE MIXING PROCESS

There are several stages in the conversion of elastomers and other compounding ingredients into rubber compounds. These are receipt of raw materials, testing, storage, weighing, feeding, mixing, batch-off, cooling, testing, storage, and dispatch. These stages can be divided into three groups: (a) material flow to the mixer; (b) mixing; and (c) material flow away from the mixer.

Fig. 6

SIKOPLAST SCREW/HOPPER

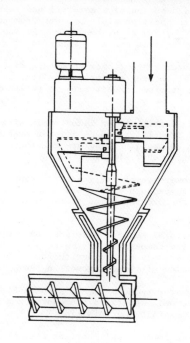

Fig. 7

M.V.X. BASIC CONFIGURATION

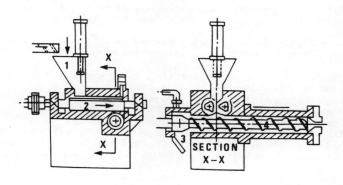

Material Flow to the Mixer

1. Storage and Handling

Proper storage and handling of elastomers and rubber chemicals is essential to achieve the best possible product from the mixing process. The following steps (courtesy of H. Long, Goodall Rubber Co.) should be taken to prevent deterioration and contamination of raw materials.

a. Unload all elastomer and rubber chemicals directly into an inside warehouse. Allow no ingredients to be stored exposed to the weather for any length of time (except perhaps sealed drums of oils and plasticizers).

b. Check material identification immediately after arrival of the ingredients. If identification is missing or not legible, apply identification to containers before the ingredient is moved into its regular, permanent, storage area.

c. Keep all elastomers, especially natural rubber and polychloroprene, away from hot spots such as radiators, heat outlets, and steam pipes. Do not expose them to radiation from fluorescent or mercury-vapour lamps.

d. Do not allow natural rubber, polyisoprene, butyl or EPDM to stay in an area where the temperature is below 5°C (40°F). Polymer viscosity may become excessively high under these conditions and this can lead to poor dispersion of the elastomer in the mixing process.

e. Keep highly unsaturated elastomers such as SBR, natural rubber, and nitrile rubber, well separated from butyl and EPDM in the storage area to avoid possible contamination.

f. Prevent chlorosulfonated polyethylene from becoming wet; store it in a dry area at all times.

g. Make sure that all containers of rubber chemicals in the warehouse are covered and sealed. Be especially careful to avoid contamination of materials in chip or pellet form. All broken or opened packages should be sent to the mixing department with complete identification for prompt use.

h. Strictly enforce the first-in, first-out rule for using ingredients, with time limits for storage of some materials.

i. Warm highly viscous plasticizers and tackifiers up to their pour temperatures before adding them to the mixer.

The five main classes of raw materials to be considered in the subject of handling are as follows:

a. Elastomers

Elastomers are normally supplied in bale form. This necessitates handling with pallets, fork-lifts and muscle as far as the feed conveyor. From here on, there should be no need for manual effort.

There are systems available that can handle four different grades or types of elastomer in bale form, weighing them simultaneously to 1% accuracy, and collecting them on a conveyor in batches up to 300 kg (660 lbs). The whole operation is controlled by a mini-computer, but this, of course, is an ideal system and most factories do not have such facilities.

b. Carbon Black

There are several justifications for bulk handling of carbon black. It is cheaper in bulk and picks up less moisture. Handling is cleaner and more efficient. As before, there are systems available for bulk handling, conveying, weighing and charging carbon black into internal mixers. However, once again, it is not unusual to find carbon black being handled manually because the usage of carbon black in many non-tire plants is not large enough to warrant expenditure for bulk handling equipment.

c. Non-Black Fillers

Whether these should be handled in bulk or not obviously depends also on usage. However, computer-controlled automatic weighing and handling is preferable if extra capital investment for the necessary equipment is financially justifiable.

d. Oils/Plasticizers

Because these are usually liquids they are the one class of raw materials that most mixing shops today handle at least semi-automatically. For those plasticizers used in large quantities, bulk handling is advantageous. Preheating is usually necessary for some of these materials in order to reduce their viscosity for proper handling.

e. Small Ingredients

An automatic weighing system for small ingredients is even more important than for carbon black. Such systems, for up to ten ingredients, occupy little space and are not very expensive. This reduces a potential source of serious error. It is very important that critical ingredients such as accelerators, antioxidants, etc. be exact because they have a profound influence on the properties of a rubber compound. An automatic weighing system also reduces the chances of using entirely wrong ingredients.

With each of the five classes of raw materials mentioned above, automatic handling systems have been recommended. However, it should be remembered that a manual system that works is preferable to a poorly designed automatic system. The installation of inadequate automatic systems can cause more problems than they solve.

2. Scheduling

Most mixing shops have a wide variety of compounds that are mixed in varying quantities and careful scheduling is important in achieving maximum productivity, prevention of contamination, and maintaining uniform quality.

Mixing Operation

The mixing operation consists of three simultaneous processes, namely simple mixing, laminar mixing, and dispersive mixing. The relative importance of each depends on the particular compound formulation (in terms of the attraction between the particles of solid additives and the flow properties of the rubber), the geometry of the mixer, and the operating conditions. In a specific case, any one of the three may be the efficiency-determining process.

Simple mixing or homogenization involves the moving of a particle from one point to another, without changing its physical shape. This increase in randomness or entropy is also called extensive mixing. If the shear forces are sufficiently large, particles may fracture (dispersive mixing), and the polymer may flow (laminar mixing). In addition, if the deformation of the elastomer exceeds its breaking strain, then it will break into super-molecular flow units.

There are four physical changes, from the point of view of the ingredients in the mix, which take place during the mixing cycle:

1. Incorporation - At the beginning of a mixing cycle, the rubber is forced or drawn into the working area between pairs of rotors and between rotors and chamber wall and the identity of the original bales or particles is destroyed. The incorporation stage is when the initially free ingredients become attached to the rubber. This is also known as the wetting stage and has two mechanisms. In the first, the elastomer undergoes a large deformation, increasing the surface area for accepting filler agglomerates, and then sealing them inside. In the second, the elastomer breaks down into small pieces and mixes with the filler and once again seals the filler inside. The former mechanism is easily observed in an open mill. The latter is not necessarily observable, because the breaking and sealing steps occur on a micro-scale.

2. Dispersion - The filler agglomerates are gradually broken down, distributed through the rubber (by simple mixing) and are then dispersed (i.e. broken down to the ultimate size) giving a fine scale of mixing. This is especially important in the case of carbon black because at this stage an intimate contact between the surface of the carbon black and the elastomer develops, resulting in bound rubber. Both the disruption of the filler aggregates and the forcing of the elastomer onto the filler surface require high shear stress. However, the shear stresses do not all result from the imposed shear field, because microscopic shear fields are generated from elongational deformations also.

3. Distribution - This process of increasing homogenization takes place throughout the mixing cycle.

4. Plasticization - In this stage of mixing, the rheological properties are modified to suit subsequent operations.

It is important to avoid overmixing. It wastes machine time and energy and can turn a profitable operation into an unprofitable one. In addition, exposure to shearing and high temperatures can result in excessive carbon black inter-reaction, viscosity increases and in some cases reversion of the rubber.

Internal Mixing

   1. Procedures

     There are three basic procedures or methods of mixing a rubber compound in an internal mixer; namely, the so-called conventional method, the rapid oil addition method, and the upside-down mix method. Many variations of these three methods are also used to suit the special characteristics of individual formulations and equipment. It is, in general, necessary to add particulate fillers early in the mixing cycle, so that good dispersion is achieved as a result of the high shear stress and high viscosity at the lower temperatures then prevailing. Similarly, the oils and plasticizers which reduce viscosity, should be added later. Upside-down procedures and variants of it are attempts to implement these ideas in practice.

     a. Conventional Mixing Method - The conventional mixing method, developed originally for natural rubber, consists of adding the elastomer first, then the dry ingredients, then the liquid ingredients after the dry materials are well dispersed in the elastomer. This method can achieve a homogenous dispersion of all ingredients, including fillers of very small particle size. However, the mixing time required is usually long, because it is more difficult to incorporate the liquid ingredients once the dry materials are dispersed. With fillers which are of low bulk-density or with fillers which cake when dry, a variation of this technique is to add part of the liquid ingredients at the same time as the dry ingredients.

     b. Rapid Oil Addition Method - The rapid oil addition method involves adding the elastomer first and the dry ingredients as soon afterward as possible. After about 1 to 2 minutes of mixing, all liquids are added together. The proper time for addition of liquids needs to be determined. Dispersion usually improves if the addition of liquids is delayed slightly; however, this will extend the mixing time. Use of this method can give very good dispersion if liquids are added at the proper time. This method often is used for compounds containing a large volume of liquid plasticizers. However, it can lead to an extended mixing cycle due to the lubricating effect of the liquids between rubber and the metal parts of the mixer.

     c. Upside-down Mix Method - This is the fastest and the simplest way of mixing. It is especially efficient and effective for those compounds containing a large volume of liquid plasticizers and large particle size fillers. This method involves adding all ingredients into the mixer before lowering the ram and commencement of mixing. All dry ingredients are added to the mixer first, then all liquids, and finally all elastomers on top. This method is not suitable for those compounds containing low structure, small particle-size carbon black, or compounds having high loadings of both soft mineral filler and oil, together with an elastomer of high Mooney viscosity.

2. Breakdown or Masticiation of Natural Rubber

   One of the more important preliminary steps in mixing natural rubber is the breakdown or viscosity reduction. Crude natural rubber as received from the plantation is high in viscosity and, for most applications, needs to be broken down to a lower viscosity prior to mixing operations. A combination of heat and work, and sometimes the addition of peptizers, usually produces a physical and chemical change reflected by a change in viscosity. The maximum effect in natural rubber is obtained either at temperatures below 55°C (130°F) or at temperatures above 130°C (270°F). Very little breakdown is obtained in the 90 to 105°C (190-220°F) region. The breakdown of natural rubber can be accomplished either on an open mill or in an internal mixer. The mill functions in the low temperature region while the mixer operates in the high temperature region of 165 to 170°C(300-350°F).

   Natural rubber is now being produced in controlled viscosity grades that reduce the need for such mastication. Many synthetic rubbers are not susceptible to such breakdown but they do not normally need to be because they can be readily manufactured in different Mooney viscosity levels. Therefore, processing requirements are usually satisfied by selecting the elastomer with the proper viscosity.

3. Two-pass Mixing

   Premature vulcanization of a rubber compound, scorch, can occur if the reaction temperature of the vulcanizing ingredients is reached before the desired time. If this temperature is reached in the mixing process before the proper viscosity and level of dispersion is obtained, then the addition of accelerators and vulcanizing agents will cause scorchiness and poor subsequent processability. Therefore, if this occurs, the batch must be mixed to the required viscosity and dispersion without the vulcanizing ingredients, emptied from the mixer and allowed to cool down. The batch is then fed back to the mixer for the addition of the vulcanizing ingredients in a second pass.

   In general, a compound requires two-pass mixing if satisfactory dispersion cannot be achieved below 120°C(250°F). Compounds containing high melting-point ingredients need a high temperature to flux such components. This precludes the addition of curatives in the first pass. Many butyl and nitrile compounds do need two-pass mixing for safe processing, usually with a 24 hour delay between passes, in order to optimize the physical properties of the end product.

4. Dump Criteria

   The most common methods of deciding when to end the mixing process have been: a preselected time, the compound reaching a preselected temperature, or the compound reaching a given temperature at a given time. The aim is to guarantee the quality of the end product, avoid overmixing and reduce variation between batches. There is an increasing body of evidence that a more precise and reproducible control of the mixing cycle can be obtained by considering the energy input at various stages in the cycle, in terms of both instantaneous power and integrated power or work input.

The changes in power consumption in a typical rubber mix are indicative of stages in the process, such as wetting, dispersion and plasticization, and can be related to the development of end product properties. Properties such as viscosity and die swell which are related to the volume fraction of rubber in the mix, reach their optimum at the end of the dispersion stages. At the beginning of the dispersion stage, the filler particles are still in agglomerates which contain rubber occluded between the particles. When subjected to shear, the entire filler agglomerate with its occluded rubber behaves as a single filler particle. As a result, a poorly dispersed mixture always has a higher viscosity and a lower die-swell than a homogenous compound. Monitoring the power usage is, in effect, only a more sophisticated way of measuring the carbon black incorporation time.

Some general conclusions can be drawn about the use of power curves and power integration as a control tool, as compared to time or temperature. Mixing to a preset time does not allow for variations in metal temperature at the start of the mix, cooling rate, or time of addition of compounding ingredients, and can result in significant batch-to-batch variation. When mixing to a predetermined temperature, as is often done with upside-down mixes with short mixing cycles, the major limitation is the accuracy with which the batch temperature can be measured. The large heat-sink provided by the mixer often makes temperature measurement inaccurate. Mixing to a predetermined power input into the batch overcomes these limitations and gives improved batch-to-batch consistency with mixes requiring longer than three minutes mixing time.

However, following the work or energy input, alone, is not sufficient. In addition, one has to establish the effect of process variables on the shape of the power curve. In other words, a recording chart which indicates both the instantaneous power and the integrated power or work done is required. Furthermore, these data should be considered as additional to the established controls of time and temperature and not a completely separate, alternative set of criteria.

5. Process Variables

There are a number of important variables or parameters in internal mixing. They are reviewed briefly as follows:

a. Shear stress – The dispersive mixing of carbon black in elastomers has been the subject of a number of theorectical analyses; the general concusion is that high shear stresses and low particle-to-particle attraction increase the rate of dispersion but that for a given particle there is a critical stress below which dispersion will not occur. The maximum shear stress occurs in the nip and is inversely proportional to the square of the gap, so this clearance is critical. However, the importance of elongational flow, which may be more efficient in particle size reduction, must not be ignored.

b. Shear Strain and Rate of Shear Strain - In general, the total
shear strain (or deformation) necessary for a particular degree
of mixing can be imposed at any rate, the shorter time required
at high rates being offset by higher power consumption and heat
generation. Shear strain rates for a variety of types and sizes
of mixers approximate to v/h, where v is the peripheral rotor
speed and h is the rotor tip clearance. Therefore, small mixers
must be run at higher rotational frequencies to give the same
shear strain rate as larger mixers. However, it should be remembered that a certain minimum shear stress has to be generated.

c. Rotor Speed - This directly affects total shear strain or deformation and thus the speed of mixing. The speed of mixing is
usually limited by the maximum allowable temperature which is
determined by the balance between heat generation and heat removal. Dispersive mixing, although dependent on shear stress,
does not seem to be directly affected by rotor speed; this is
probably due to the dominance of elongational flow, which also
creates high shear stress.

d. Ram Pressure - The function of the ram is to keep the ingredients
in the mixing area, so increased ram pressure would not be expected to influence mixing efficiency. However, in practice,
high ram pressure, up to 0.55 MPa (80 psi), has definite advantages, especially for high viscosity mixes because high ram
pressures decrease voids within the mixture and increase shear
stress by reducing slippage. In addition, the effect of increasing pressure is to increase the contact force between the rubber
and the rotor surface, thus increasing the critical stress so
that flow begins at a lower temperature. In general, 0.3-0.4 MPa
(40-60 psi) are required for filler incorporation, 0.4-0.55 MPa
(60-80 psi) for elastomer blends or natural rubber breakdown.
Higher ram pressure can lead to mechanical problems with dust
seals.

e. Temperature - Probably the most important, and often the most
neglected, factor in mixing is temperature control. The rate at
which the stock is heated and cooled, and the length of time
that it is kept at each temperature, has a profound effect on its
subsequent performance. The many variables involved include batch
size, temperature and flow rate of the heating or cooling medium,
rate of heat transfer, and work input to the stock. Care must be
taken to ensure that the temperature control capabilities of the
equipment are not exceeded. The equipment should be inspected
periodically to ensure that the heat control mechanisms continue
to operate efficiently. Scale deposits in piping and on heating
and cooling surfaces prevent sufficient heat transfer and should
be removed.

A major concern in most mixing operations has been to control
the temperature at the end of the mixing cycle, and so it has
been normal to use cold or even chilled water as a coolant. With
the advent of internal mixers with more efficient heat exchange
capability, cold water can be too efficient a coolant, and at the
beginning of mixing the rubber slips on the cold metal surfaces.
This problem can be avoided by maintaining the cooling water at
such a temperature that the rubber adheres to the rotors and deforms readily. The result is more consistent mixing and a slight
reduction in mixing time.

Milling was the original method used to mix rubber stock and is still used for specialty compounds, small batches, and in small operations where the production volume does not warrant expenditure on an internal mixer.

In mill mixing, temperature control is very important. Cooling is usually accomplished by flooding or spraying the inside of the mill rolls with water, or circulating water through channels drilled in the roll walls. Chilled water is used where it is available. Compound temperature is adjusted by regulating the rate of flow of the water through the rolls. Steam heating is used where a temperature increase is required.

Roll temperature suitable for mixing a given compound depend upon the nature of the elastomer and such factors as the types and quantities of fillers and plasticizers to be incorporated. Nitrile and lightly-loaded EPDM compounds are usually milled with roll temperatures in the range 10-30°C (50-90°F); chloroprene compounds at 20-40°C (70-110°F) and butyl and highly-loaded EPDM compounds at 60-80°C (140-180°F). For butyl and EPDM compounds, the front roll should be approximately 10°C (20°F) cooler than the back roll because these elastomers tend to release from the hotter roll.

Mixing is caused by the shearing action in the nip between the two rolls. Originally, mills had a roll speed ratio of 1.4:1.0, the faster roll at the back, to provide efficient breakdown of natural rubber. With the advent of synthetic rubbers and viscosity-stabilized standard Malaysian and Indonesian rubbers, this friction ratio has been reduced to 1.12:1.0 and now the fast roll is often at the front because most synthetic rubbers band more easily on the faster roll.

In mill mixing the elastomer is first added to the nip, about 6 mm (0.25 in) wide, at the top of rolls. A band of elastomer then comes through the nip and is formed preferably around the front roll. Depending on the elastomer used, varying degrees of difficulty may be encountered in forming the band at the beginning. But after a few passes a band will form and be fed back into the nip continuously. The elastomer is then cut back and forth twice to assure proper blending and to allow the elastomer in the bank to go through the nip. It is important for efficient mixing to maintain a rolling bank on the mill during incorporation of ingredients. All dry ingredients except the fillers and the cure system are then added into the nip and the compound is cross-cut back and forth twice to assure good dispersion of these dry ingredients throughout the batch.

The next step is to open the mill slightly and add the fillers slowly to the batch. In order to prevent excessive loading of fillers at the center of the mill, strips of compound are cut from the end of rolls several times during this operation and thrown back into the bank. When most of the fillers have dispersed in the compound, the liquid and the remaining fillers are added slowly and alternately to the batch. When no loose filler is visible, the batch is cross-cut back and forth twice more to assure good dispersion of fillers and plasticizers. It is often a useful procedure to "pig" roll the batch and feed the "pigs" back into the nip at right-angles as a part of the cross-blending process.

The next step is to open the mill more and add vulcanizing agents to the batch. When the vulcanizing agents are well dispersed, the entire batch is cut back and forth at least five times to assure thorough crossblending before being sheeted off the mill.

There are various practical problems which arise when handling rubber compounds on two-roll mills. These are discussed later in this section under Material Flow from the Internal Mixer.

Mill mixing is a slow operation, (about 30 minutes/batch vs. 8 minutes or less in an internal mixer), which requires constant physical effort from a mill operator. It is not only time-consuming but difficult to control because it so heavily depends upon the skill of the operator. The internal mixer is much more widely used in the industry because of its versatility, rapid mixing, and large through-put. Environmental regulations make the handling of powdered ingredients on an open mill even less likely in the future, unless used in a costly masterbatch form.

Major Mixing Problems

Most problems of mixing are mainly concerned with (1) dispersion, (2) scorchiness, (3) contamination, (4) poor processability at the sheeter mill, and (5) batch-to-batch variation. The cause of these major problems are many and various. In most cases, it is more difficult to identify the cause of a problem than to find a solution to it. Corrective action is usually simple once the exact cause of a problem is known. The follwoing tables (courtesy of H. Long, Goodall Rubber Co.) provide a check-list of common causes of major mixing problems.

TABLE I

POSSIBLE CAUSES OF POOR DISPERSION

A. **Mixing Procedure**

1. Insufficient mixing time.
2. Dump temperature too low or too high.
3. Simultaneous addition of acidic and basic materials (such as stearic acid and ESEN retarder together with zinc oxide and magnesia).
4. Insufficient breakdown of elastomers.
5. Improper order of addition of ingredients.
6. Fillers added too late in the mixing cycle.
7. Simultaneous addition of small particle-size carbon black and resins or viscous oils.
8. Insufficient time to disperse metallic oxides.
9. Adding liquid plasticizers after the batch has begun to tear or crumble.
10. Batch size too large or too small.

B. **Workmanship**

1. Failure to follow established mixing procedure.
2. Allowing agglomerates of oily and dry materials to stick to ram and sides of hopper.
3. Use of wrong rotor speed.
4. Compound removed too soon from sheeter mill.
5. Failure to use overhead blender at sheeter mill.

C. Equipment

    1. Ineffective control of mixer temperature.
    2. Insufficient ram pressure.
    3. Excessive wear of armoured parts in mixing chamber.
    4. Ineffective control of sheeter mill roll temperature.
    5. Malfunction of overhead blender at sheeter mill.

D. Materials

    1. Over-aged and partly gelled elastomer.
    2. Cold EPDM or butyl rubber.
    3. Frozen natural rubber.
    4. Insufficiently pre-masticated natural rubber.
    5. Excessive moisture in fillers (caking).
    6. Viscous ingredient added at temperature below its pour point.
    7. Use of wrong ingredients.

E. Compound Design

    1. Use of elastomers with considerable difference in Mooney viscosity.
    2. Plasticizers incompatible with the elastomers.
    3. Too many ingredients in hard pellet form.
    4. Too large an amount of small particle-size fillers.
    5. Use of resins with excessively high melting point.
    6. Insufficient liquid plasticizers.
    7. Excessive loading of fillers and plasticizers.

TABLE II

POSSIBLE CAUSES OF SCORCHINESS

    1. Insufficient cooling of mixer.
    2. Curing system acting too quickly.
    3. Dump temperature too high.
    4. Accelerator added at wrong time into the mixer.
    5. Poor dispersion of accelerators and/or vulcanizing agents.
    6. Resin build-up on rotors.
    7. Retarders omitted.
    8. Incorrect weighing of ingredients.
    9. Use of too high a rotor speed.
  10. Initial loading temperatures too high.
  11. Too large an amount of small particle-size fillers
  12. Insufficient liquid plasticizers
  13. Stacking compound while it is still hot and wet.

TABLE III

COMMON CAUSES OF CONTAMINATION

1. Physical contamination of elastomers and rubber chemicals by dust, dirt, grit, and other materials.
2. Chemical contaminatin of butyl and EPDM by other elastomers, such as natural rubber and nitrile.
3. Using scoop indiscriminately for different ingredients.
4. Using wrong ingredients.
5. Oil seepage from faulty oil seal in mixer.
6. Left-over ingredients from previously used tote pans.
7. Residual compound sticking to rotor, dump door, hopper and ram. This problem is reduced if a clean-up batch is run through periodically..
8. Residual compound sticking to dump chute, mill pan and guides, and overhead blender.
9. Residue buildup at dust rings.
10. Generally poor housekeeping in area surrounding the mixer and the sheeter mill.

TABLE IV

POSSIBLE CAUSES OF POOR PROCESSABILITY AT SHEETER MILL

1. Failure to use specified mill roll temperatures.
2. Ineffective control of mill roll temperatures and friction ratio and speed.
3. Mooney viscosity of the compound is too low.
4. Excessive amount of tackifiers.
5. Too high a loading of tacky fillers (such as clay).
6. Too large an amount of viscous plasticizers.
7. Lack of proper processing aids in formulation.
8. Insufficient or excessive loading.
9. Wrong choice of elastomer viscosity.
10. Poor dispersion.
11. Compound prone to scorch.
12. Compound left on mill too long.

TABLE V

COMMON CAUSES OF BATCH-TO-BATCH VARIATION

1. Variation in initial loading temperature.
2. Variation in flow and/or temperature of cooling water.
3. Variation in ram pressure.
4. Errors in weighing of ingredients.
5. Lot-to-lot difference of compounding ingredients.
6. Use of substitute ingredients.
7. Variation in dump time and /or temperature
8. Different ways of handling compounds at sheeter mill by different operators.
9. Variation in crossblend time.
10. Different level of dispersion.

Material Flow From the Internal Mixer

The normal procedure for handling the product from a batch mixer is to dump it from the mixer onto a mill. The purpose of the mill is twofold: it cools the batch and by banding on the mill roll, changes its physical shape so it can be sheeted or stripped off and fed to a conveyor. If a travelling stock-blender is installed at the mill, both cooling and further homogenization are much more efficient.

The majority of mills in the rubber industry have fixed speed, fixed friction ratio and a manually adjustable gap setting for the nip. Also, for ease of stripping, the front roll is usually at the slower speed. These features became standard because they were effective for natural rubber and for SBR. However, many of the other synthetic rubbers are much more difficult to handle on standard mills, transferring to the fast roll or sagging, bagging, or crumbling on passage through the nip. Techniques to overcome these problems include altering the critical slip forces between rubber and rolls by spraying milk on the front roll or soap on the back roll, and adjusting the nip distance and temperature based on past experience.

The behavior of a particular compound on the sheeter mill depends on the balance between its viscous and viscoelastic properties. If the stresses caused by deformation in the nip exceed a certain critical value, then in the time of revolution of the roll (2 to 4 seconds normally), the material can relax and sag in a process akin to melt-fracture in extrusion. The stresses (or stored energy) may be high enough to initiate tears. The surface speed of the loaded roll determines the time the material has to sag and the time the tears have to spread. So a large difference in speed between the rolls, a narrow nip and the material on the slower roll can lead to bagging. It has too much time to relax. Unfortunately, the reverse can be true; if the material is transferred to the fast roll the time to relax is shorter and the stresses do not relax enough but build up with further passes through the nip resulting in tearing and crumbling.

There are four regions of mill behavior depending on the operating temperature and the particular elastomer involved. Figure 8 shows the change from Region 1 to Region 4 as the temperature is increased. It is only in Region 2 that stable milling and adequate mixing take place.

Whether, at a given temperature, the material goes to the slow roll or the fast roll, or even drops down without banding depends on the size and speed of the mill and the rheological properties of the material. However, in general, materials tend to go to the fast roll when the nip opening is very small. When the nip opening is increased to a certain size, the material goes to the front roll. At the transition point, the material can band on neither roll, but drops down without banding. Figure 9 illustrates the effect of nip opening on behavior of rubber on a mill.

Thus a factory having a wide variety of rubber compounds to handle on the same mill requires that mill to have (1) independent speed control on both rolls, (2) widely variable speed on both rolls, (3) independent temperature control on both rolls, and (4) hydraulically operated nip adjustment. This enables roll speed, friction ratio and temperature to be adapted to each individual compound instead of struggling to handle numerous compounds of many different elastomers under the same milling conditions.

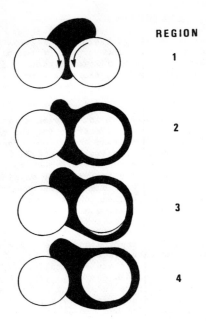

Fig. 8   Effect of temperature on behavior of rubber on a mill

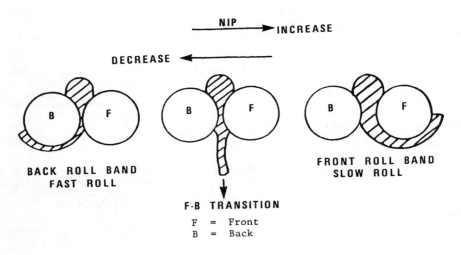

Fig. 9   Effect of nip opening on behavior of rubber on a mill

A dump extruder is only of value when the compound has to be strained or when a virtually continuous operation is involved. It avoids splices but does not achieve the same regularity and consistency as a mill and a stock-blender.

The subsequent batch-off system has several requirements: (a) quick cooling, (b) ability to handle stock in slab, sheet, or strip form, (c) ability to handle all types of stock, (d) low final temperature, 20°C (70°F) even in the middle of a thick sheet, (e) application of anti-tack, (f) packaging of absolutely dry stock automatically.

The relationship between the mixer and the feed and takeoff systems can be simply defined. The output should be limited by the mixer and not by either the feed or takeoff system. This may seem obvious, but it is surprisingly common in the rubber industry for the mixer to sit idle between mixing of different compounds because the raw materials handling system is inefficient. It is equally common for the mixer to be idle between batches because the takeoff system is a bottleneck.

Continuous Mixing

Continuous mixing is not usual in the rubber industry. However, interest in continuous mixing has grown because a series of interconnected processes from raw rubber to finished product should lead to savings in time, labor, and energy. Semi-continuous and fully continuous systems of mixing are only viable with long runs of a limited number of compounds. Semi-continuous mixing is the term used to describe a system in which batches from an internal mixer are discharged into an extruder, Transfermix or Farrel Continuous Mixer. These extruders are finishing mixers and their use results in shorter residence times of the stock in the internal mixer.

Fully continuous mixing requires the use of elastomer in powder or particulate form. A limited range of elastomers is commercially available in such form, others may be granulated or powdered in-house by the processor.

There are two main routes that can be followed in processing powdered rubbers. These involve (a) using heavy-duty mixers and, (b) by-passing such mixer (see Figures 10 and 11). The economics of processing powdered rubber are so dependent on the type of rubber, the compound formulation, the mixing equipment, the processing equipment, and the end use, that there is no general answer to the question of whether the savings obtainable in processing offset the premium normally charged for powdered rubber over the price for bale form. The generally slow development of the technology is probably due to the lack of clear-cut evidence for the cost effectiveness of processing powdered rubber, together with a natural reluctance to adopt new and unproven technology for mixing, the most crucial process in the rubber industry.

The advantages claimed for using powdered rubber are:

1. Shorter mixing cycles.
2. Less power consumption.
3. Less plant maintenance.
4. Less capital intensive plant.
5. Better ultimate dispersion.
6. Shorter heat history.

Fig. 10

PROCESSING OF POWERED RUBBER VIA HEAVY DUTY MIXERS

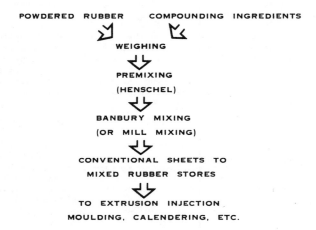

Fig. 11

PROCESSING OF POWERED RUBBER BY-PASSING HEAVY DUTY MIXERS

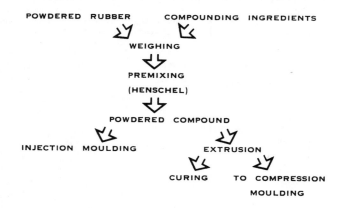

There are two commercially available systems for mixing powdered rubber, the Bayer Process and the Farrel-Bridge Process. The first step in the Bayer Process is mixing in a Papenmeir turbo-rapid intensive mixer to produce a homogenous, free-flowing mixture in powder form in the shortest time, with the least expenditure of energy and the lowest heat build-up. To process this material through vented extruders or injection molding machines, a new processing step was developed between initial mixing and final production in order to compact the powder mix from specific gravity 0.5 to the approximate specific gravity of the final mix. This step, using a Sikoplast Screw/Hopper, produces a heterogeneous but compact, continuous strip, suitable for feeding extruders or molding machines. Extruders with 20-24 L/D ratio can achieve outputs between 140 and 160 kg/h (30-350 lbs/h) of thoroughly dispersed profile and hose stocks.

The Farrel-Bridge Mixing, Venting, Extruder (or M.V.X.) uses a premixed feed stock. In order to produce an intimate shearing/smearing action with turbulence, the machine has two drive motors - one driving the mixing section and the other driving a polymer pump to extrude a finished profile.

SUMMARY

The intent of this chapter is to provide the newcomer to the industry, especially one who does not have a technical background, with some insight into mixing of rubbers. Mixing is of crucial and fundamental importance to the rubber industry. Elastomers have to be extended with plasticizers, reinforced with fillers and have important additives, such as accelerators and curatives, thoroughly distributed before they can be shaped and vulcanized to give an end-product with adequate properties. All these cannot be achieved without effective mixing.

The chapter deals with mixing equipment and the mixing process. The first section describes the equipment used in mixing rubber compounds. The equipment includes internal batch mixers, mixing mills, continuous internal mixers and mixing extruders.

The second section describes the mixing process and deals with material flow to the mixer, the mixing operation itself and material flow from the mixer. The mixing process is discussed, as are the physical changes which take place during the mixing cycle. The three basic mixing procedures, conventional, rapid oil addition and upside-down, are described, as is the basic procedure of mill mixing. A set of five trouble-shooting charts on major mixing problems are provided. There is a final brief section on continuous mixing of powdered rubber. For those who desire further reading for more details on the subject of mixing, a list of literature references is provided.

64

GENERAL REFERENCES

1. Evans, C. W., "Powdered and Particulate Rubber Technology"
    Applied Science Publishers Ltd., London (1978)

2. Funt, J. M.,   "Mixing of Rubbers", The Rubber and Plastics
    Research Association of Great Britain (1977)

3. Gessler, A. M., Hess, W.M., and Medalia, A.I., "Reinforcement of
    Elastomers with Carbon Black", Plastics and Rubber
    Processing, 3 (i) March 1978 p1 (ii) June 1978
    p37 (iii) September 1978 p109 (iv) December 1978 p141

4. Johnson, P.S., "Developments in the Application of Science to Rubber
    Processing - A Review", Elastomerics, 113(12),43 (1981)

5. Long, H.,   "Mixing of Rubber Compounds", Goodall Rubber Co. (1980)

6. Matthews, G., "Polymer Mixing Technology" Applied Science Publishers
    Ltd., London (1982)

7. Morrell, S.H., "Mixing of Rubber Compounds", Progress of Rubber
    Technology, 41, 97 (1978)

8. Norman, R.H., and Johnson, P.S., "Processability Testing", Rubber
    Chem. Technol., 54, 493 (1981)

9. Palmgren, H., "Processing Conditions in the Batch-Operated Internal
    Mixer", Rubber Review 1975, Rubber Chem. Technol. 48,
    462 (1975)

10. Wiedmann, W.M., and Schmid, H.M., "Optimization of Rubber Mixing in
    Internal Mixers:, Rubber Chem. Technol. 55, 363 (1983)

WORK ASSIGNMENT NO. 3

CHAPTER 3. MIXING EQUIPMENT AND THE MIXING PROCESS

INSTRUCTIONS: Read each question carefully, select one, and only one, appropriate answer to complete each statement.

1. The major components of an internal mixer are

___(a) chute, rolls, and mill-pan
___(b) hopper, ram, rotors, chamber, and door
___(c) pelletizer, screw, chamber, and door
___(d) screw, barrel, head, rolls

2. One of the prerequisites for getting the best possible product from the mixing process is

___(a) proper storage and handling of elastomers and rubber chemicals
___(b) fast discharge of batch from the mixer
___(c) automatic loading of ingredients into the mixer
___(d) none of above

3. Several important processes occur simultaneously during mixing. They are

___(a) squeezing, coating, and moving
___(b) homogenization, laminar flow, and dispersion
___(c) moving, heating, and cooling
___(d) none of above

4. From the point of view of the ingredients, the following physical changes occur during a mixing cycle

___(a) incorporation, dispersion, distribution and plasticization
___(b) entering, contacting, flowing, and dumping
___(c) contacting, squeezing, and moving
___(d) none of above

5. The mixing method consisting of adding the elastomers first, the dry ingredients, then the liquid ingredients after the dry materials are well dispersed in the elastomer is known as

___(a) the conventional method
___(b) the rapid oil addition method
___(c) the upside-down method
___(d) none of above

6. The upside-down mixing method is efficient and effective for those compounds

___(a) containing a large volume of liquid plasticizers and large particle size fillers
___(b) containing low structure, small particle size carbon black
___(c) containing high loading of both soft mineral filler and oil, together with an elastomer of high Mooney viscosity
___(d) none of above

7. The maximum effect on masticating crude natural rubber for viscosity reduction is obtained

___(a) either at temperature below 55°C (130°F) or at temperature above 130°C(270°F)
___(b) at temperature between 90 and 105°C (190 to 220°F)
___(c) only at temperature above 130°C (270°F)
___(d) none of above

8. A major reason for two-pass mixing is

    ___(a) to prevent scorch, or premature vulcanization of a rubber compound
    ___(b) to increase Mooney viscosity of a rubber compound
    ___(c) to improve physical and chemical properties of the end product
    ___(d) none of above

9. In order to keep the ingredients in the mixing area in its chamber and in-
    crease the shear stress for dispersive mixing, an internal mixer must pro-
    vide

    ___(a) adequate ram pressure
    ___(b) high rotor speed
    ___(c) effective temperature control
    ___(d) a large feed hopper and a small discharge door

10. A major disadvantage of mill mixing is

    ___(a) it is not only time-consuming, but also too dependent upon the skill
        of the operator
    ___(b) it is difficult to prevent rapid rise of stock temperature
    ___(c) it provides no shearing action
    ___(d) none of above

11. A common, and often overlooked, cause of poor dispersion and scorchiness is

    ___(a) specific gravity of the stock too low
    ___(b) batch size too large
    ___(c) dump temperature too low
    ___(d) tensile strength of the stock too high

12. Residual compound sticking to rotor, dump door, hopper and ram has been a
    common cause of contamination. Another cause of same is

    ___(a) insufficient breakdown of elastomers
    ___(b) adding viscous ingredient into mixer at temperature below its pour point
    ___(c) use of resins with excessively high melting point
    ___(d) residual compound sticking to dump chute, mill pan and guides

13. Batch-to-batch variation in mixed compound is seldom caused by

    ___(a) variation in initial loading temperature
    ___(b) variation in flow and/or temperature of cooling water
    ___(c) variation in ram pressure
    ___(d) variation in size of ingredient tote pans

14. One of the basic requirements for good processability at the sheeter mill is

    ___(a) inclusion of a large amount of viscous plasticizers in the compound
        formulation
    ___(b) high loading of tacky fillers to hold the batch together
    ___(c) effective control of mill roll temperatures and speed
    ___(d) leaving the stock on sheeter mill as long as possible for drastic re-
        duction of Mooney viscosity.

15. Fully continuous mixing requires the use of rubber in powder or particulate form. Semi-continuous mixing is the term used to describe a system in which mixed compound from an internal mixer is discharged into an extruder. Semi-continuous and fully continuous mixing systems are most viable in

____(a) mixing operation involving a very large number of compounds
____(b) mixing operation involving the use of numerous different elastomers
____(c) long mixing run of a limited number of compounds
____(d) short mixing run of a large number of compounds containing many ingredients in liquid form

EXTRUSION - EQUIPMENT AND PROCESS

A. James Lambright

Monsanto Company
Akron, Ohio 44314

INTRODUCTION

Extruders have been described as machines which force rubber through a nozzle or die to give a profiled strip of material. They are divided into two types: those in which the pressure required to force the rubber through the die is produced by a ram, and those in which the pressure is produced by a screw. Ram-type extruders are limited to specialized machines such as a Barwell preformer. Screw-type extruders are most widely used in the rubber industry.

Extruders have been used in industry for about 150 years. In 1845 ram extruders were invented to cover wires with gutta percha. In the 1880's, screw extruders were invented and used to process components for pneumatic tires. Other devices of lesser economic importance for polymer melt have also been developed. In the 1880's, Willoughby Smith, an Englishman, used rotating rolls to feed a gear pump for continuous extrusion of gutta percha. Iddon of England used feed-rolls to force rubber into a tube that had a die fixed to the other end. During the 1950's Bryce Maxwell developed a "normal stress pump". In this apparatus melt is fed to a gap between a rotating disc and a stationary member that has a die in the center.

Ram Extruders

Early in the nineteenth century, railroads were expanding their lines and telegraphy was recognized as the best way to communicate between stations. The advent of telegraphy and the need for electrically insulated wires provided the initial stimulus for finding a material with water-resistance properties and developing a device to coat wires with it. A water-proof electrical insulation was essential for the wires in contact with the ground. The need for an insulating material stable in the presence of moisture was recognized as one of the technical problems of the day.

The challenge was met quickly with the application of gutta percha, a new material which Dr. William Montgomerie found in Malay. In Britain, the Gutta Percha Company, set up by Charles Hancock and Henry Bewley, focused on serving the telegraphy industry. In 1845, Henry Bewley and Richard Brooman developed a ram extruder to manufacture gutta percha thread. Referring to Figure 1, a roll of gutta percha was introduced into a cylinder, B, and the piston was forced down by hand. The gutta percha softened at the lower end of the die box, C, (see Figure 2) which was heated by steam in the hollow chambers, F, escapes from the pressure through the orifices, E, in a series of threads.

Brooman's patent seems to be the first recorded description of extruding a thermoplastic material. The process was developed somewhat further in Bewley's patent of the same year in which the extruder was modified for the manufacture of flexible syringes, tubes, hose, etc. The diagram appended to the patent indicates the manner in which it operates (see Figure 3).

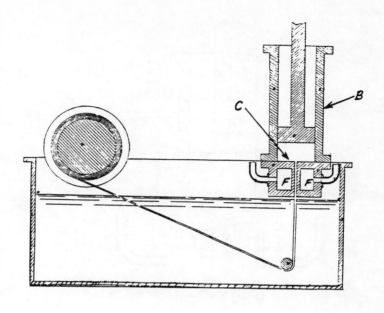

FIGURE 1

SECTION THROUGH BROOMAN'S EXTRUDER

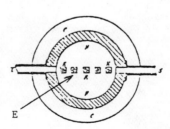

Fig. 2   Sectional plan of Brooman's die box

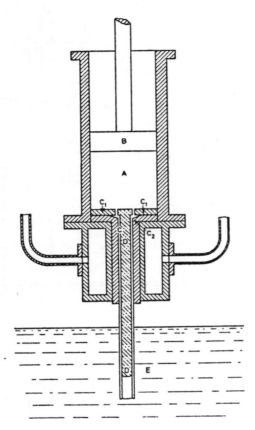

Figure 3

Section of Bewley's Extruder

Bewley's partner, Charles Hancock, adapted the machine for wire covering. He passed the copper conductor through the die box as the gutta percha was forced out, thus covering the conductor with a layer of insulant. The first submarine cable, laid between Dover and Calais in 1851, was covered by this method.

Screw Extruders

The ram extrusion technique was not efficient enough for mass production of cable and tubing. The need for a continuous process rather than the intermittent process of ram extrusion seemed clear. However, it was not until 1887 that Willoughby Smith, an employee of Gutta Percha Co., patented an "apparatus for covering or insulating wire". The invention was on the processing of gutta percha and it provided for a continuous feed from a hopper through hot-feed rolls into a chamber fitted with a gear pump. The Smith machine was used for gutta percha cabling until the 1950's when the naturally produced insulant was completely replaced by polyethylene.

The screw extruder was developed in the 1870's and 1880's. Its inventor is unclear. Priority has been claimed by William Kiel, John Prior and John Royle in the United States, and by Mathew Gray, A. G. DeWolfe and Francis Shaw in England. Evidence also suggests this invention was anticipated in Germany. The Phoenix Gummiwerke has published a drawing of a screw dated September 18, 1873. V.M. Hovey, in a paper on the history of extrusion equipment, has adduced strong circumstantial evidence supporting the contention that Mr. A. G. DeWolfe was insulating wire by means of a screw extruder in possibly 1866.

The screw extruder is important because it continuously converts feed to a finished form, such as a rod, tube, or profile. Feed can be in the form of strip or granules. The apparatus doing the conversion is an Archimedian screw which fits inside a barrel. Along the barrel are a number of collars that form heating/cooling zones. Feed material is forced forward by the rotating screw. As it moves forward, the feed is softened by the frictional heat developed through the shearing action of the screw, supplemented by the heat conducted from the barrel wall. By the time the feed reaches the end of the screw, it is in a viscous state that can be forced through an orifice or die and formed into the desired shape.

A considerable source of power must be made available to drive the material forward and to develop the heat needed. Thus, for a modern 4-1/2" cold feed extruder, a motor of about 150 horsepower is required.

The development and growth of the screw extruder is linked with the patent of Mathew Gray in 1879. Gray used a pair of heated horizontal rolls as part of the feed system and claimed that "a uniform pressure of the compound against the die will be maintained". This feature remains an important consideration in the production of good quality extrudate.

John Royle of Paterson, N. J., built the first extruder in North America in 1880. In Germany, the first screw extruders were imported from England and the United States. Paul Troester Maschinenfabrick of Hanover quoted the dimensions of their first machine in feet and inches.

By the early years of the 20th century, a variety of hot feed screw extruders were already in use. Feed stock was warmed using a two-roll mill and a strip was fed to the screw extruder. In the mid-30's, extensive work on the extrusion of polyvinyl chloride (PVC) led to the development of cold feed rubber extruders. The shift from the use of hot compound occurred because PVC could not be processed using the hot strip feed method. Unlike rubber, PVC could not be processed to arrive at the extruder at a constant temperature. Variation in temperature of the PVC feed strip led to inconsistency in behavior inside the barrel, unsteady pressure at the die, and loss of control on product uniformity.

Paul Troester took the first systematic approach to plastic extrusion in the 1930's. Features such as increases in length to diameter (L/D) ratio of the barrel and screw, electrically heated barrels and dies, building the barrel and screw from Nitralloy, and pellet form for feed were studied in detail during this period.

There have been many more developments and refinements in the design and operation of extruders during the past three decades. Modern extruders are capable of producing good quality extrudates at high speed with a large variety of material. Today, extrusion is a very important basic process in the manufacture of rubber products.

MAJOR COMPONENTS OF SCREW EXTRUDER

In its simplest form a screw extruder consists of three components: (1) a feed screw operating within a barrel, (2) a head, and (3) a die or a die plate. An electric motor turns the screw through a reduction gear. Rubber compound enters at the feed hopper, is pushed along the barrel where it builds up pressure and temperature, and exits at the die where it takes the shape of the die.

Feed Screw and Barrel

A feed hopper is provided to receive the rubber compound and guide it down into the "feed flights" of the screw. The compound may be supplied hot, in the form of intermittent or continuous strip, or it may be supplied cold in the form of a strip or pellet.

The barrel along the "feed flights" may be undercut to assist the feed. A driven feed-roll positioned parallel to the screw may be provided to pull feed into the screw (see Figures 4 & 5). In some cases, the rubber compound is supplied as the discharge from an internal mixer in which case a power operated ram is used to push the compound into the screw flights.

If the feed volume is gradually increased, a point will be reached at which the extruder will choke and feed will regurgitate or "back-up" into the feed hopper. There is an upper limit to the rate of feed for a particular screw speed, and usually the best conditions for extrusion are obtained when compound is fed at about 90% of the amount to choke the machine. The rate of feed must be determined for each compound and screw speed.

The screw should preferably have a lower volume in the flights at the discharge end. This is achieved by (1) a reduction in pitch of the screw, (2) a reduction in the depth of the base of the screw, (3) a reduction in overall diameter of the screw and barrel, or (4) an increase in the number of starts in the screw. Methods (2) and (4) are the most economical and commonly used. The screw must be full at the discharge end to avoid changes in swell of the extrudate

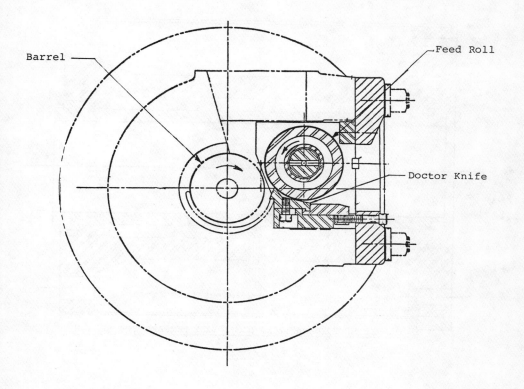

Barrel

Feed Roll

Doctor Knife

EXTRUDER FEED-ROLL

Figure No. 4

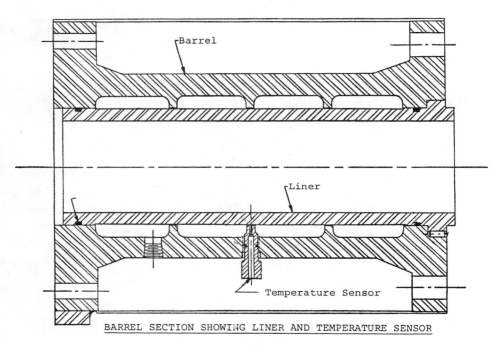

BARREL SECTION SHOWING LINER AND TEMPERATURE SENSOR

Figure No. 5

and to maintain uniform output.

A vacuum device can be fitted in the barrel to remove gases or other volatile matter from the compound. Vacuum extruders are used to make articles for low pressure vulcanization processes, such as open steam, hot air, molten salt and fluidized bed. The removal of entrapped air and volatile matter reduces chances of porosity developing during vulcanization.

Head

The purpose of the head is to equalize the pressure, to transport compound to the die, and to hold the screen pack, pressure and temperature sensors, and spider if used (see Figure 6). Rubber compound must move smoothly to the die, and ideally at equal pressures and speed. Any points where compound does not move are known as "dead spots". Compound can cure in these "dead spot" areas then break away to give bits or "nibs" of scorched compound in the extrudate. The head's design must satisfy the following requirements:

1. The head must alter the cross section of flow giving it a shape corresponding to the cross section of the extruded product.

2. Configuration of the annular gap in the extruder head which shapes the compound must take account of the alteration in shape to which the compound is subjected as a result of high elastic recovery

3. Geometrical dimensions of the annular gap and the angle of discharge must insure maximum output without any "elastic turbulence".

4. Configuration of the channels in the extruder head through which the compound flows must be such that there is no risk of forming zones of stagnation.

5. The extruder head must create sufficient resistance to develop, at the delivery end of the screw, a back pressure necessary for effective mixing and homogenization of the compound.

Die

The die forms the compound into the desired shape. Rubber compounds exhibit significant die swell as they exit the die. This die swell makes die design semi-empirical. For each compound the amount of die swell is dependent upon the shear rate and viscosity of the compound. Die swell should be determined at production speed to duplicate shear rate and viscosity. Measurements made with a capillary rheometer can be used to predict die swell at various shear rates.

BASIC PRINCIPLES OF EXTRUSION

The rubber extruder is a single screw machine where the screw rotates in a tightly fitted barrel thereby transmitting mechanical energy into the rubber compound. As the temperature of the rubber increases, the plasticity is lowered to such a level that the rubber can be shaped by passing through a die located at the end of the barrel. The flights on the screw and the inner surface of the barrel form a conduit or flow channel. Figure 7 shows the geometry of the flow channel and descriptive symbols for the screw and barrel. These symbols are used throughout this chapter.

76

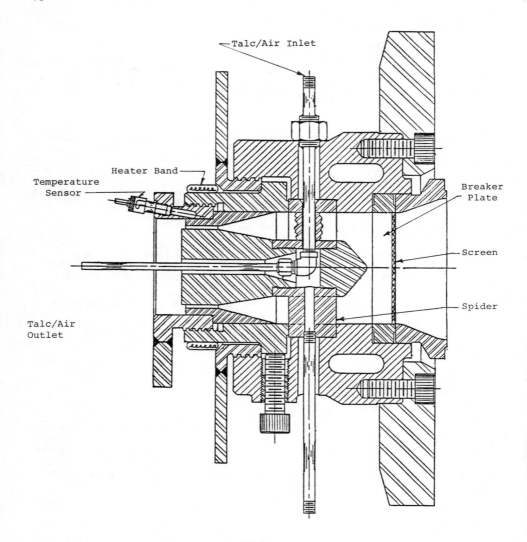

EXTRUDER HEAD WITH TUBE DIE

Figure No. 6

FIG. 7   DESCRIPTIVE SYMBOLS FOR AN

EXTRUDER FLOW CHANNEL

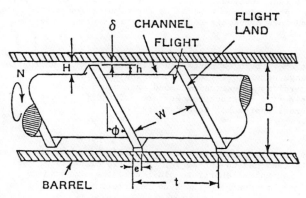

D = INSIDE BARREL DIAMETER
h = FLIGHT DEPTH
H = RADIAL DISTANCE FROM THE SCREW
     ROOT TO THE BARREL SURFACE
W = CHANNEL WIDTH
Ø = NOMINAL LEAD ANGLE (OR HELIX ANGLE)
e = FLIGHT THICKNESS IN THE SCREW, AXIAL WIDTH OF FLIGHT LANDS
δ = RADIAL CLEARANCE BETWEEN THE FLIGHT LAND OF THE
     PRESUMED-CENTER SCREW AND BARREL
N = ROTATIONAL SPEED OF THE SCREW, REV./SEC.
t = AXIAL LEAD LENGTH OF SCREW FLIGHT OR PITCH
n = NUMBER OF FLIGHTS
μ = AVERAGE VISCOSITY
L = EFFECTIVE LENGTH OF SCREW CONSIDERED

The material movement toward the discharge end of the open-end extruder is a function of the frictional forces in the flow channel due to rotation of the screw in the stationary barrel. In order for the material to move in the axial direction, the frictional force at the barrel must be greater than the sum of the flight and channel frictional forces. If the coefficient of friction between the material and screw is much larger than the coefficient of friction between the material and barrel, the material will turn with the screw, within the stationary barrel, and the axial velocity of the elastomeric plug would be zero. In reality, the elastomeric plug moves partially in the circumferential direction and partially in the axial direction.

A simple extruder screw has three distinct sections, namely the feed section, the transition or metering section, and the compression section. A screw for a non-vented cold feed extruder is shown in Figure 9. Each screw section performs a distinct function. The feed section transports material from the hopper. The transition section heats and mixes the material. The compression section homogenizes and builds up pressure necessary to force material through the die.

EXTRUDER DESIGNS

A well designed extruder for high performance is capable of handling rubber compounds with a wide range of viscosity and processing characteristics, achieving good homogeneity regardless of extrusion speed, and providing high output rate without causing rapid rise in stock temperature. The differences in extruder design reflect different approaches toward these goals.

Cold Feed Extruder

As the name implies, a cold feed extruder is generally fed rubber compound at room temperature. The feed can be in the form of strip or pellets. The screw must transmit sufficient mechanical energy to plasticize the compound to near minimum viscosity (μ) as well as to overcome the head restriction (P).

The cold feed extruder receives cold feed at near maximum viscosity and reduces the viscosity to the equivalent of hot feed within a 30-120 second time frame. Figure 8 shows a cold feed non-vented extruder.

Screws used in cold feed extruders require special considerations in design. To accomplish the extra mastication necessary, the flight depth (h) must be small and the screw length (L) must be long. A large drive motor and gear box are required to supply and transmit the mechanical energy to the screw. The shallower flight depth (h), the higher starting viscosity (μ) of the compound, and the longer screw (L) have a combined effect that makes the cold feed extruder less sensitive to flow variations with changes in head pressure (P). Plastication is accomplished in the transition section. Reduction in the flight depth (h), high compression ratios, an increase in the number of starts, are the variables used to achieve high shear and high output. Figure 9 shows a typical screw for non-vented cold feed extruders.

Hot Feed Extruder

In general, an extruder which is fed rubber compound at a temperature above ambient, may be considered to be a hot feed extruder (see Figure 10). Many of them are still being used today. A hot feed extruder receives rubber compound at near minimum viscosity (μ), and must overcome the head restriction (P), with a minimum temperature rise and hold time. This is necessary because the compound has already been at an elevated temperature for a period of time during milling.

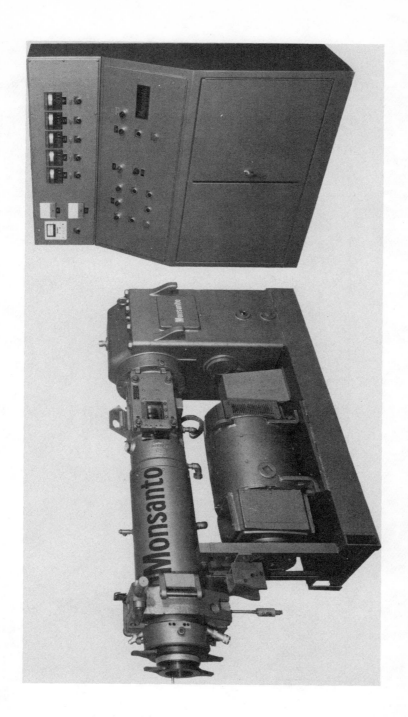

Fig. 8   Cold feed non-vented extruder.   (Courtesy of Monsanto Company)

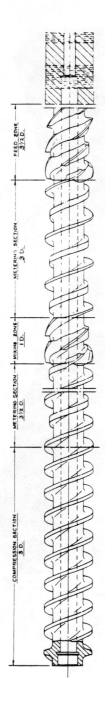

80

SCREW FOR NON-VENTED COLD FEED EXTRUDER

<u>Figure No. 9</u>

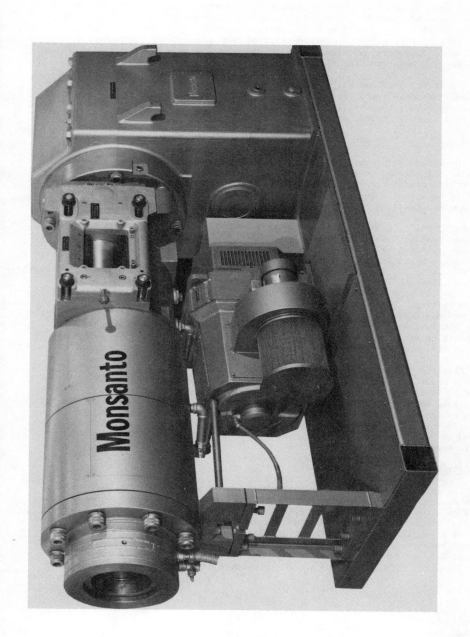

Fig. 10   Hot feed extruder.   (Courtesy of Monsanto Co.)

A major goal in hot feed extruder design is to minimize the temperature rise of the compound through the extruder. The flight depth (h) of the feed screw must be fairly high to hold down the energy imparted to the compound and to keep its temperature low. Unfortunately, as head pressure (P) increases output decreases. Therefore, hot feed machines are most suitable only for applications requiring low head pressure (P).

The modern hot feed extruder is in the range of 5:1 to 8:1 ^{L}/D. 5:1 for the lower pressure operations and 8:1 for the higher pressure operations. The longer the screw, the easier it is to achieve a balance of pressure flow. Figure 11 shows a typical screw for hot feed extruder.

Vented Cold Feed Extruder

The vented or vacuum cold feed extruder was developed to expel unwanted gases from the rubber compound in order to cure extrudates satisfactorily at atmospheric pressure. The screw in a vented extruder has two distinct zones. The first zone has three sections - feed, transition, and metering. The second zone has two sections - transition and metering. A dam separates the two sections.

As shown in Figure 12 each of these sections performs a distinct function. The feed section moves material from the hopper or feed box into the barrel. Heating and fluxing take place in the transition section. Homogenizing and build-up of pressure occur in the metering section. In the dam section, small axial grooves cut in the dam surface serve as dies. A vacuum pump connected to a port located below the exit side of the dam maintains a low pressure zone. Material exits the dam zone in the form of many thin strands and enters the second transition section. The combination of thin strands, high temperature, and low pressure are conducive to the release and escape of trapped gases. Escape of trapped gases and further heating and fluxing occurs in the second transition section. Homogenizing and buildup of pressure necessary to force material through a die is done in the second metering section.

Plugging of the vent port with compound occurs when head pressure rises to a level where the first zone pumps at a higher rate than the second zone. Temperature profiling can be of some assistance to reduce the pumping rate in the first zone and increase the pumping rate in the second zone. Increasing the ^{L}/D ratio in the second zone is a very effective way to increase the pumping rate in the second zone. A combination of 8:1 ^{L}/D in the first zone and 12:1 ^{L}/D in the second zone is a good balance for extrusion of most compounds. Figure 13 shows a cold feed vented extruder.

Pin Extruder

The pin extruder represents the latest innovation in extrusion machinery. Screw designers have determined that rotating laminar planes are generated around the flow channel of a simple conveying screw and there is little exchange of material between the layers. The warm layers of material that contact the screw and barrel surfaces remain stratified. The cold rubber at the core is slow to warm-up because it is insulated from the warm outer layer due to the low thermal conductivity of rubber. This effect is present along the whole length of the screw, causing difficulties in attaining optimum homogenization of the material.

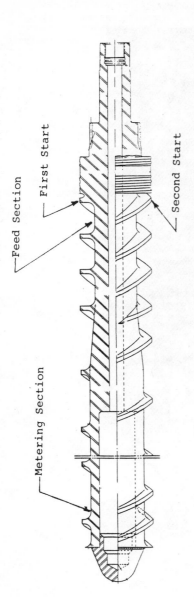

Feed Section

First Start

Second Start

Metering Section

Fig. 11   Typical screw for hot feed extruder

Fig. 12   Screw for vented cold feed extruder

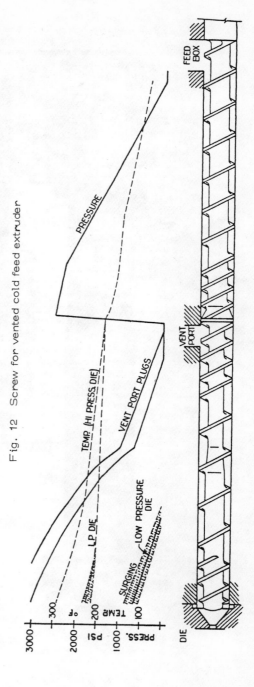

Fig. 13   Cold feed vented extruder.   (Courtesy of Monsanto Company)

The uneven temperature profile is manifested in the cross section of the extrudate as corrugated surfaces as well as unacceptable dimensional variation. This undesirable effect grows as the flight depth, pitch angle, and diameter of a conventional screw with constant pitch and root diameter increases. The larger the depth of the screw channel the more difficult it becomes to uniformly homogenize the rubber compound through friction from the barrel and screw surfaces (see Fig. 14 and 15). An extension of the L/D ratio with screw diameters greater than 4-1/2" improves extrudate quality but rarely does it increase output.

Pins mounted in the barrel provide an effective way to interrupt or split the laminar planes and improve homogenization wtihout using high shear rates. Slipping on the barrel wall is also prevented by the pins. Eight to twelve pins are arranged radially in 6 to 10 rows (see Figure 16). The first pin row is located near the feed inlet where the screw filling sequence has been completed. These pins hold the cold rubber compound radially so that the conveying lands convey the compound axially. A mixing zone such as shown in Figure 17 is located immediately downstream of the last row of pins. This mixing zone further homogenizes the compound.

TEMPERATURE CONTROL

Extruders having metal surfaces at uncontrolled temperatures will do an uncontrolled amount of work on the rubber compound. High stock temperatures, poor dispersion, and wide viscosity variations are probable problems resulting from the absence of control over the metal surface temperature.

The transfer of heat from one material to another can be described as a function of the temperature differences, the thickness, the amount of surface area, and the thermal conductivity of the material involved. The relative thermal conductivity of steel is about 200 times that of rubber.

To remove frictional heat through the screw and barrel it is necessary to transfer the heat from the rubber to the steel. To achieve a good flow of heat, new surfaces of the rubber must be exposed to the metal surfaces. This condition is called turbulent flow. To achieve turbulence in the rubber, it is necessary for the rubber to grip the metal surfaces, enabling shear to take place. If rubber slides on the steel surface, more frictional heat is generated at the surfaces of heat transfer.

The grip of the rubber depends on the roughness of the surface, the lubrication of the surfaces and the temperature of the rubber and metal. The best temperature is the lowest possible temperature which will give a sufficiently high coefficient of friction.

Both hot feed and cold feed extruders are designed to optimize temperature control. In general, cold feed extruders require more sophisticated temperature control systems. The range of temperatures that may be individually controlled by the temperature control system at different parts of the extruder is called the temperature profile.

In the cold feed extruder, the zones separately controlled are usually the die, head, one or more barrel zones, feed zone, and the screw. In the vented extruders there is usually an additional zone of control, the vacuum zone.

Fig. 14   Cross section of a normal conveying screw channel

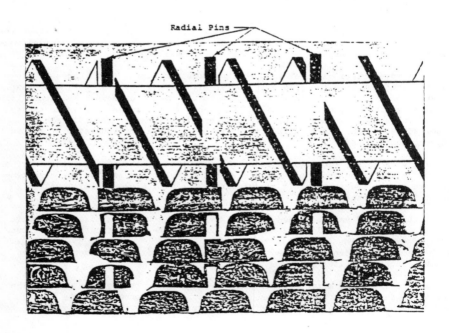

Fig. 15   Cross sections over 3 pin rows of a QSM screw channel

Figure 16

Cross Sections of Pins Showing
Radial And Axial Arrangements

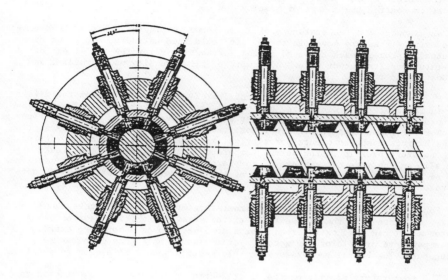

Figure 17

Cross Section Showing Pins and Mixing Zone

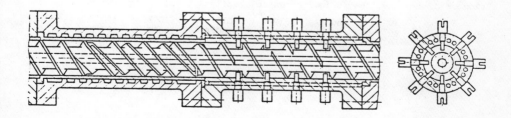

The frictional heat introduced by the screw is usually so great that a large proportion of the energy put in by the motor must be removed by cooling the screw and barrel. Zone temperatures are not the same as the temperature of the rubber compound passing through that particular zone. This is due to the comparatively small amount of surface area, relative to volume, exposed in each zone and to the elapsed time the material takes to pass through the zone.

Temperature control is accomplished by a temperature control system that uses thermocouples to sense the temperature and an electronic temperature controller to control the amount of heating and cooling.

An example of a temperature profile is shown in Figure 18 for an EPDM compound using a standard screw in the 3.5 in. cold feed extruder. It is necessary to actually process each compound in the extruder to determine the effect of temperature on its output rate, uniformity of flow, quality of extrudate, and extrudate temperature.

Figure 19 shows two temperature profiles, T_1 and T_2. Note that the difference in temperature between screw and barrel is greater for profile T_1. Temperature profile T_1 gave an excellent output rate. However, uneven extrudate flow was observed indicating insufficient mastication. Inspection of a cross section of the extrudate showed minute porosity and spiralling outward from the center. In temperature profile T_2 the barrel temperatures are raised 10°F to create more slip on the internal surface of the barrel. The results were more mastication of the stock, improved uniformity of the extrudate and a reduction in output rate.

For cold feed vented extruders, temperature profiling techniques should be applied separately to the two sections of the screw; the first section being treated as a cold feed extruder and the second section as a hot feed extruder. The temperature profile of the second section should be set to give maximum throughput. The barrel temperature in this section should be as low as possible.

The temperature profile of the first section should be set to maintain an output rate that does not cause regurgitation or flooding in the vacuum port. Increasing the barrel temperature will increase mastication and reduce throughput.

The vacuum zone is treated like the die. The temperature should be high (200–250°F) to create slip on the barrel surface. For the most complete removal of volatiles one should aim to achieve the maximum surface area exposure in the evacuated area past the dam.

Screw temperature is usually set higher than the barrel temperature. It has a strong effect on extrudate temperature. Increasing the screw temperature does not always raise the extrudate temperature. For many compounds the extrudate temperature decreases when the screw temperature is raised.

In the process of establishing proper temperature profile for optimum extrusion of a compound, the following control settings should be tried:

| Screw | 90°F | 150°F | 210°F | 210°F | 210°F | 150°F | 90°F |
| Barrel | 90°F | 90°F | 90°F | 150°F | 190°F | 190°F | 190°F |

Fig. 18

TEMPERATURE PROFILING

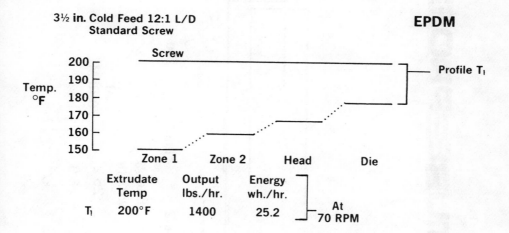

3½ in. Cold Feed 12:1 L/D
Standard Screw

EPDM

	Extrudate Temp	Output lbs./hr.	Energy wh./hr.	
T_1	200°F	1400	25.2	At 70 RPM

Fig. 19

TEMPERATURE PROFILING

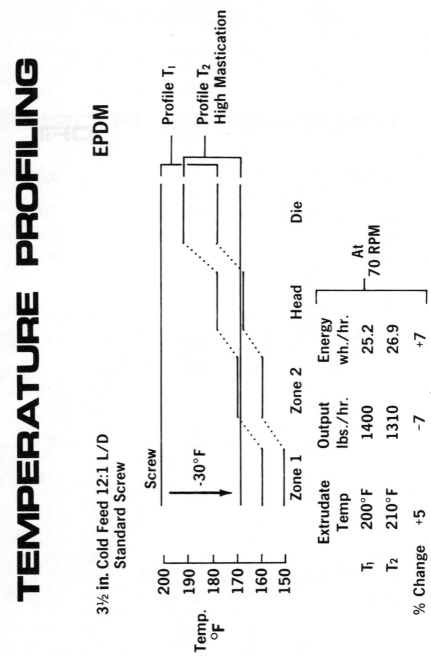

EPDM

3½ in. Cold Feed 12:1 L/D
Standard Screw

Screw

-30°F

	Extrudate Temp	Output lbs./hr.	Energy wh./hr.
T_1	200°F	1400	25.2
T_2	210°F	1310	26.9
% Change	+5	-7	+7

At 70 RPM

Zone 1 Zone 2 Head Die

Temp. °F
200
190
180
170
160
150

Profile T_1

Profile T_2
High Mastication

Output rate, extrudate temperature, and extrudate quality should be determined for each setting. Only after this study has been completed can the optimum temperature profile be determined.

Temperature control of the feed section may improve uniformity of the output rate. Some compounds tend to ball in the feed zone and causes starving at the feed port. A temperature setting between 110 and 140°F works well with most compounds. Feeding of stiff compounds is usually improved when the temperature is controlled at 120-140°F.

EFFECT OF EXTRUSION PROCESS

Output rate, extrudate temperature, Mooney viscosity, and scorch time are affected by the extrusion process. Maximum output is limited by the maximum permissible heat history of the compound (scorch time). The effects of extrusion processing on an SBR compound with a moderate Mooney viscosity (35 Mooney units at 250°F) is shown in Fig. 20.

Mooney viscosity of the extrudate dropped from 35 to 33 Mooney units (MU) due to the additional mastication at the extruder. However, the Mooney viscosity changed very little as screw speed increased from 20 to 70 rpm. Processing safety as measured by Mooney scorch, (t_5) at 250°F, is reduced only slightly.

At low screw speeds, output rate is nearly directly proportional to screw speed (rpm) for most compounds. As the screw speed increases toward the high end, the output rate decreases for most compounds. Output rate is normally given in terms of pounds per hour or pounds per rpm.

Extrudate temperature rises as screw speed increases. The actual temperature rise is affected by screw design, head pressure, and the properties of the compound being processed. Based on studies, the output rate for the non-vented extruder is about double that for the vented extruder. The rise of extrudate temperature is higher at the vented extruder.

Table I shows a comparison of output rates for three types of extruders. The data was obtained from extrusion of a rubber compound possessing good processing characteristics at equal screw speed (rpm).

COMMON EXTRUSION PROBLEMS

Complex manufacturing processes are seldom trouble-free. Extrusion is no exception. Among the common processing problems are those relating to output rate, dimensional stability, heat generation, and rough extrudate.

Output Rate

For a given size of extruder the factors having the greatest effect on output rate are screw design, temperature profile, head pressure, and compound formulation. Output can vary by a factor of two, depending upon screw design. High mastication screws give the lowest output. Temperature profile can affect output by as much as 20% or more. A temperature profile study should be made for each compound to establish the optimum temperature profile. Prior to making a temperature profile study, each zone of the temperature control system should be checked to assure that all components are functioning properly. Output will decrease as head pressure increases. A pressure sensor should be located in the head to monitor pressure. Die's should be designed to develop minimum head pressure. Output is very dependent upon the properties of the compound being processed. A well

Fig. 20   Effect of Extrusion Process
on Mooney Viscosity and Scorch Time

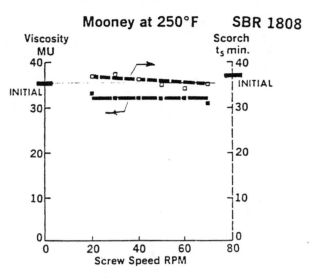

TABLE I

EXTRUDER
OUTPUT COMPARISON

Maximum output lbs./hr. at equal rpm.

Extruder Screw Diameter		RPM.	Hot Feed	Cold Feed	Cold Feed Vacuum
in.	**mm.**				
2.5	60	95	410	330	200
3.5	90	70	900	1100	530
4.5	120	59	1910	1800	990
6.0	150	51	2990	3080	1540
8.0	200	42	4620	5060	2750

FOR EASY-TO-PROCESS COMPOUNDS.

designed compound can improve output 10% or more. Scorch time of the compound must be sufficient to permit extrusion at maximum screw speed.

Dimensional Stability

Dimensional stability of the extrudates is dependent upon many factors. A few are discussed below:

(1) Take-Away - The strength of the rubber extrudate is relatively low as it exits the extruder. Take-away equipment that includes take-off conveyors, water baths, take-up reels, etc. must be properly designed. Drive motors should be variable-speed with fine speed adjustment. Stress applied to the extrudate must be constant. Cooling should be sufficient to lower the temperature of the extru-date and allow it to develop normal "green strength".

(2) Screw Speed Control - Output is nearly directly proportional to screw speed. If screw speed fluctuates or drifts, the dimensions of the extrudate will change because output is not constant. Speed of the main drive motor should vary less than 1%. D.C. drive systems should be set up to give this level of speed control. Electric power supplied to the drive motor should be free of surges. A speed meter should be mounted on the control panel to monitor speed accuracy. Digital meters are preferred over analog to reduce reader's judgement errors. Since surges may not be evident with meters, installation of speed recorders is very desirable.

(3) Feed - Output will change if feed to the extruder fluctuates. A uniform feed strip coupled with a power driven feed-roll and temperature control on the feed zone enhance the uniformity of output. A slightly flooded feed hopper is better than a starved feed hopper. The size and number of feed strips should be adjusted to maintain a small ball in the feed throat.

(4) Temperature Control - Output will fluctuate if the control system permits temperature variations in the controlled zones. Each temperature controller should be tuned to maintain a temperature uniformity of $\pm 1°F$.

The operator should check temperatures periodically because solenoid and pumps do fail at times.

(5) Compound - Output rate and die swell are very dependent upon compound design and compound uniformity. If output or die swell changes right after starting a new skid of feed stock, a change in compound or batch-to-batch uniformity is suspect. Mooney scorch should be determined for both the feed stock and the extrudate.

Heat Generation

Temperature build-up in the extrudate can result in scorch. It is affected by extrusion speed, type of screw, head pressure, and compound formulation. The compounder and the engineer must work together to solve this problem. Reducing screw speed, adjusting temperature profile, using a less-mastication screw, and reducing restriction at the die are directions the engineer can take. Modifying the compound to reduce viscosity, adding prevulcanization inhibitors, and changing the cure system are alternatives the compounder can pursue.

Rough Extrudate

Surface roughness of the extrudate not caused by scorchy compound is either due to air entrapment or insufficient mastication. Both causes are related to screw design and screw speed. Adjusting the temperature profile to increase mastication, changing to a screw design for more mastication and additional breakdown of the compound in the mixer are solutions to this problem. In some cases polishing the inner surface of the die or increasing the length of the die land will reduce surface roughness.

SUMMARY

The development of extrusion equipment is a continuing process. During the past 150 years this development has brought us from labor intensive ram extruders to modern self-feeding cold feed extruders. In recent years the emphasis of development has been directed toward screw designs for self-feeding, more effective mixing and higher output rates. In the years ahead we will see further development of cross-flow mixing, co-extrusion, and incorporation of microprocessors to control the extrusion process.

Extrusion is another primary operation in the manufacturing process for rubber products. It is an important part of rubber technology. For those who desire further reading on the subject, a list of literature references is provided.

GENERAL REFERENCES

1. Blow, C.M. ed., "Rubber Technology and Manufacture", Butterworth & Co., London, England (1971)

2. Boguslawski, J.J., "Basic Fundamentals of Extrusion and Mixing Theory", Rubber Chem. Technol., $\underline{45}$, 1421 (1972)

3. Christy, R.L., "The Extruder – Compound Interface", Rubber World, $\underline{184(6)}$, 38 (1981)

4. Christy, R.L., "Hot vs. Cold Feed Extrusion", Rubber World, (i) $\underline{180(4)}$, 100, (ii) $\underline{180(6)}$, 30 (1979)

5. Ellwood, H., "Temperature Control", European Rubber Journal, Feb. 1977

6. Harms, E.G., "Pin-type Cold Feed Extruder: Capability in Rubber Processing", Elastomerics, $\underline{109(6)}$, 33 (1977)

7. Johnson, P.S., "Developments in Extrusion Science and Technology", Rubber Chem. Technol., $\underline{56}$, 575 (1983)

8. Kaufman, M., "The Birth of the Plastics Extruder", Plastics and Polymers, June 1969, England

9. Lambright, A.J., "New Techniques in Extrusion Technology", Akron Rubber Group Meeting, Jan. 1979

10. Proceedings of Educational Symposium No. 8, "Extrusion of Elastomers", ACS Rubber Division Meeting, May 1982

11. Smith, D.H. and Christy, R.L., "Modern Extrusion Equipment", Rubber Chem. Technol. $\underline{45}$, 1434 (1972)

12. Tadmor, Z. AND Goges, C.G., "Principles of Polymer Processing", Wiley-Interscience, New York (1979)

13. Tadmor, Z. and Klein, I., "Engineering Principles of Plasticating Extrusion", Van Nostrand Reinhold Co., New York (1970)

14. Technical Literature – QSM Cold Feed Extruder with Cross Flow Mixing Barrel – Paul Troester Maschinenfabrik, Hannover, Germany, Feb 1979

WORK ASSIGNMENT NO. 4

CHAPTER 4. EXTRUSION - EQUIPMENT AND PROCESS

INSTRUCTIONS: Read each question carefully, select one, and only one, appropriate answer to complete each statement.

1. Extruders are machines which

____(a) force rubber through a nozzle or die to give a profiled strip of material
____(b) force rubber through the clearance between two parallel rolls rotating in opposite directions
____(c) shear rubber between two rotors revolving in opposite directions at slightly different speeds
____(d) none of above

2. The major advantage of a screw extruder over a ram extruder is that

____(a) it was invented earlier and its technology was perfected and well-known
____(b) it is a continuous process instead of an intermittent process
____(c) it develops no frictional heat through the shearing action of the rotary screw
____(d) none of above

3. The basic form of a screw extruder consists of

____(a) hopper, ram, rotors, chamber, and door
____(b) feed hopper, screw, barrel, head, and die
____(c) cylinder, piston, chamber, and die
____(d) none of above

4. In order to avoid variation in die swell and to maintain uniform output in extrusion

____(a) rubber compound should be fed at about 50% of the amount to choke the extruder
____(b) the barrel of the extruder must be fully filled with rubber compound at the discharge end
____(c) rubber compound must move at an accelerating speed from the feeding hopper toward the head and die
____(d) none of above

5. The amount of die swell in extrusion is dependent upon

____(a) the shear rate of the extruder and the viscosity of the compound
____(b) the specific gravity of the compound
____(c) the tensile strength and elongation of the compound
____(d) none of above

6. Because it receives feed stock with near minimum viscosity at an elevated temperature, a hot-feed extruder

____(a) must minimize the temperature rise and the hold time for the stock to avoid scorch
____(b) must raise head pressure to increase output
____(c) must have high screw speed to avoid excessive frictional heat
____(d) none of above

7. Plugging of the vent port with rubber compound will occur in a vented cold-feed extruder if

____(a) stock feeding is too slow and insufficient ("starving")
____(b) head pressure is too high
____(c) screw speed is too fast
____(d) none of above

8. In a pin extruder, the pins mounted in the barrel provide an effective way to

____(a) heat the stock inside the barrel
____(b) improve homogenization of stock in the barrel
____(c) increase head pressure
____(d) none of above

9. The temperature profile in extrusion is

____(a) the range of temperatures individually controlled by a control system at different parts of an extruder
____(b) the difference in temperature between the feed stock and the extrudate
____(c) the difference in temperature between the extruder head and the extrudate
____(d) none of above

10. The optimum temperature profile should be determined by the following factors

____(a) feed stock temperature, specific gravity, and color
____(b) feed stock temperature and extrudate temperature
____(c) extrudate temperature, extrudate quality, and output rate
____(d) none of above

11. The output rate of an extruder is not greatly affected by

____(a) the Mooney scorch and Mooney viscosity of the compound
____(b) the head pressure
____(c) the resilience and tensile strength of the compound ✓
____(d) the screw design

12. In a cold-feed extruder, the extrudate temperature increases as

____(a) the Mooney viscosity of the compound decreases
____(b) the screw temperature increases
____(c) the screw speed increases
____(d) none of above

13. The dimensional stability of the extrudate is seldom affected by

___(a) stress applied to it by take-away equipment
___(b) cooling efficiency of take-away equipment
___(c) fluctuation of stock feeding and screw speed
___(d) the compound's resistance to compression set

14. Scorching of extrudate usually cannot be avoided by changing

___(a) stock-feeding speed
___(b) screw speed
___(c) head pressure
___(d) temperature profile

15. Surface roughness of the extrudate is not likely to be caused by

___(a) air entrapment or insufficient mastication
___(b) high screw speed
___(c) improper temperature profile
___(d) insufficient cooling at take-away equipment

CHAPTER 5

CALENDERING - EQUIPMENT AND PROCESS

William A. Allee

Intercole Bolling Corporation
Cleveland, Ohio 44127

INTRODUCTION

The first patent for a calender was issued to Thomas Hancock in 1825 and was used to manufacture rubberized cloth. Later in 1836, Edwin Chaffee designed and built a calender in Roxbury, Massachusetts that weighed 30 tons and cost $30,000. This so-called "Chaffee's Monster" was eventually acquired by Charles Goodyear who transferred it to the Naugatuck India Rubber Company. Calenders are generally very durable. Many calenders in operation today are nearly 100 years old.

According to one dictionary, the definition of the verb "calender" is "to press (as cloth or paper) between rollers or plates so as to make smooth or to thin into sheets". Therefore, in rubber terminology a calender is a machine which continuously produces sheet goods in a variety of widths, thicknesses and profiles from elastomeric materials, sometimes incorporating reinforcing elements such as textiles, wire and the like. In its simplest form, a calender closely resembles a mill. However, it is much more carefully designed and precisely constructed in order to achieve effective control of product thickness.

A rubber calender in basic form consists of two or more hardened and accurately machined metal rolls rotating in bearing journal boxes which are set in rugged iron frames. At least one roll is equipped with screwdowns to control thickness of processed material. Adjacent pairs of rolls rotating in opposite directions form a "nip" where the material being processed is squeezed into sheets or is laminated to form the desired product. The drives for the rolls include constant or variable-speed motors and reduction gearing to achieve roll surface speeds required by the processing requirements of the materials. A calender, depending on the number and the design of its rolls, is capable of sheeting, frictioning, coating, profiling and embossing.

Rubber calenders are made in a number of roll configurations, horizontally and vertically, and in sizes ranging from laboratory units to giants weighing many tons. However, the three-roll vertical calender with 24-inch(diameter) x 68-inch (face length) rolls and the four-roll "Z" and "L" with 28-inch x 78-inch rolls are typical of the machines used for mass production of tires, belting, sheeting and the like. The three-roll calenders have been widely used for processing of mechanical rubber goods. The four-roll calenders are popular in tire plants. The four rolls permit simultaneous application of rubber compound on both sides of tire cord fabrics. Two-roll calenders are used to produce strips and profiles, often in combination with extruder feeding, in which case they are commonly referred to as "Roller Dies".

CALENDERING OPERATIONS

Calenders are used in five separate operations in the manufacture of rubber products. These important operations are sheeting, frictioning, coating, profiling, and embossing.

Sheeting

This basic operation utilizes a two-roll calender in horizontal or vertical configuration. The feed material, either in strip or "pig" form, is fed into one side of the nip and is flattened, thereby emerging as a sheet which is pulled from the roll by some manual or mechanical means. Because of its versatility, the three-roll calenders are now more widely used for sheeting as well as other basic calendering operations (see Figure 1, A and B). Thickness control is accomplished by use of the screwdowns and may be further refined by automatic control systems using thickness sensors. It should be noted here that the force required in the nip to flatten the feed material causes deflection of the rolls, however slight. If some corrective steps are not taken, the product thickness will vary across the sheet resulting in excessive variations of the product and possibly excessive use of expensive materials. In order to overcome these problems, three basic techniques are used to achieve uniform thicknesses:

1. Grinding or "crowning" of the roll faces to compensate for deflection. The roll are mechanically ground so that the diameter at the center is larger than that at the ends of the roll face. Under load, the "crowned" rolls deflect so that the gap between them is more uniform.

2. Roll "crossing" whereby the roll axis can be mechanically deflected from a planar relationship. This effect will create a progressively greater gap between the rolls from center to ends. Because roll crossing is a deliberate misalignment of the horizontal axis of the rolls, it is also known as "axis skewing".

3. Roll "bending" whereby the roll is physically bent by the application of force to the outside of each roll journal bearing. Positive bending causes an increase in roll convexity while negative bending causes an increase in concavity.

In order to minimize air entrapment and blistering, the thickness of each sheet is generally limited. To build up the required thickness of the final sheet, two or more plies of calendered sheet are usually laminated on the bottom roll of a three-roll calender.

Frictioning

Frictioning involves rubbing or wiping an elastomeric compound into a substrate of textile or metallic cords which may or may not be held together by "pick" threads or fill yarns, or the substrate may consist of a "square woven" fabric like "hose ducks" or "belt ducks" discussed in Chapter 9.

Usually a three-roll calender is employed wherein the rubber sheet is formed between the upper and middle rolls while the resulting sheet is simultaneously being frictioned into the substrate between the middle and bottom rolls. In this operation the upper and middle rolls may be moving at "odd" or "even" surface speed, but the middle and bottom rolls will be run at "odd" or unequal surface speeds so that the rubber is effectively wiped into the substrate being carried on the bottom roll. (see Figure 1-B)

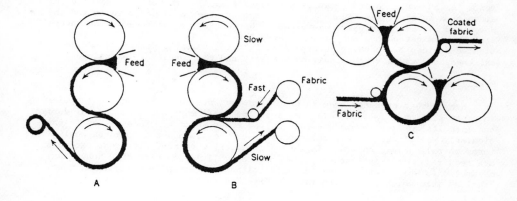

Fig. 1   Basic calendering operations

A.   Sheeting
B.   Frictioning
C.   Double coating

Coating

A coating or skim-coating operation is similar to that described for frictioning except that the middle and bottom rolls will run at "even" surface speed so that the rubber sheet is merely laid and pressed against the substrate. This is particularly true of a multi-pass operation where the substrate will have previously been frictioned. The coating operation may produce a heavy deposit or merely a thin "skim" coat depending upon the product requirement. Generally, multi-purpose calenders such as a three-roll unit, are equipped with "even" and "odd" gearing arrangements so that a number of combinations on roll speed ratios are possible.

A more complex form of coating calender is the four-roll "Z" or "L" arrangement. A four-roll calender can simultaneously apply a rubber coating onto both sides of a fabric. (see Figure 1-C). In effect, the No. 1 and 2 rolls and the No. 3 and 4 rolls form pairs where two rubber sheets are produced. The sheets are then laminated to a substrate between the No. 2 and 3 rolls. Very sophisticated devices are usually incorporated into the calender design to control thickness and width of the individual sheets and the resulting laminate.

Profiling

Many rubber products require uncured components which are not rectangular in cross section. In such cases, at least one roll may have a peripheral design cut into its surface to produce the desired cross section. This method is particularly useful when long production runs are possible but becomes expensive in terms of roll change and roll inventory necessary when many different sections are required. In this instance, the calender roll may consist of a heavy basic mandrel onto which may be clamped solid cylindrical or split cylindrical steel "shells" into which the appropriate profile design has been cut.

Embossing

Some rubber products are made from uncured components which must have a surface design that cannot be economically formed by subsequent molding. One such example is the cover strip around the sole of canvas shoes. The method of producing such strips is similar to that described under "Profiling" in that the required design is engraved into the calender roll or "shell" as a mirror image of the design itself.

CALENDER DESIGNS

Through advancement in machine design, calenders are available today with rolls in various diameters, face lengths, and configurations plus sophisticated devices to effectively control process temperature and product dimensions. Figure 2 shows the many possible arrangements of calender rolls as well as standard sizes available and commonly used in the rubber industry. Obviously there are other variations for special applications. The arrangement of the rolls is generally determined by: (1) the resolution of separating forces between rolls and roll deflection, (2) ease of rubber stock feeding, (3) space requirements for calender mounted attachments such as trim knives and gauging sensors, and (4) space requirements for auxiliary attachments.

In Figure 2, the top row of two-roll arrangements (Line A) illustrates the basic positioning of rolls common to all calenders. The vertical arrangement (A.1) simplifies take-away of the sheet but makes strip or "pig" feeding difficult. Horizontal arrangement (A.2) solves the feeding problem but complicates take-away of the sheet. A practical compromise is the slant arrangement (A.3) which is usually incorporated into large double coating calenders such as shown on Line F.2 and F.3.

Figures 3 to 5 show calenders of different design commonly used in the rubber industry. Figure 6 illustrates a roller die extruder.

CALENDER AUXILIARIES

The rubber supply in the nip, called the bank of a calender, must be fed constantly by some means to prevent tears and holes in the resulting sheet. The ideal bank is relatively small and is continuously effecting a rolling action from end to end of the nip. In most instances, the rubber compound is warmed up on an adjacent mill and is then either fed to the calender nip in the form of a continuous strip or in the form of rolled "pigs" which the operator manually removes from the mill. In some installations the strip feed material is supplied from an adjacent extruder. As previously mentioned in the introduction, the calender may be integrally coupled to an extruder as shown in Figure 6.

Depending upon the type of product being processed, other auxiliary equipment may include:

1. Fabric let-off stands to accommodate rolled goods under accurate tension and speed control.

2. Wire-spool creel rooms in which a multiplicity of spools of reinforcing wire are paid out, oriented into a flat sheet-like alignment and guided into the calender laminating nip under accurate tension and spacing control.

3. Festooners consisting of multiple-pass movable roller devices similar to an elevator hoist rigging - which can store or pay out a fabric during stopping of certain parts of the line, yet with the calender operating at normal speed.

4. Heating and cooling drums.

5. Heating and dipping units for fabric entering the calender.

6. Windup units for the calendered material. These can consist of speed/tension coordinated spindle units for incorporating a reusable "anti-stick" liner between wraps of the material. They can also be belted-conveyor tables where windup with a liner is accomplished on a surface-driven central core.

7. Thickness gauging equipment for the final product. One widely used system employs a sensor taking advantage of the emission characteristics of the isotope Strontium 90. This system is commonly called a Beta Gauge. The degree of process management from such systems can range from a mere readout of thickness to complete control of the calender and its auxiliaries. However, for any given process the economics of total equipment cost vs. benefits in quality and materials savings must be evaluated.

CALENDERS — STANDARD SIZES

Roll Diameter	Conventional Normal Journal Diameter	Conventional Normal Face
10	6.5	20
12	8	24
14	9.25	30
16	10.5	36
18	12	48
20	13.25	54
22	14.5	60
24	16	68
28	19	78
30	20	84
32	21.5	92
36	24	96

Inches used in all dimensions.

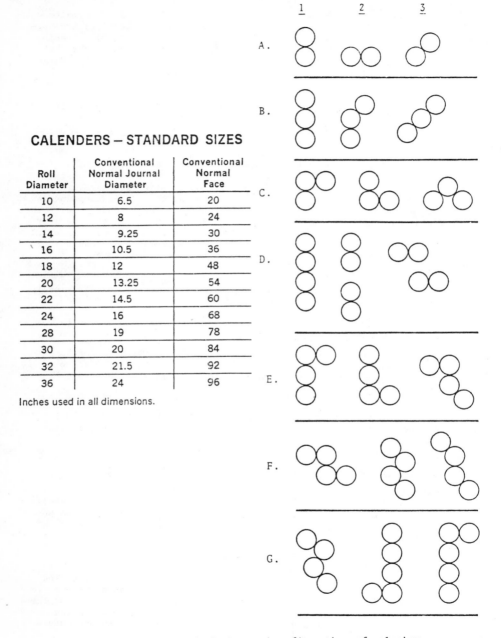

Fig. 2   Standard sizes and configurations of calenders

Fig. 3 24" x 68" three-roll calender with 120° inclined top roll (courtesy of Intercole Bolling Corp.)

Fig. 4   24" x 68" four-roll inclined "Z" calender.   (Courtesy of Intercole Bolling Corp.)

Fig. 5   24" x 69" four-roll inverted "L" calender.   (Courtesy of Intercole Bolling Corp.)

Fig. 6   15" extruder with 20" x 42" roller die   (Courtesy of Intercole Bolling Corp.)

8. Temperature Controls. Temperature control of calender roll surfaces is extremely important. During startup of the calender, the rolls must be brought up to the proper operating temperature, say 200°F. However, during operation the squeezing and shearing action of the rolls on the rubber results in heat which must be removed from the rolls to prevent rubber scorching. Here again, quality and cost considerations dictate the degree of sophistication in equipment. The basic calender roll is usually made of cast iron. During the casting process the roll surface temperature is cooled at a required rate to become very dense and hard, enabling subsequent mechanical grinding to give the desired surface finish. Even though the roll is cast with a hollow core, any heat transfer liquid which is circulating within this core is separated by a matter of inches from the surface upon which the rubber will reside. Therefore, a lag in heat transfer exists which must be considered in the design of the temperature control system. More expensive and efficient calenders utilize "drilled" rolls which have a number of rifle-drilled holes just under the chilled surface. As a result of high velocity circulation of the heat transfer fluid in these holes, response time is greatly reduced and accurate temperature control is more assured. A combined pumping and heat exchange unit used for temperature control is referred to as a TCU.

9. Trim knives. They are used to remove excess rubber from the outer margins of a calendered sheet or to provide discreet widths of sheet material emerging from a nip.

10. Safety equipment. The importance of this element of calendering equipment cannot be overemphasized. Without dwelling on details, it should be obvious that the potential is real for people being injured in the many nip points in a calender installation. The safety equipment required is contained in the American National Standards Institute, Inc. Standard B28.1-1967, Safety Specifications for Mills and Calenders in the Rubber and Plastics Industries. This standard has its roots in work initiated in 1924 by the Rubber Section of the National Safety Council and is now adopted by the Occupational Safety and Health Administration (OSHA). The standard should be required reading on a repetitive basis for anyone concerned with calender and mill installations, operations, and maintenance.

COMMON CALENDERING PROBLEMS

Inasmuch as the rubber compounds which are fed to the calendering equipment are not chemically altered by the process itself, this section concerns itself mainly with those variables which can be controlled by the equipment. Should problems arise which cannot be corrected by the equipment itself, the solutions probably lie elsewhere, such as mixing and compound design. Needless to say, a rubber compound's processability is very much influenced by its formulation and how well it was mixed.

Basic calendering problems obviously vary with the class of material being processed and the type of equipment being used. However, there are many common calendering problems. They and their possible causes are as follows:

Problem	Possible Causes
1. Off-gauge material	a. Incorrect crowning of rolls
	b. Excessive wear in roll journal bearings
	c. Improper operation of pullback and zero-clearance devices
	d. Improper use of roll-crossing or roll-bending devices
	e. Faulty gauging equipment
2. Stock blisters	a. Inadequate temperature control (roll temperature too high)
	b. Too large feed bank
	c. Lack of, or improper use of "pricker" roll
	d. Improper stock warm-up (excessive breakdown)
	e. Sheet gauge too thick
3. Holes in sheet	a. Bank of rubber too small or too large. Should have a rolling bank.
	b. Inadequate temperature control
	c. Improper stock warm-up (insufficient breakdown)
4. Scorched stock	a. Inadequate temperature control (roll too cold or too hot)
	b. Bank too large
	c. Nip opening too big
	d. Running speed too fast
	e. Stock on warm-up mill too long
5. Stock too dry or too tacky	a. Inadequate temperature control (roll too cold or too hot)
	b. Improper feed temperature
6. Excessive scrap and rework	a. Trim knives not properly set or maintained
	b. Improper startup temperature control
	c. Defective stock guides

Problem	Possible Causes
7. Localized crushing or distorting of fabric	a. Improper roll crowns
	b. Improper crown control
	c. Improper screwdown operation
	d. Too much bottom roll pressure
	e. Improper tension on fabric
8. Coat peeling	a. Improper temperature control (roll temperature too low or too high)
	b. Improper crown or crown control
	c. Not enough screwdown pressure
	d. Fabric too cold
9. Friction pick-off	a. Improper running speed
	b. Improper roll temperature
10. Cold checks	a. Improper stock warm-up (insufficient breakdown)
	b. Improper roll temperature (too low)
11. Crows feet	a. Excessive squeezing between center and bottom roll

SUMMARY

Calendering is one of the fastest and most uniform ways to produce flat rubber products in high volume. It is basically a continuous extrusion process between a pair of counter-rotating cylindrical rolls. Depending on the number and the design of its rolls, a calender is capable of sheeting, laminating, frictioning. coating, profiling, and embossing operations.

Calenders are available with two or more rolls mounted in different configurations. The three-roll calenders have long been widely used in the manufacture of mechanical rubber goods because of their versatility, while the four-roll calenders are popular in tire plants because they permit simultaneous application of rubber compound on both sides of tire cord fabrics.

Like mixing and extrusion, calendering is a primary operation in the manufacturing process for rubber products. It is an important part of rubber technology. For those who desire further reading on the subject of calendering, a list of literature references is provided.

GENERAL REFERENCES

1. Blow, C.M., ed., "Rubber Technology and Manufacture", Butterworth & Co., London, England (1971)

2. DelGatto, J.V. and Hague, S.R., "Machinery and Equipment for Rubber and Plastics", Rubber World, Bill Brothers, New York, (1970)

3. Klingender, R.C., "Processing", 14th Annual Akron Rubber Group Lecture Series, Ohio, (1977)

4. Kulgren, G.V., "Modern Calender Processing Equipment", India Rubber World, 120, 323 (1949)

5. Lake, C.G., "Calendering", 16th Annual Akron Rubber Group Lecture Series, Ohio, (1979)

6. Paslay, P.R., "Calendering of a Viscoelastic Material", J. Appl. Mechanics, 24, 602 (1957)

7. Perlberg, E., "How to Select A Calender", Rubber Age, (104 (4)), 43 (1972)

8. Schildnecht, C.E., ed., "Polymer Processes", Interscience Publishers, Inc., New York, (1956)

9. Tadmor, Z. and Gogos, C.G., "Principles of Polymer Processing", Wiley-Interscience, New York, (1979)

10. Willshaw, H., "Calenders In Rubber Processing", IRI and Lakeman, London, England (1956)

WORK ASSIGNMENT NO. 5

CHAPTER 5.   CALENDERING – EQUIPMENT AND PROCESS

INSTRUCTIONS: Read each question carefully, select one, and only one, appropriate
answer to complete each statement.

1. Calender is a machine used mainly to continuously produce

_____ (a) tubing
_____ (b) shoe sole
_____ (c) sheet goods ✓
_____ (d) cement

2. A calender resembles most closely

_____ (a) an internal mixer
_____ (b) a mill ✓
_____ (c) an injection molding machine
_____ (d) a press

3. The basic form of a rubber calender consists of

_____ (a) screw and barrel
_____ (b) platens
_____ (c) cylindrical rolls ✓
_____ (d) cavity molds

4. Calender is not capable of

_____ (a) sheeting
_____ (b) tube forming ✓
_____ (c) frictioning
_____ (d) "skim-coating"

5. "Roller dies" are used to produce rubber strips and profiles. "Roller dies"
    consist of

_____ (a) a two-roll calender in combination with extruder feeding ✓
_____ (b) a 3-roll vertical calender in combination with a 2-roll calender feeding
_____ (c) a two-roll calender in combination with open mill feeding
_____ (d) a two-roll calender in combination with internal mixer feeding

6. The word "nip" is used in calendering to describe

_____ (a) the wedge shaped entrance formed between adjacent rolls ✓
_____ (b) each plate near roll end for keeping the rubber stock on the calender
_____ (c) the rubber supply on the calender
_____ (d) the pinching action of the windup unit for the calendered material

7. The deflection of calender rolls during processing is mainly caused by

_____ (a) too much tension on the fabric being processed
_____ (b) the excessive amount of feed material on the calender
_____ (c) the force required in the nip to flatten the feed material ✓
_____ (d) the high speed of taking way the calendered material

8. A 3-roll calender is usually employed for frictioning. Frictioning on a calender involves

____ (a) coating a fabric with rubber stock at least 1/8 inch thick
____ (b) depositing a coat of liquid cement on a fabric for adhesion promotion
____ (c) forcing the rubber among and into interstices between fibers of a fabric through wiping with roll pressure between the middle and bottom rolls
____ (d) producing a surface design on sheet material

9. When a 3-roll calender is used for frictioning, the surface speed of the bottom roll is usually

____ (a) equal to the middle roll
____ (b) slower than the middle roll
____ (c) faster than the middle roll
____ (d) none of above

10. A 3-roll calender is also employed for coating or skim-coating. A coating operation is similar to frictioning operation except

____ (a) the middle and bottom rolls run at even surface speed
____ (b) all three rolls run at different surface speed
____ (c) the surface speed of the bottom roll is faster than that of the middle roll
____ (d) none of above

11. Profiling and embossing operations are similar in that

____ (a) a four-roll calender is required
____ (b) the cross section of the calendered material is always rectangular
____ (c) the design is usually engraved into a cylindrical "shell"
____ (d) none of above

12. Calenders are available with various roll configurations. Calender rolls may be arranged vertically, horizontally, in "L" design, or in "Z" design. One of the important factors in selecting roll arrangement is

____ (a) ease of feeding stock and taking-off calendered material
____ (b) how many rubber compounds requiring calendering operation
____ (c) the chemical resistance of the rubber compounds involved
____ (d) the tensile strength of the rubber compounds involved

13. Off-gauge material processed by calendering is not likely caused by

____ (a) incorrect crowning of rolls
____ (b) improper use of roll-bending or roll-crossing devices
____ (c) use of wrong rubber compound
____ (d) excessive wear in roll journal bearings

14. "Stock blisters" problem at calender is usually not related to

____ (a) size of rubber feed bank at nip
____ (b) inadequate temperature control
____ (c) improper use of pricker roll
____ (d) tensile strength of the stock

15. Temperature control of calender roll surfaces is extremely important. However, it is not likely the cause of

_____ (a) holes in sheet
_____ (b) stock too tacky
_____ (c) off-gauge sheet ✓
_____ (d) air entrapped in stock

CHAPTER 6

MOLDING - EQUIPMENT AND METHODS

John G. Sommer

GenCorp, Research Division
Akron, Ohio 44305

INTRODUCTION

It is an unusual rubber product that isn't molded. Molding is defined by
Webster as the act or process of shaping in or on a mold, or anything cast in a
mold. In this chapter, molding of thermoplastic rubber will not be considered.
Thus, the discussion will be restricted to rubber which is crosslinked during
the molding process. Crosslinking is the act of connecting together the extremely long rubber molecules in a rubber composition. Generally this is done at high
temperatures.

Crosslinked molded parts are successfully used in a wide variety of consumer,
industrial and engineering applications. To meet the different needs of these
applications, many different types of rubber have been developed. Different rubbers and the materials used to form parts vary considerably in their characteristics.

Some materials used to mold polyurethane compositions might have very low
viscosity, about like castor oil. Viscosity is a measure of the resistance to
flow. Most rubber used for molding has a much higher viscosity, about like cheddar
cheese.

In units of Pascal-seconds (Pa·s), castable materials for polyurethane have a
viscosity of about one. High viscosity rubber has a viscosity of about 100,000
Pa·s. The 100,000 ratio for the two different materials greatly affects the
choice of the molding method and equipment.

Another factor is the presence or absence of other materials in a molded
product. Some products are all rubber, while others are complex composites such
as rubber/metal or rubber/textile. Hence, variations in the rubber itself, combinations of it with other materials, economics, and other factors, all play an
important role in selecting molding equipment and methods.

The purpose of this chapter is to review the equipment and methods used in
molding rubber. This is done while broadly considering the effect of material
viscosity on molding behavior.

GENERAL DISCUSSION

There is a difference and a similarity between molding behavior of low-and
high-viscosity meterials. Low-viscosity materials become rubberlike only after
they react with one another in a mold. In contrast, high-viscosity materials,
like natural rubber, are rubberlike before they enter a mold. Low- and high-
viscosity materials are similar because they both crosslink within a mold. Table
I shows molding methods for these materials.

116

Table I

MOLDING METHODS

Material Viscosity	Method
Low	Casting
	Manual
	Machine
	Reaction Injection Molding (RIM)
High	Compression
	Transfer
	Injection
	Bladder

The in-mold time for these different processes varies more than a thousand-fold. Times are as short as 30 seconds, and as long as 24 hours[1].

Figure 1 provides a useful and general overview of the relationship among in-mold time, molding method and viscosity. This figure does not take into account part size which significantly affects in-mold time.

Materials having intermediate viscosity (like a caulking compound) are generally avoided in molding. Reasons for this are that they are difficult to handle and that they show a strong tendency to trap air during processing and molding; the retained air is often evident as porosity in a molded part.

Sometimes a low viscosity material is cast and allowed to react partially, increasing its viscosity[2]. This higher viscosity material can then be molded by high pressure methods such as compression or transfer[2]. High molding pressure acts on this high viscosity material and squeezes out the air, minimizing porosity. Thus a part initially molded by casting might be molded finally by compression.

Compression molding is normally done between rigid metal plates. Bladder molding is a variation of compression molding where the material to be molded is squeezed against a rigid mold surface by a flexible rubber bladder. Bladder molding is important because virtually all tires are molded this way and tires account for about two-thirds of all rubber used.

Flow Behavior - Rubber must flow or deform in order to fill the cavity in which it is molded. One of the ways it deforms is in shear. Shear flow can be visualized by sliding the cards in a deck of cards upon one another as shown in Figure 2. In this figure:

v = velocity, cm/sec

t = thickness, cm

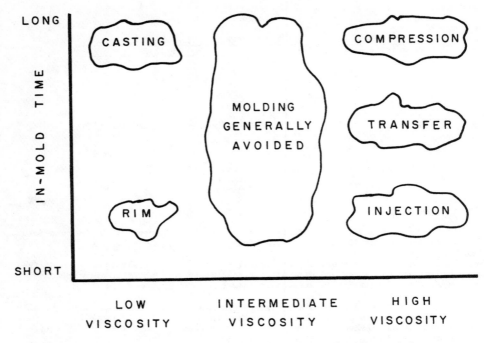

Fig. 1   In-mold time as a function of viscosity and molding method.

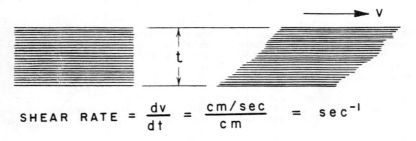

$$\text{SHEAR RATE} = \frac{dv}{dt} = \frac{cm/sec}{cm} = sec^{-1}$$

Fig. 2   Concept of shear rate.

and shear rate is defined by the change in velocity per unit thickness to give shear rate in units of reciprocal seconds, s^{-1}.

During injection molding, rubber often flows through a channel in its path to a mold. Shear flow in a channel can be compared to extending the antenna on a portable television set or extending the elements of a telescope. Instead of flat cards sliding upon one another (Figure 2), concentric tubes slide past one another on their common axis. Again the shear rate between tubes is in units of s^{-1}.

Flow in a channel or in a mold is quite complicated and the mode of flow can vary. For example, extensional or stretching flow might occur in tapered sections. In this chapter, flow is assumed to occur in shear. If water flows in a channel at sufficiently low shear rates, a "particle" of water moves in a straight line path; this behavior represents laminar or viscous flow. But if the shear rate is increased to some critical value, flow becomes unstable and a "particle" of water moves in an erratic or turbulent manner.

In the range of shear rates associated with laminar flow, water has a constant viscosity value. Fluids behaving in this way are described as Newtonian fluids. Figure 3 shows that viscosity is independent of shear rate for Newtonian fluids. For a Newtonian fluid like water in the laminar range, the rate of flow is directly proportional to the applied pressure. Therefore, doubling the pressure doubles the flow rate.

Again referring to Figure 3, the axis for viscosity is broken. This was done because the viscosity of a typical high viscosity rubber is about ten million times higher than that of water; thus water and rubber cannot reasonably share a common viscosity axis on a linear basis.

In Figure 3 rubber viscosity, relative to that of water, responds quite differently to a change in shear rate. Rubber viscosity decreases sharply with increasing shear rate, i.e., it is non-Newtonian. Because of this relationship, increased pressure on rubber disproportionately increases its flow rate relative to water. This happens because higher shear rates reduce rubber viscosity and cause it to flow faster for a given pressure change.

For example, an increase in pressure of 25% on rubber might cause the flow rate of rubber to increase by 50% or more. This effect is dramatic and is used to great advantage in injection molding where shear rates are very high.

Rubber is molded using methods in which shear rates vary considerably. To put this in perspective, the viscosity of rubber is shown in Figure 4 over a shear rate range of one million[3]. This range of rates causes the viscosity to change by a factor of about 10,000. The effect of temperature is also shown because a range of temperatures is used for molding and crosslinking rubber. Particularly at high shear rates, the temperature of flowing rubber is increased by viscous heating.

The temperature range shown (100-150°C) causes considerably less change in viscosity during molding than does the change in shear rate. This is true only if no crosslinking occurs. If crosslinking occurs while rubber is flowing, viscosity increases sharply and flow will virtually stop. Thus a mold cavity should be filled completely with rubber before crosslinking commences.

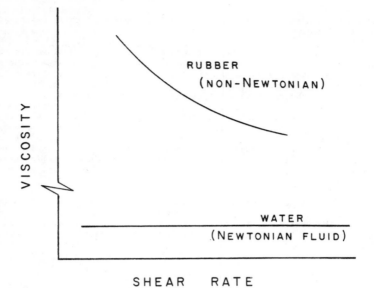

Fig. 3 Newtonian and non-Newtonian behavior.

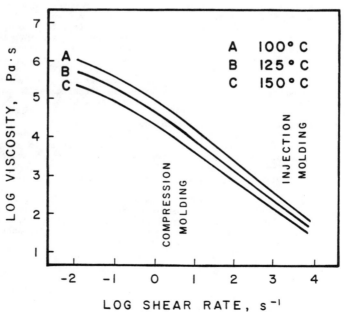

Fig. 4 Effect of temperature and shear rate on viscosity.
(After Reference 3)

Included in Figure 4 are the shear rates associated with two important molding methods, compression and injection. Compression molding is typically done over a shear rate range[4] of about 1-10 s^{-1}. Injection molding is usually done in a range of about 1,000-10,000 s^{-1}. Transfer molding, another important molding method, is done in a range intermediate between compression and injection.

The important point is that the viscosity of a rubber may be more than 100 times lower when it is being injection molded compared to when it is being compression molded. Thus the rate at which the rubber moves, i.e., the shear rate, critically affects the ease with which rubber flows during molding.

The rate of flow during compression molding is similar to the flow or shear rate that occurs in a Mooney viscometer, about 1 s^{-1}. Hence, the Mooney viscometer should provide viscosity data relevant to compression molding. Since injection molding is done at considerably higher rates, the Mooney viscometer is a poorer predictor of injection molding behavior. For this reason, the viscosity of rubber compounds for injection molded rubber is sometimes measured at injection shear rates by high-rate viscometers. These are better able to predict viscosity and therefore injection molding behavior.

HIGH VISCOSITY MATERIALS

The equipment and methods for compression, transfer, injection and bladder molding of high-viscosity materials are discussed in terms of molds, presses and processes. Emphasis is placed on injection molding because it is a newer and more complex method than compression, transfer or bladder molding.

Compression Molding - Compression molds vary considerably in size, shape and complexity, and they might contain as many as 360 cavities. A simple, single-cavity compression mold is shown in Figure 5. A cylindrical, uncured rubber preform is shown in its cavity prior to mold closure. The rubber preform is shaped to approximately fit the cavity. Because the preform doesn't fit the cavity exactly, it will keep the top plate above the cavity plate.

During mold closure, rubber is squeezed between the top plate and the land and the excess flows into the flash groove. Typically the volume of the flash groove is 10-20% of cavity volume[5].

However, if the rubber preform is too large, excess rubber will flow past the flash groove toward the dowel pins. If the rubber gets into the clearance between the dowel pins and the hole into which they fit, mold opening and closing becomes difficult. Thus, the dowel pins should be sufficiently remote from the flash groove to avoid contact of rubber with dowel pins.

The purpose of dowel pins is to obtain proper register among mold plates and to prevent the mold plates from being assembled improperly. To prevent improper assembly, the dowel pins can be arranged so the mold can be assembled and closed only in the desired manner.

Because a simple cylindrical part is shown in Figure 5, register among plates is not as important as if the part were more complicated. For example, a mold pin could be affixed to the top or bottom plate and project into the cavity to form a concentric hole in the rubber cylinder. If wall thickness of the hollow cylinder was critical, register would have to be maintained between pin and mold wall to obtain the desired wall thickness.

A molding press, to be discussed shortly, provides the force necessary to close the mold. The closed mold is shown in Figure 6. Excess rubber has flowed past the land into the flash groove. The thickness of flash above the land and the volume of flash in the flash groove will vary. The variable thickness flash between the land and top plate causes closure dimensions that are less accurate than fixed dimensions for compression molded parts.

After the molding cycle is completed, the mold is opened. Opening is aided by placing a pry bar in the slot in the cavity plate.

The need for a separate cavity plate is dependent upon the shape of the rubber part being molded. As the height/width ratio of a molded part increases, part removal from the mold becomes more difficult. For example, the rubber cylinder in Figure 6 can be pushed from the cavity plate only after both top and bottom plates are removed from the cavity plate. A three-plate mold is required because of the large area of contact between the walls of the rubber cylinder and the mold cavity wall.

In contrast, a thin rubber sheet can be molded easily in a simple two-plate mold. There is relatively little surface area of the molded part in contact with the cavity walls. Hence, the cavity plate and bottom plate could be a single metal plate rather than two separate plates shown for the cylinder in Figure 5.

It was mentioned above that flash should be kept to a minimum because it causes variations in the closure dimension. But sometimes thick flash is desirable, as shown in Figure 7. This flash permits rapid demolding of all parts as a continuous sheet. The individual parts can then be cut from the sheet by a die. Hence, compared to demolding of individual parts from mold cavities, demolding parts as a sheet saves time.

Compression molds vary considerably in size and a small one can be manually slid in and out of the press (Figure 8). As size increases, a mold eventually becomes too large and heavy for a press operator to manipulate. Large molds can be attached to press platens so that they are opened and closed by the press. Normally molds are heated by direct contact with press platens (Figure 8). Some molds are heated by steam or hot fluid that circulates through channels in a mold.

It takes considerable force to close a mold containing high viscosity rubber. For the majority of non-tire or mechanical molded parts, hydraulic pressure provides the force to close a press. The two major types of molding press in use today are the four-post press and the side-plate press; the four-post press is most popular[6]. A schematic diagram of a four-post press with a mold in place is shown in Figure 8. The mold is purposely shown undersized for the press and the reason for this is discussed under "Molding Problems and Corrective Action".

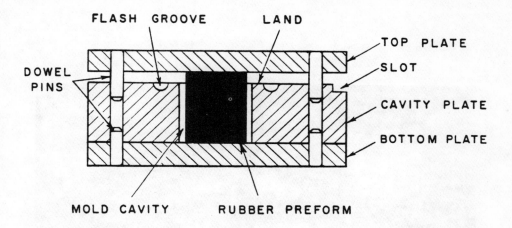

Fig. 5 Compression mold containing a rubber preform before closing mold.

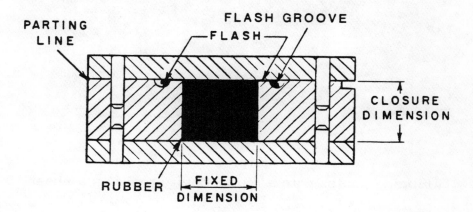

Fig. 6 Compression mold after closing.

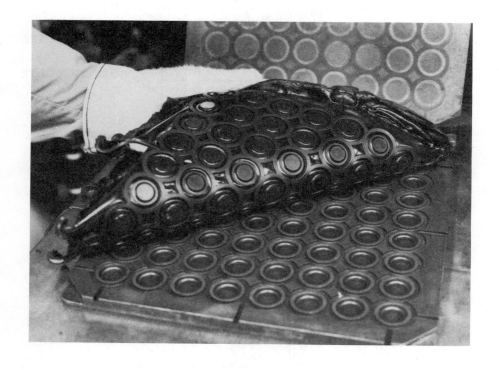

Fig. 7
Stripping parts from a multi-cavity mold as a sheet.

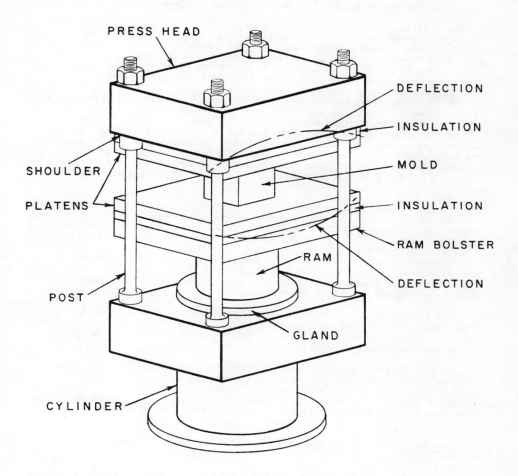

Fig. 8 Four-post molding press.

In Figure 8 the press head is attached to the cylinder by four posts. In operation, hydraulic fluid under high pressure is supplied to the cylinder. A packing gland prevents leakage of fluid between cylinder and ram. This fluid pushes the ram upward against the ram bolster and provides pressure to the mold.

For a typical press with a 66 cm (26 in.) diameter ram under 13.8 MPa (2000 psi) hydraulic pressure, the force is 4.6 MN (531 tons). Unless the ram bolster and press head are sufficiently rigid, they will deflect excessively because of the high force (see Figure 8). This deflection can distort platens and mold plates and cause excessive flashing. Thus, rigidity must be provided by the ram bolster and press head since very little rigidity is provided by the press platens.

The function of the platens is to heat the mold uniformly. The source of this heat is generally steam, but hot fluid or electric heating is also used. With electric, resistance heating is most common, but induction heating is also used. To minimize undesirable heating of the ram bolster, ram and press head, insulation is used between the lower platen and ram bolster and between the upper platen and the press head. This insulation is especially important for the ram bolster. If the ram bolster becomes too hot, heat transfers through the ram into the gland and hydraulic fluid. This heat accelerates deterioration of the packing gland and the hydraulic fluid in the cylinder.

In Figure 8 the press has only one opening (called the daylight) for accepting a mold. Daylight usually is specified as the distance between the top of the ram bolster and the bottom of the press head[6]. To determine the opening available for a mold, platen and insulation thickness must be subtracted from the daylight.

While only one daylight is shown in the press in Figure 8, two or more daylights are often provided in a press. Multiple daylights permit using two or more molds simultaneously in a press. With two daylights, the center platen heats the bottom of the top mold and the top of the bottom mold.

Four platens are shown in the large side-plate press shown in Figure 9; thus three molds could be used simultaneously in this press. The major difference between the side-plate and four-post press is the use of steel plates in place of the posts as structural members.

Yet another press design is the "C" frame which allows unobstructed access to the daylight from the front and both sides. This type of press is gaining in popularity[6], and an example of a large "C" frame press is shown in Figure 10. It is 10.1 m (33 ft.) long and has seven daylight openings, each 18 cm (7 in.) deep. Nine separate rams provide a total closing force of 5.1 MN (575 tons) to give a platen pressure of 3.4 MPa (500 psi).

Transfer Molding - In one sense, transfer molding is a variation of compression molding. In transfer molding, a plunger compresses a rubber preform in a pot as shown in Figure 11. The rubber is heated by contact with the plunger face and pot. When sufficient force is applied to a mold by a press, rubber flows through the sprue and into the mold cavity (Figure 12).

Fig. 9   Side-plate molding press.
(Courtesy of Adamson Division of Wean United, Inc.)

Fig. 10   C-Frame molding press.
(Courtesy of Pathex Canada Limited)

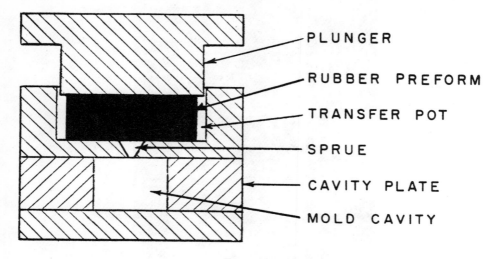

Fig. 11
Transfer mold showing preform in transfer pot before closing mold.

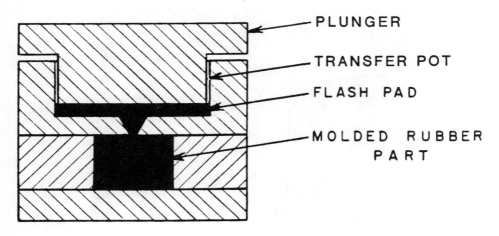

Fig. 12   Transfer mold after closing.

Clearance between the transfer pot and plunger is important. This clearance should be small enough to minimize flow of rubber between plunger and the wall of the pot. But it should be large enough to prevent binding between plunger and pot wall. A clearance of about 0.12 mm (0.005 in.) is suggested[5].

An important feature of a transfer mold is the depth of engagement of the plunger and pot. The plunger should engage the pot deeply enough to minimize tilting of the plunger in the pot.

The sprue is round in cross-section and becomes narrower as it approaches the mold cavity. Because the sprue is narrowest just above the molded part, the sprue breaks there when the flash pad is removed from the transfer pot. Thus the major portion of the sprue remains affixed to the cured flash pad (see Figure 12) and is removed with the flash pad.

Another important consideration for transfer molds is the ratio between the area of the plunger face and the projected area of the cavity or cavities. The area of the plunger face must be larger than this projected area. If it is not, flash will form between the cavity plate and the plate containing the transfer pot. To avoid this problem, make the area of the plunger face about 30 to 50% larger than the projected cavity area[5].

Discussion up to now has been limited to a single-cavity transfer mold; now a multi-cavity mold is considered. A cavity plate for a nineteen-cavity mold[7] is shown in Figure 13. The cavities are cylindrical in shape, 28.7 mm (1.129 in.) diameter by 12.7 mm (0.5 in.) high. A square preform was used in the pot and each cavity was fed by four sprues. Sprue diameter was 1.6 mm (0.062 in.) at the cavity entrance.

Pressure transducers were located in the bottom plate (not shown) of the mold, under the cavities marked "C" and "O" in Figure 13. A third pressure transducer was located in the center of the plunger face in contact with the rubber in the transfer pot. By this arrangement, pressure transducers monitored changes in pressure during mold closing.

Figure 14 shows the pressure at the plunger face and in the two cavities as a function of time[7]. This figure shows the expected sharp rise in pressure (P) at the plunger face when the mold closes. Then this pressure decreases as rubber flows into the sprues above the cavities. At about 8 seconds, the outer cavity (O) fills and its pressure rises. It is only after the pressure rises significantly in the outer cavity that the pressure increases in the central cavity (C), at about 29 seconds. Then the pressures at the three locations tend to equalize after about 60 seconds.

The cavities and their respective sprues were identical, and the distance between sprues and their respective cavities was identical. Even so, the central and outer cavities did not fill at the same time. More uniform filling time would be expected with a Newtonian fluid like water.

As with compression molds, large transfer molds are unwieldly. For larger transfer molds, the plunger can be attached to the upper platen of a curing press. The cavity plate can then be taken from the press for removal of parts. Part removal might be done by hand or it might be automated. Ordinarily, transfer molds are used with four-post and side-plate presses.

Fig. 13
Cavity plate for a transfer mold showing location
of pressure transducers (Marker "C" and "O").

131

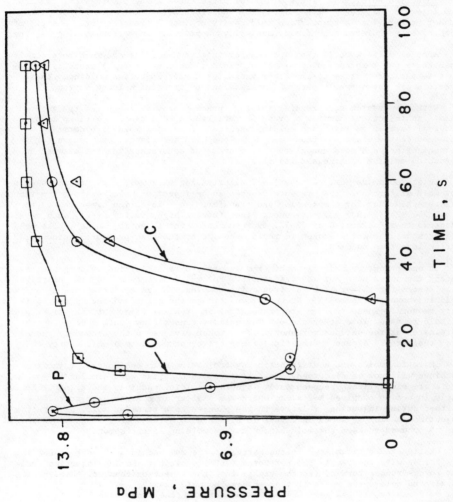

Fig 14   Pressure as a function of time for Plunger Face (P), Outer Cavity (O), and Central Cavity (C).

In the above examples of transfer molding, transfer of materials was directly from transfer pot to cavities. A runner system might be used to distribute rubber; a distribution system is described later in the section on injection molding.

Injection Molding - There are major differences among compression, transfer and injection molding. With compression and transfer, it is necessary to place a rubber preform into a compression mold cavity or into a transfer pot. A strip of rubber, or granulated rubber, automatically supplies an injection molding machine.

Another difference is that systems for injection molding are much more complex than those for compression or transfer molding; there are several controls to adjust temperature, pressure and other variables during injection molding. These controls are not normally part of compression and transfer molding systems.

With compression and transfer molding, presses provide the force to close a mold. In injection molding, a press is referred to as a clamp. A clamp is an integral part of an injection molding machine. Injection molds are normally attached to the clamp and thus open and close with the clamp. One reason for attachment between mold and clamp is the need for accurate alignment between an injection molding machine and its mold.

Injection molds must be capable of withstanding extremely high pressures without mold distortion. The pressure reached in an injection mold is about ten times greater than that for compression and transfer, i.e. injection pressures up to about 200 MPa (29,000 psi) are used. Therefore, a high quality steel, such as 4140 hardened to a Rockwell C of 28-32, is recommended for injection molds[8]. The mold plates should be thick enough to resist bending at the high pressures encountered during injection molding.

In operation, preheated rubber from a nozzle on an injection molding machine enters the sprue of a hot injection mold. For multi-cavity molds, the distribution system for this rubber is often quite complex. A system for an eight-cavity mold is shown in Figure 15. Rubber flows through the sprue and enters four primary runners. These runners are trapezoidal in cross-section, but they might also be half-round or some other shape. The primary runner flows into a drop, which terminates at the secondary runner. The rubber divides in the secondary runner to feed the gates. A gate is the final restrictive pathway into a mold cavity.

Injection molds and a distribution system having been considered, injection machines will now be discussed. Just as early automobiles were similar to wagons, there are similarities between early injection molding machines and transfer molds. Early injection machines had a ram which was smaller in diameter and traveled farther during injection, relative to the plunger on a transfer mold. A ram-type injection machine is shown in Figure 16 attached to a two-plate, single-cavity mold. The clamp used to keep the mold closed during molding is not shown.

Heating fluid circulates in the barrel of the ram machine. Rubber is fed into its throat with the ram in the retracted (left) position. During injection, this ram forces rubber forward (to the right) into the injection chamber, through the nozzle and mold sprue where it then enters the mold cavity. Before rubber enters the mold cavity, it has been heated by contact with the inner barrel wall. Then the rubber becomes hotter as it passes through the nozzle and sprue at very high shear rates.

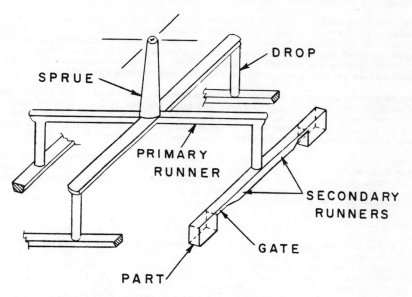

Fig. 15 Distribution system for an injection mold.

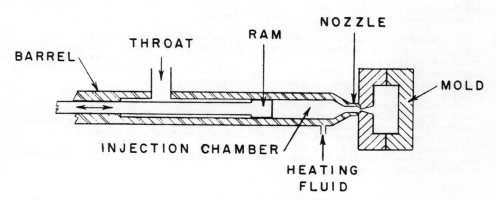

Fig. 16 Ram type machine for injection molding.

For the simple mold shown in Figure 16, the sprue also serves as a gate. When a separate gate is used (Figure 15), rubber temperature rises significantly as rubber passes through the gate. The gate is small and it restricts rubber flow.

The upper temperature reached by rubber while in the injection chamber of a ram type machine is limited to the temperature of the chamber wall. This wall transfers heat relatively slowly to the rubber by conduction. Because this process is slow, the temperature of the rubber is less uniform than desirable. This deficiency, among others, led to the greater popularity of the reciprocating screw machine; this machine provides greater temperature uniformity and machine flexibility.

The reciprocating screw machine is illustrated in Figure 17. Its throat, barrel, injection chamber, nozzle, heating fluid and mold are nearly identical to counterparts in the ram machine. The main difference is that the reciprocating screw machine is fitted with a screw which rotates inside the barrel. This screw not only rotates, it also moves back and forth on its axis like the ram in Figure 16.

Rubber is fed into the throat of a reciprocating screw machine, where it then contacts the rotating screw. The screw plasticizes (softens) the rubber and transports or pumps it to the front of the injection chamber. Rubber accumulates there because the screw retracts (moves to left) to provide the needed volume in the injection chamber. When a sufficient volume of rubber accumulates, the screw moves toward the mold and fills the mold with rubber. Thus the screw acts as both a pump and a ram.

The screw develops less pressure and does not meter rubber as accurately as a ram. These undesirable features occur because the clearance between ram and barrel wall (Figure 16) is typically less than between screw and barrel wall (Figure 17). The clearance between ram and wall can be as little as 0.05 mm (0.002 in.)[9]. With this small clearance, less leakage of rubber occurs during injection; hence, higher injection pressure and more accurate shots are obtainable with the ram-type machine, compared with the screw-type machine.

The reciprocating screw does work on the rubber in the barrel and raises rubber temperature above the barrel temperature; the higher temperature reduces rubber viscosity as seen in Figure 4. This capability of the reciprocating screw machine has been combined with the higher injection pressure capability of the ram machine. Figure 18 shows a machine with a separate screw and ram.

In this machine, the screw does not move back and forth on its axis; it only rotates, heating and pumping rubber to a 3-way valve. The heated rubber flows through the valve into the injection chamber. A ram then forces rubber from the injection chamber into a mold. Hence, the best features of a ram machine and a reciprocating screw machine are combined in a single machine.

Arrangements of the components of an injection molding machine fall into three basic categories, namely: horizontal, vertical and multiple-station rotary. The reciprocating screw type machine in Figure 17 is an example of a horizontal machine. A vertical machine is shown in Figure 18 (screw/ram machine). A vertical machine can be equipped with a sliding platen which permits moving the lower half of the mold to the operator; this movement facilitates removal of rubber parts and loading of inserts into the mold by the operator.

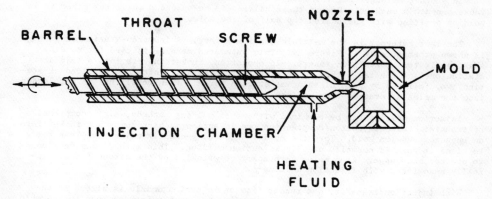

Fig. 17 Reciprocating screw machine for injection molding.

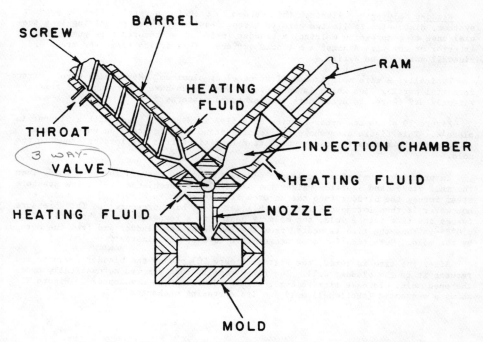

Fig. 18 Injection molding machine with separate screw and ram.

In another arrangement, two bottom halves for a mold can be located on a shuttle table beneath a machine. One of these halves can be unloaded while the other is in molding position with the shared top half of the mold.

The last category is the multiple-station rotary. A fourteen-station machine[10] is shown schematically in Figure 19. This automated machine is used for molding shaft seals that contain an insert. In operation, rubber injects into a mold at station one and the table then rotates counterclockwise. Parts are demolded at station two, followed by mold cleaning at station three. Then metal inserts are loaded into the molds at station four and the cycle is repeated.

Injection molding can be combined with other molding methods, e.g., compression or transfer. With injection/compression, an injection machine pumps hot rubber into an open compression mold. Then the mold is closed, generally using much less force to close it than is normally used in injection molding. This method was developed to protect shoe uppers from being torn apart or wrinkled by the strong forces typically associated with injection molding[11].

With injection/transfer, hot rubber from an injection nozzle is placed in the pot of a transfer mold. Then a plunger transfers hot rubber from the pot to the mold cavities as described earlier. With both injection/compression and injection/transfer molding, cycle times are shorter than for regular compression or transfer molding. Rubber entering the mold is preheated and this rubber therefore crosslinks in a shorter time.

Bladder Molding - Although this method is used for several different product systems, discussion is limited here to tires. Basically, bladder molding is a special case of compression molding; a bladder inside of an uncured tire pushes the exterior of the tire against a hot mold surface. This action forms the tread and sidewall patterns on a tire.

Typically, a tire mold is made from steel or aluminum. Most molds have a circumferential parting line which is on center. Some molds have a parting line that is slightly off center to accomodate complex tread patterns.

Figure 20 shows the cross-section of a tire in a curing press with a bladder in place[12]. This figure also shows the loading stand used to store an uncured tire, along with the automatic loader which transfers tires from the loading stand to the mold.

In practice, the automatic loader places an uncured tire in the open mold. Then the mold closes and a piston raises the bladder from the bladder well; low pressure steam forces the bladder into the uncured tire as shown in Figure 20[12]. Steam or hot water is then introduced into the bladder under high pressure[13]. This pressure forces the tire into a mold; the mold is heated to a temperature of about (177°C) 350°F[12]. Thus the tire is heated from the inside by the bladder and from the outside by the mold. Cure time for a passenger tire is about 16 minutes[12].

After the tire is cured, the piston (Figure 20) pushes the bladder downward and returns it to the bladder well. The cured tire is then removed automatically from the open mold. To ease tire removal, segmented molds were developed[12]. Figure 21 shows a segmented (sectional) mold and its operating mechanism.

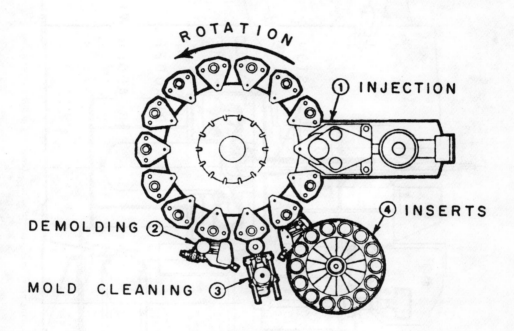

Fig. 19

Fourteen-station machine for injection molding shaft seals containing an insert. (Courtesy of Rubber Chemistry and Technology.)

138

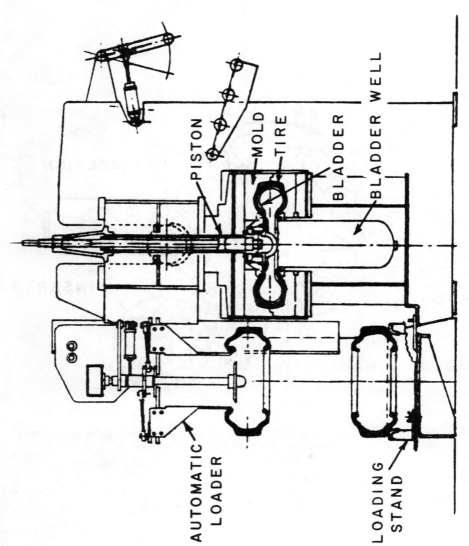

PISTON

MOLD

TIRE

BLADDER

BLADDER WELL

AUTOMATIC LOADER

LOADING STAND

Fig. 20   Tire curing press with tire in mold.   (Courtesy of NRM Corporation)

Fig. 21
Segmented (sectional) tire mold.
(Courtesy of NRM Corporation)

Figure 22 shows a segmented mold in place in a tire press. For best results, the two sidewall sections of the segmented mold should close to the final cure position before tread segments move toward the tire[12]. These segments must move into the tread area in exact symmetry with one another. Automatically controlled mechanical linkages accomplish the desired movement. The bladder shown in Figure 22 has only partly entered the tire. In transitioning from the bladder well into the tire, the bladder turns inside out. With another design of tire curing press, the bladder does not do this. Instead, a center post inserts and removes the bladder from the tire. A vacuum on the bladder reduces its diameter so that the bladder can be inserted in the opening available in a tire. Once there, pressure is applied to the bladder during molding as described above.

LOW VISCOSITY MATERIALS

The equipment and methods used to mold low viscosity (liquid) materials differ substantially from those used for high viscosity materials. Quite low pressure, generally less than 0.34 MPa (50 psi), is used to mold liquid materials. This means that molds for liquid materials do not have to be as rigid and strong as the metal molds typically used for high viscosity materials. Thus molds for liquid materials can be lighter and sometimes they are made from non-metallic materials like silicone rubber or epoxy resin.

Another difference between low and high viscosity materials is the time before crosslinking occurs. After reactants for a liquid system are mixed, crosslinking might occur in minutes or even seconds. Hence, the liquid must be quickly cast in a mold after mixing to insure that it is still mobile. Such haste is not necessary with most high viscosity rubber compositions; they are usually stable for days, and even months, before they crosslink or scorch in storage.

Among liquid materials for molding, polyurethane, or simply urethane, is most common. The simplest urethane system consists of an isocyanate and a polyol blend. These components start reacting after they are mixed, causing the viscosity of the mix to increase. The rate of increase of viscosity for hand mixes is usually slow enough for them to be cast into a mold before increasing viscosity becomes a problem. Generally this time is several minutes; it depends upon the amount of material to be cast, reaction rate, complexity of the mold, number of cavities, and other factors.

However, with reaction injection molding (RIM), the viscosity increases sharply only several seconds after the components are mixed. Thus the mixture must be transported to the mold very rapidly to avoid too great an increase in viscosity while the mixture is flowing. The RIM method is considered later following discussion of hand casting and machine casting methods.

Casting - This is the simplest method used to mold liquid materials. Reactants can be mixed by hand and then cast into a mold and crosslinked. Care must be taken during hand mixing and casting to minimize air entrapment. Air causes voids or bubbles in cast parts.

For casting large parts or many small parts, a machine is usually used to mix reactants. Machines mix large quantities quickly and they provide more uniform mixing than hand mixing. Roller skate wheels are an example of a molded urethane part made at high production rates (1500 per hour) by machine mixing[14]. The mix

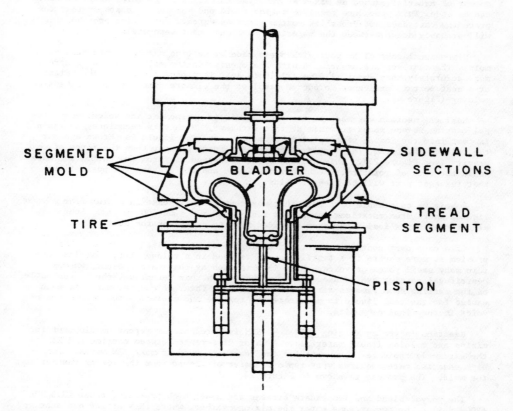

Fig. 22 Curing press containing a segmented mold. (Courtesy of NRM Corporation)

from the machine is cast directly into open molds through a flexible tube using shot sizes accurate to one gram. A rapid demolding cycle partly accounts for the high production rate; the molding cycle can be as short as 90 seconds.

Large parts can be made by both hand and machine casting. If a sufficient amount of material cannot be mixed at one time to fill a large mold, multiple casts can be made. This procedure requires making rapid and successive casts so that the preceding cast does not crosslink to too great an extent. Otherwise poor bonding will probably occur between the materials that were cast separately.

Dimensional control is poor with parts made by casting material into an open mold. The cast surface associated with the opening in the mold cannot be controlled more accurately than about ±1.6 mm (±1/16 in.)[2]. Thus poor control of the height of a cast part is analogous to poor control of the closure dimension in compression molding (Figure 6).

Earlier, mention was made of the problem of air entrapment and voids; centrifugal casting is one means to minimize this problem[2]. With this technique, a liquid is cast into the inside of a rotating drum. Because the liquid is thrown against the wall of this drum, the liquid experiences a force greater than the force of gravity (see Figure 23). This action forces entrapped air from the part. The more rapid the rate of rotation, the higher the force and the greater the possibility that the cast part will be free of voids.

A belt is an example of a part that was centrifugally cast in a drum from a liquid, where drum rotational speed was $6.67-11.67$ s^{-1} (400-700 rpm)[15]. Four electric elements inside the drum provided heat to crosslink the belt.

If a cast part contains inserts, trapping of air is a likely problem. This problem is more severe if a textile insert is used in a molded part; textiles contain many small pores or voids. When inserts such as these are present, vacuum centrifugal casting can be used to advantage. With this technique, the vacuum pulled on the casting drum removes air from the textile. This, of course, makes it much easier for the cast liquid to penetrate the textile and minimizes the occurrence of voids in the final composite.

Reaction Injection Molding (RIM) - RIM is a relatively recent development for mixing and molding liquid materials. A major difference between casting and RIM is the extremely rapid reaction rate for the reactants used to make RIM parts. This high reaction rate requires very rapid transfer of liquid from the mixing chamber to the mold. The process is shown in Figure 24.

The polyol blend and isocyanate streams are under high pressure, about 13.8 MPa (2000 psi). The two streams enter the mixing chamber, where they strike one another at very high velocities, causing turbulence. This turbulence results in thorough mixing of the streams, and the mixture then flows into the runner at low pressure. From the runner, the mixture flows through the gate into the mold cavity to form the molded part.

In Figure 24, the parting line of the mold (not shown) is in the plane of the paper. Relatively low forces are needed to keep the mold closed because molding pressure is typically only about 0.34 MPa (50 psi) or less. This low molding pressure permits the use of light clamps for RIM.

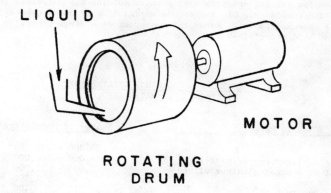

LIQUID

MOTOR

ROTATING
DRUM

Fig. 23   Centrifugal casting of liquid materials.

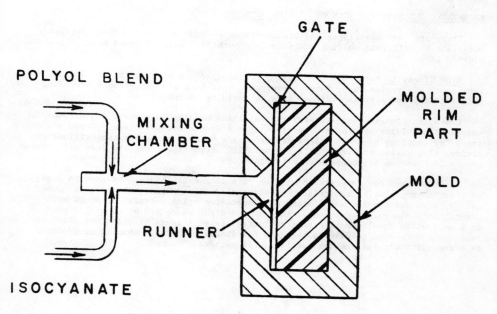

GATE

POLYOL BLEND

MIXING
CHAMBER

MOLDED
RIM
PART

MOLD

RUNNER

ISOCYANATE

Fig. 24   Schematic diagram for RIM.

144

The use of low molding pressure also permits molding RIM materials in non-metallic molds, even rubber molds[16]. Of course, the useful life of molds depends upon the mold material chosen. Table II shows the number of demoldings typically obtained with different mold materials[16].

Table II

TYPICAL NUMBER OF DEMOLDINGS OBTAINED WITH
DIFFERENT MOLD MATERIALS

Mold Material	Number of Demoldings
Steel	50,000 – 200,000
Electroplated copper/nickel	10,000 – 100,000
Cast or wrought aluminum alloys	5,000 – 50,000
Epoxy resin	50 – 1,000
Silicone rubber	10 – 100

Thus if only a few moldings are needed, silicone rubber could be considered. For a large number, a metal mold would probably be selected.

With RIM, the clamp containing a mold is often tilted. A tilted mold allows air to flow ahead of the rising mixture during mold filling; to release this air during molding, vents must be properly located in a mold.

ADVANTAGES AND DISADVANTAGES OF MOLDING METHODS

There are many advantages and disadvantages to consider when molding different materials by different molding equipment and methods. Only selected factors are considered here.

High Viscosity Materials - These materials produce high forces in molding equipment. To resist these forces, equipment must be rigid and strong; providing this rigidity and strength raises costs for molding equipment.

Comparing compression, transfer and injection molding, equipment and methods for compression molding are the simplest; this is a pronounced advantage. Other advantages for compression are a tolerance for a wide variety of rubber compositions and minimal flow during molding. This minimal flow accounts for the low residual strains generally observed in compression moldings.

Disadvantages for compression molding are long cycle times, the need to load each cavity separately, and relatively short mold life. This short life is caused mainly by manual opening and closing of compression molds outisde the press with ensuing mold damage. For example, this damage might be caused by closing a press on a mold while dowel pins are improperly registered (Figure 5). Another disadvantage for compression molding is the need for shaped preforms. Shaping of preforms is often difficult for complex cavity configurations.

In compression molding, inserts in a mold cavity tend to be displaced during molding because they are positioned in an open mold. This open-mold condition can be contrasted to transfer and injection molding, where rubber enters a closed mold containing an insert. A closed mold holds inserts in place in transfer and injection molds in the mold-closing direction. Hence, inserts in transfer and injection molding are less likely to cause mold damage relative to compression molding.

Comparing compression and transfer, transfer molding tends to be more tolerant of non-parallel press platens than compression. Relative movement between the plunger face and the bottom of the transfer pot accomodates some non-parallelism in a transfer mold (Figure 11). Use of non-parallel platens with compression molding tends to cause greater flashing on one side of the mold (Figure 6). The top plate of a compression mold might not remain parallel to the cavity plate if press platens are not parallel.

Again comparing compression and transfer, scrap loss caused by the flash pad (Figure 12) is generally much greater than the flash (Figure 6) that occurs with compression. The volume provided for flash in the flash grooves of a compression mold is about 20% maximum[5]. With transfer, flash pad loss might be 50%[17].

It is possible to reduce this large scrap loss by use of a special transfer mold in which the transfer pot is kept below vulcanization temperature. Hence, rubber normally scrapped as flash pads can be used to make rubber parts. These special molds are more complex and expensive than their counterparts which produce flash pads.

Transfer and injection molding share several advantages relative to compression. One advantage is that preheated rubber enters transfer and injection molds. The higher temperature of this preheated rubber shortens the molding cycle (especially for injection) relative to compression.

Better adhesion of rubber to inserts is another advantage for transfer and injection. Better adhesion generally results from a fresh rubber surface. A fresher rubber surface is provided by transfer and injection relative to compression. But care must be taken to prevent rubber from wiping adhesive from an adhesive-coated insert.

Among different types of injection molding machines, there are relative advantages and disadvantages. With a vertical type machine, the parting line of the mold is horizontal (Figure 18); this is an advantage if inserts are used. The inserts are held in place in the lower portion of the mold by gravity. Hence, there is less potential for mold damage caused by improperly positioned inserts. Also, a vertical machine occupies less floor space than a horizontal machine.

Horizontal machines can be used for injection molding parts containing inserts. Such a machine was discussed earlier (Figure 19)[10].

Injection molds are normally attached to a clamp on an injection molding machine. These molds are usually less subject to damage relative to compression molds. If damaged, injection molds are quite expensive to repair because of their greater complexity.

With injection molding, the ratio (molded part weight/distribution system weight) varies considerably. If the part weight is very small, the weight of the distribution system (Figure 15) might well exceed the weight of saleable parts[8]. This factor is a considerable disadvantage, especially if an expensive material is molded.

In the above methods, rubber is molded against rigid surfaces. Because of a tire's complex shape, it is extremely difficult to mold the interior surface of a tire with a rigid member. Hence a flexible member, a bladder, is used to form the interior surface of a tire. The capability to bladder mold tires in large quantities in automated equipment (Figure 20) is an advantage. A shorter-than-desirable life for bladders is often a disadvantage.

Low Viscosity Materials - Equipment for molding low-viscosity (liquid) materials is generally lower in cost than that used for high-viscosity materials[2]. Some open molds for casting are simple to fabricate, light in weight, low in cost, and are therefore useful for making only a few parts.

An uneven top surface is a disadvantage for a part that is cast in an open mold. This surface might require trimming to meet a specified tolerance. Cast liquid materials sometimes require a long molding cycle, partly because of the long pot life that must be provided to avoid gelation before casting.

Centrifugal casting, and especially vacuum centrifugal casting, shortens cycle time and minimizes trapped air. Rapid distribution of the cast material by a rotating drum (Figure 23) accounts for the shortened time. Another advantage to centrifugal casting is the ability to form thin walls in a part and to push material into small openings in a rotating mold.

With RIM, the very rapid reaction between the isocyanate and polyol blend is a distinct advantage; this reaction causes a rapid temperature rise in the mixture and raises the temperature throughout the part. This higher temperature accelerates the reaction rate permitting short molding cycles. Thus, much of the needed heat is provided by the reacting materials in the RIM mold.

With compression molding of high viscosity materials, the mold provides virtually all the needed heat. Heat transfer into rubber from its mold is a slow process; thus cycle times are long for thick parts.

While there are relative advantages and disadvantages for the different equipment and methods, none of them are without occasional problems.

MOLDING PROBLEMS AND CORRECTIVE ACTION

It is no surprise that problems occur when one considers the variety of materials, methods and equipment involved in molding. Selected molding problems are reviewed below along with possible corrective action.

Dimensions and Appearance - Mold lubricants are widely used to provide easy release of rubber parts from a mold. With continued use, some of these lubricants form a deposit on the mold which eventually causes an indentation in molded parts. To avoid this appearance problem, molds must be kept clean, and several cleaning methods are available[18]. Most of these methods require removing a mold from its press; then the mold is cleaned by methods such as particulate blasting, or by ultrasonic or chemical means.

One method permits cleaning a mold in place in a press, by vulcanizing a special cleaning composition in a dirty mold[18]. This method is especially useful for parts which have undercuts, because the surface of the mold forming the undercut is often difficult to clean by other means.

Critical parts like O-rings must be functional and have a desirable appearance[17]. If a gate is used during molding, it should be small and located to provide a satisfactory molded surface. Considerations such as these are especially important during design of a mold; an improperly designed mold is often expensive to modify.

Flash is evident on many rubber parts, especially parts made by compression molding. If flash is objectionable, it can be removed by methods such as hand trimming or buffing.

Flash can be also removed by tumbling parts together at a temperature low enough to make the rubber brittle. Dry ice or liquid nitrogen can provide the low temperature needed for deflashing. Because flash is generally thin, it becomes brittle before the bulk of the rubber part. During deflashing, the brittle flash breaks near the part surface as it tumbles against another part.

Non-parallel press platens sometimes cause uneven flash thickness on compression molded parts (Figure 8). Overtightening the nuts on the press posts can cause this non-parallelism. Overtightening compresses the shoulder on a post and changes the dimension between the press head and ram bolster[19]. This problem can be corrected by equalizing the shoulder-to-shoulder distances on the posts. The shoulder should have sufficient surface area to resist yielding when the nuts on the posts are tightened[19].

Again referring to Figure 8, more contact area between mold faces and press platens lessens deflection in the press head and ram bolster. Most platens are designed to have the mold uniformly distribute its load over at least 80% of the platen area[19]. Because the mold shown in Figure 8 is much too small for the press, it significantly increases deflection of press components.

Molds that are too small for presses can cause permanent metal distortion. This distortion can occur in the mold or platens. Thus, there are several reasons to properly match mold size and press size.

Porosity - Porosity is a problem that occurs with both liquid and high viscosity materials that are molded by several methods. There are two major sources of porosity. One is trapped air and the other is moisture.

If moisture is present in a polyol blend, it reacts with isocyanate to form carbon dioxide gas, and the gas causes porosity. To minimize the formation of carbon dioxide, moisture must be removed from the polyol blend before it is mixed with an isocyanate.

Moisture causes porosity in high viscosity materials for a different reason. High molding temperatures convert moisture into vapor. If the degree of crosslinking in a part is inadequate to resist the pressure of this vapor, porosity will occur. Porosity can be minimized by curing (increasing crosslinking) for a sufficient time period before opening a press.

Incorporation of calcium oxide in a rubber composition is another approach to reduce porosity. Calcium oxide selectively absorbs moisture in a composition. To further minimize moisture-caused porosity, store raw materials under dry conditions and expel any moisture present by mixing at sufficiently high temperatures.

Trapped air causes porosity in both liquid and high viscosity materials. With liquid materials, raising temperature reduces viscosity; reduced viscosity helps to release air[1]. Also, surfactants can be incorporated to reduce viscosity[20].

With high-viscosity materials, increased viscosity sometimes aids removal of air during molding. Viscosity can be increased by modifying a formulation or by reducing molding temperature. Higher viscosity provides higher forces for squeezing air out during molding.

A variety of venting techniques are used to remove air during molding. With tires, for example, air removal from the inner tire surface is aided by ridges molded into the surface of the bladder which contacts the tire (Figure 22)[12]. These ridges form a flow path for escape of air.

For release of air from the outside surface of the tire, vent holes are drilled into a mold. These holes are open to atmosphere on the outside of the mold; they might also be connected to a manifold that serves as a common vacuum source. Special lubricants applied to the inner and outer tire surfaces before molding also help air to escape.

Removal of air is sometimes a problem with injection molding because rubber enters a mold cavity rapidly. Rapid entry of rubber compresses the air in the cavity and sharply increases air temperature. If venting is inadequate, air temperature becomes high enough to degrade a rubber surface. To avoid this effect, provide a sufficient number and size of vents for molds. Locate these vents so they release air at an acceptable rate.

A vacuum source is sometimes attached to a vent to remove air from an injection mold cavity. An example of this is shown in Figure 25 for a molded diaphragm[21].

Release - The ease of release of rubber from molds varies considerably. Release is affected by factors such as the material being molded, cavity surface finish, and shape and complexity of a molded part.

It is not surprising that liquid urethanes tend to stick in a mold cavity. They are widely used as adhesives. To minimize this problem, apply an effective release agent uniformly to a cavity surface before molding.

High viscosity rubbers, like natural rubber and EPDM, usually release from molds much easier than urethanes. Even so, release agents are often used with natural rubber and EPDM to aid their flow and release, especially for parts having a complex shape.

The material used in a mold cavity and its surface finish affect release of molded parts. Release is aided by a cavity surface having a desirable finish. For example, parts release more easily from a chromium plated surface than from a steel surface[5]. For most rubber products, an acceptable surface roughness is in the range 0.25-0.50 μm (10-20 micro-inches)[5].

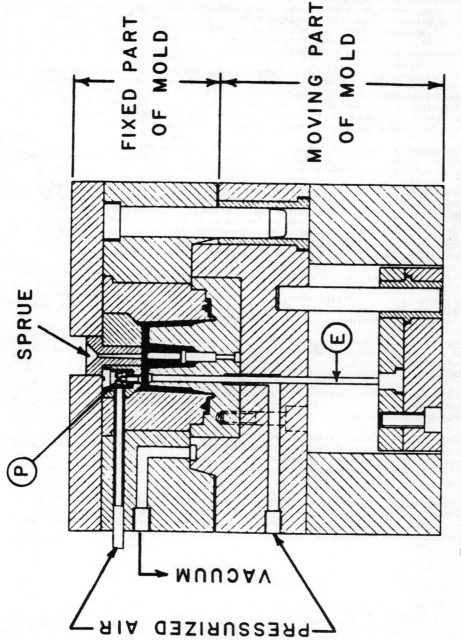

Fig. 25   Injection mold showing system for automatically ejecting parts.
(Courtesy of European Rubber Journal)

The surface area of a molded part also affects ease of release. If a large surface area must be released in shear, then a release agent containing a silicone fluid can be used. This type of release agent is also a good lubricant. Hence, a lubricating release agent aids removal of the rubber cylinder in shear from the cavity plate shown in Figure 6. This shape part should be relatively easy to remove because of its simple shape and smooth surface.

If a part is thin and complex in shape, release and removal is more difficult. An example[21] of a part like this is shown in Figure 25. Automatic part removal is accomplished by applying air pressure to the piston marked "P" when the mold opens. Then the ejection pin, marked "E", moves up and strips the diaphragm from the moving part of the open mold in about one second. Another technique to remove rubber parts from molds is to contact them with a rotating brush.

Composites - Rubber is frequently combined with other materials to form a composite. Composites like tires might be formed prior to molding; composites like bonded rubber/metal parts might be formed during molding.

The uniformity of tires is affected not only by the molding process, but also by storage conditions prior to molding[12]. For example, an uncured tire might be exposed to uneven temperatures while it is on a loading stand (Figure 20). The part of the tire closest to the mold can become up to 8°C warmer (15°F) than the rest of the tire[12]. This temperature difference can cause unequal cure rates and uniformity problems in finished tires. To minimize uneven heating, insulation can be installed between the molding press and the tire on its loading stand.

When bonded rubber/metal composites are molded by injection, another problem can occur. Rubber injected into a mold might impinge upon the adhesive surface of an adhesive-coated metal and wipe adhesive from the metal. Loss of adhesive causes poor rubber-to-metal bonding. To avoid this problem, locate the gate so that rubber does not impinge directly upon adhesive-coated metal.

Shrinkage - Shrinkage is the difference between the dimensions of a mold cavity and those of a rubber part, when both are measured at room temperature. For high-viscosity materials, shrinkage is as low as 0.52% and as high as 3.9%[1]. A typical value is 1.5%[5].

For dense urethanes, shrinkage is in a range of about 1.8 to 2.2%[22]. Shrinkage for RIM urethane is typically about 1-2%. RIM urethane normally has a cellular interior with a dense skin.

Shrinkage is affected by factors such as curing temperature and the level of filler in a composition. Sometimes curing temperatures are raised to shorten molding cycles. This higher temperature causes higher shrinkage in a cured part. If this higher shrinkage is a problem, it can be lowered by increasing the level of filler in a composition.

Higher filler loadings reduce shrinkage. The upper limit of filler is limited by factors such as allowable viscosity for the composition and specification requirements. Hence, in making a change to correct a molding problem or any other problem, consideration must be given to the overall effect of the change.

Backrinding - Backrinding describes the torn or gouged appearance of some vulcanizates at a mold parting line[23]. Backrinding is caused by the continuing thermal expansion of rubber in a mold after crosslinking occurs at the parting line. This expansion forces crosslinked rubber into the opening at the parting line and causes this crosslinked rubber to rupture.

Both molded part geometry and rubber composition affect backrinding. Backrinding becomes more severe as the surface area/mass ratio decreases for a molded part. Hence, backrinding is most severe for a sphere or ball where this ratio is minimum.

Lowering cure temperature reduces backrinding, as does preheating a rubber compound before placing it in a mold cavity. Molding the minimum weight of compound required for a given part also reduces backrinding.

SUMMARY

Equipment and methods for molding rubber materials are discussed in terms of the crosslinkable materials that are molded. The viscosity of these materials varies from extremely high, like cheese, to very low, like castor oil. This large difference in viscosity significantly affects the choice of molding equipment and methods for these materials.' Other factors must be considered such as:

- Economics
- Complexity and specifications for a molded part
- Number of parts to be molded
- Allowable part tolerances

While some molding problems can be identified relatively easily and then corrected, others are difficult and costly to correct. For example, it might be necessary to alter or redesign molds if they do not fill properly; this can be quite expensive.

To maximize success in molding, materials, methods and equipment must be chosen carefully. Then the proper controls must be placed on the molding operation to insure continuing success.

REFERENCES

1. J. G. Sommer, Rubber Chem. Technol. 51, 738 (1978).

2. W. M. Haines, Elastomerics 110 (9) 26 (1978).

3. J. D. Byam and G. P. Colbert, presented at a meeting of the Rubber Division of the American Chemical Society, Chicago, IL, May 3-6, 1977.

4. G. P. Colbert, Akron Rubber Group, Inc., Technical Symposiums, 1978-1979, p. 66.

5. S. W. Schmitt, Neoprene Bulletin NP-450.1, "Molding Neoprene".

6. F. J. Persichilli, Rubber World 180 (4) 102 (1979) July.

7. Unpublished work, H. N. Grover and J. G. Sommer, The General Tire & Rubber Co.

8. W. D. Fleming, Rubber Age 107 (2) 49 (1975) Feb.

9. J. A. Jannet, Elastomerics 112 (2) 22 (1980) Feb.

10. H. J. Rienzner, Rubber Chem. Technol. 48, 263 (1975).

11. M. A. Wheelans, European Rubber Journal 163 (1) 13 (1981) Feb.

12. G. E. Isaksson, "Methods of Curing Tires", presented at the 16th Annual Lecture Series sponsored by the Akron Rubber Group, University of Akron, Akron, OH, April 30, 1979.

13. G. F. Morton and G. B. Quinton, in Rubber Technology and Manufacture, C. M. Blow, Ed., Newnes-Butterworths, London, 1977, p. 365.

14. Anon., Rubber World 174 (5) 25 (1976) Aug.

15. J. F. Coleman, J. of Elastomers and Plastics 8, 185 (1976).

16. U. Knipp and W. E. Becker, in Reaction Injection Molding, W. E. Becker, Ed., Van Nostrand Rinehold Company, New York, 1979, p. 233.

17. H. G. Gilette, Rubber World 157 (1) 67 (1967) Oct.

18. J. G. Sommer, H. N. Grover and P. T. Suman, Rubber Chem. Technol. 49, 1129 (1976).

19. H. A. Trishnan, India Rubber World 123 (6) 673 (1951) Mar.

20. E. N. Doyle, "The Development and Use of Polyurethane Products", McGraw-Hill Book Company, New York, 1971, p. 313.

21. M. Egli, European Rubber Journal <u>160</u> (2) 17 (1978) Mar.

22. P. Wright and A. P. C. Cumming, "Solid Polyurethane Elastomers", Maclaren and Sons, London, 1969, p. 202.

23. J. G. Sommer, presented at a meeting of the Rubber Division, American Chemical Society, Indianapolis, IN, May 8-11, 1984.

WORK ASSIGNMENT NO. 6

CHAPTER 6.   MOLDING EQUIPMENT AND METHODS

INSTRUCTIONS: Read each question carefully, select one, and only one, appropriate answer to complete each statement.

1. Beside the viscosity of the material being molded, the choice of a molding method is affected by:
____ (a) the tensile strength of the molded part
____ (b) the color of the molded part
____ (c) tolerances required for molded parts
____ (d) none of above

2. Compression is a major method for molding high-viscosity material. Another major method for same material is
____ (a) casting
____ (b) transfer
____ (c) RIM (reaction injection molding)
____ (d) none of above

3. Bladder molding is important because
____ (a) molding between bladders is an advantage
____ (b) virtually all tires are made by this method
____ (c) extremely high molding pressures are used
____ (d) none of above

4. Extremely high pressure used in injection molding results in
____ (a) poor surface appearance
____ (b) lower viscosity caused by higher flow rates
____ (c) long service life for molds
____ (d) none of above

5. The Mooney viscometer is most effective in predicting behavior of
____ (a) RIM
____ (b) casting
____ (c) injection molding
____ (d) compression molding

6. Closure dimensions are less accurate for compression molding than for transfer or injection molding because
____ (a) the thickness of flash formed in compression molding is usually greater and more variable than for the other methods
____ (b) compression molds are larger than other molds
____ (c) compression molds have a rougher surface finish
____ (d) cure cycles are shorter

7. Compared to transfer molding, compression molding has the advantage of
____ (a) a wider tolerance for different rubber compositions
____ (b) shorter molding cycles
____ (c) better insert-to-rubber bonding
____ (d) ability to easily hold an insert in required position in mold cavity

8. Thick flash is sometimes desired in compression molding because
___ (a) it reduces material cost
___ (b) many molded parts can be simultaneously removed from a mold as a sheet
___ (c) closure dimensions are better controlled
___ (d) cure cycles are shorter

9. Clearance between the vertical surfaces of a plunger and pot in a transfer mold shoud be such that
___ (a) cure cycles are not too long
___ (b) the mold does not open at the parting line during molding
___ (c) non-black as well as black compounds can be processed
___ (d) excessive flow of rubber between plunger and pot is avoided and binding is prevented between plunger and pot

10. In comparison to the ram injection machine, the screw injection machine
___ (a) provides higher molding pressures
___ (b) has the advantage of raising the rubber temperature above the barrel temperature by doing work on it
___ (c) is the less popular
___ (d) all of above

11. Injection molding becomes economically unfavorable if
___ (a) too much rubber is used in its distribution system
___ (b) short cure cycles are used
___ (c) a very large number of the same parts are made
___ (d) high mold temperatures are used

12. Vacuum centrifugal casting possesses which of the following advantages
___ (a) longer curing cycles
___ (b) reduction in the amount of trapped air
___ (c) capability to handle high viscosity materials
___ (d) none of above

13. Molded parts prepared by the RIM process have very short molding cycles because
___ (a) the liberation of heat (and the associated temperature rise) is initiated very shortly after the material components are mixed
___ (b) the surface of molds is smooth
___ (c) molding pressure is low
___ (d) heat is rapidly transferred from the mold to the RIM mixture

14. In order to produce molded parts with good appearance and consistent dimensions
___ (a) the molds must be kept clean
___ (b) the cure cycles must be short
___ (c) the molds must be much smaller than the press platens
___ (d) the rubber used must have high resistance to flow

15. The major causes of porosity problems are
___ (a) use of high viscosity material and application of mold release
___ (b) moisture and trapped air
___ (c) low molding temperature and long curing cycle
___ (d) none of above

CHAPTER 7

VULCANIZATION - METHODS AND EQUIPMENT

ROBERT A. GARDINER

HI-TECH EXTRUSION SYSTEMS, INC.
NORTH STONINGTON, CONN   06359

INTRODUCTION

Vulcanization is an irreversible process during which an elastomeric compound
is, through chemical crosslinking in its molecular structure, converted from a
thermoplastic to a thermoset having improved elastic properties. The processing
of vulcanizable elastomeric compound is divided into two steps. The first step is
the shaping or configuring of the product while the material is still in its
thermoplastic state. The second step is chemical conversion of the shaped material
into its final thermoset state.

The term vulcanization is derived from the early days of the discovery that certain natural polymers could be treated in the presence of heat and sulfur, resulting
in a merterial possessing very unique properties of extensibility, elasticity,
reasonable thermal stability and impermeability to water and air. From the days of
mythology, the god Vulcan was identified as the god of fire and brimstone, brimstone
being what is known today as sulfur. Hence, the unique polymer conversion from
thermoplastic to thermoset, whether or not conducted in the presence of sulfur, has
been known as vulcanization.

VULCANIZABLE ELASTOMERS

All vulcanizable elastomers have one thing in common, that of a degree of unsaturation within the polymer structure. Quite simply, this is defined as the presence
of double bonds between carbon atoms periodically along the carbonaceous skeleton
of the polymer to be processed. The elastomers in this state possess plastic-like
properties, although not necessarily the useful properties that the thermoplastic
might have. In particular, the material will soften with heat and return to its
original state when cooled; a process that can be repeated assuming that no other
side effects or reactions are introduced concurrently.

Due to this behavior, elastomers can be mixed with other ingredients effectively.
Shape can be formed to precise detail by forcing this material through a configured
die on a continuous basis under pressure wherein the process is known as extrusion.
Up to this point, there is no fundamental distinction between the processing
characteristics of plastics and that of elastomers.

Once the material has been shaped, the thermoplastic is simply cooled, which
completes the essence of the process. The vulcanizable elastomer, on the other hand,
must have the vulcanizing reaction completed, before the product is coold to finish
the comparable process. The vulcanizing reactions are those which promote attack of
the carbon-to-carbon double bonds. During vulcanization these bonds are broken and
allowed to react with other materials such as sulfur-bearing ingredients wherein
adjacent polymer chains are attached to one another, or to promote additional single-
bond links to carbon units on adjacent polymer chains giving a similar result of
crosslinking. Once this reaction takes place, the process is as irreversible as

that reaction through which the elastomer itself was produced. Therefore, vulcanization can be considered a permanent change to the elastomeric material.

The actual chemical reactions in vulcanization that can and do take place are many, and are quite complex. Since this discussion is an overview, it is sufficient to present only the simple essence of vulcanization.

BASIC VULCANIZATION SYSTEMS

In vulcanization there are two basic reactions of major commercial significance. One of the reactions involves crosslinking of sulfer-bearing materials incorporated into the elastomeric compound and promoted by the presence of appropriate catalytic agents and internal conditions such as pH and other similar factors, and supported by the addition of energy in the form of heat.

The other basic reaction is created by the attack of free radicals upon the unsaturated polymer, which results in the carbon-to-carbon crosslinking alluded to earlier in the discussion. In this case, it takes energy to produce the free radicals, which in turn produce the desired end result. Although the common approach to the production of free radicals is the thermal decomposition of certain peroxides, there are mechanisms such as electron beam radiation wherein free radicals can be produced without heating the polymer structure, or, in theory, adding any ingredient to the elastomeric compound for the purpose of vulcanization.

The other fundamental that should be understood is that the vulcanization process takes place in conformity to the Arrehenius equation:

$$\log K = -E/2.303\ RT + C$$

k = the reaction rate constant
E = activation energy
R = gas constant
T = absolute temperature
C = constant

This equation in essence states that the greater the amount of heat (or energy), the faster the vulcanizing reaction will take place. Since all of the more common methods of vulcanization involve thermal energy, it can be stated that the higher the vulcanization temperature, the faster the process can be completed. To that end, a graphic representation of a typical reaction is illustrated in Figure 1.

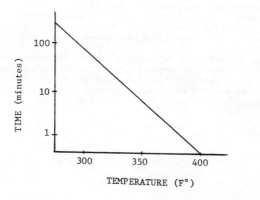

Figure 1

THERMAL ENGERY FOR VULCANIZATION

There is one major physical phenomena that must be contended with in the practical application of thermal vulcanization; and that is heat transfer. Just as the chemical reaction is a time-dependent temperature-interrelated phenomena, the process of heating the part to be vulcanized also has dependence on a number of factors that impact the rate of temperature rise as well as the uniformity of vulcanization throughout the part. Basically, the vulcanization process is that of applying heat at a certain temperature for a certain period of time.

Since thermal energy is most commonly used in the promotion of vulcanization, the methods by which this energy is applied to the elastomeric material, constitute an important part of rubber technology.

Saturated Steam Method

By far, the most common thermal energy used in vulcanization has been saturated steam. Saturated steam is readily generated in the plant and has a very high energy content per pound. Although not totally free from oxygen, it has oxygen content so low that polymer oxidation at elevated temperature is not a problem. Therefore, it can be considered an inert environment for the vulcanization or curing process.

Saturated steam does have a major hindrance, namely its temperature is directly related to the pressure in the vulcanization process. Table I is an abbreviated steam tabe showing this relationship. Pressure to a reasonable degree can be desirable in the thermal vulcanization process. It produces a more compacted end product because the pressure resists the volatility of various components within the elastomeric composite and/or the vaporization of vulcanization by-products.

With respect to rate of heat transfer, saturated steam can be assumed to have essentially an infinite heat transfer coefficient, that ability to heat the product surface. In English units, this term is given in BTU/hr-sq.ft/°F, or the amount of heat per hour that can be applied to the surface of the product per degree of temperature difference between that of the heating media and the product itself.

Heated Gas Method

Heated air is the next more common thermal energy used in vulcanization, although its use is generally confined to continuous processes. Heated air must be used only with polymers where oxidation will not inhibit the curing process or degrade the polymer structure. It has a generally low heat transfer coefficient. However, air can be heated practically to much higher temperatures than steam. Noting that the heat transfer coefficient are dependent on the temperature gradient between the media and the product surface temperature, much of the inefficiency of heated air can be diminished simply by taking advantage of its high temperature capability.

Heated air is much more easily contained and re-used than saturated steam. The process can be readily vented for removal of contaminants. The product emerges from processing clean, free of media contamination and water spotting. Heated air can readily be compressed. It can provide an elevated pressure for vulcanization, although the use of high pressure is not a very common practice.

TABLE I

<u>TEMPERATURE OF SATURATED STEAM AT VARIOUS PRESSURES AT SEA LEVEL</u>

PRESSURE psi	TEMPERATURE °F	°C	PRESSURE psi	TEMPERATURE °F	°C
0	212.0	100.0	80	323.8	162.1
5	227.1	108.4	85	327.6	164.2
10	239.4	115.2	90	331.2	166.2
20	258.8	126.0	100	337.8	169.9
30	274.1	134.5	125	352.9	179.8
40	286.7	141.5	150	365.9	185.5
50	297.7	147.6	175	377.4	191.9
55	302.6	150.3	200	387.9	197.7
60	307.4	153.0	225	397.2	202.9
65	311.7	155.4	250	406.1	207.8
70	316.0	157.0	300	421.0	216.1
75	320.1	160.0	350	436.5	224.7

A method essentially identical to heated air is that of heated nitrogen. Since air is approximately 80% nitrogen, from a performance perspective, there is little difference between the two. The main reason for the use of nitrogen for vulcanization is to prevent oxidation of sensitive elastomers, to provide a compressed source of gas for cure systems operating at elevated pressures, and in some cases, to achieve higher operating temperatures wherein oxidizing effects may limit the applicability of heated air. There are some instances where other low cost gases such as carbon dioxide may be utilized for similar reasons.

Heat Transfer Fluid Method

There have also been a variety of heat transfer fluids and pseudo-fluids used in the vulcanization process. These fluids must be totally inert to the elastomeric composite over the entire operating range of temperatures of the process. This further implies that no material will be absorbed into the product, no surface reactions are involved, and no other undesirable side effects are found. Further, the media itself must undergo no changes during continual processing. It must retain its properties throughout the necessary temperature cycling involved.

Some of the more successful materials used for heat transfer in vulcanization processes are inorganic eutectic salt mixtures, certain organic glycerides, and minute inorganic particles fluidized by heated air, which act as dry pseudo-liquid in the majority of its properties. These heat transfer materials have moderate heat transfer coefficients and are desirable from that property alone. They are generally used in continuous vulcanization processes, more commonly, but not exclusively non-pressurized, and provide reasonably rapid temperature rises and moderate vulcanization speeds.

Both the glycerides and the eutectic salts have specific temperature limits of operation that must be observed. They are further characterized by their water solubility which facilitates their removal from the product once the process is complete. Fluidized particles, which can operate at much higher temperatures, must be removed from the product by physical means.

The products vulcanized with heat transfer fluids and pseudo-fluids must be postcleaned. There is appreciable loss of materials used for heat transfer in these vulcanization processes. This loss can have a major impact on operational cost.

Direct Energy Transfer Methods

The next new methods to be discussed are direct energy transfer methods of vulcanization. They are not necessarily more effective. Infrared heating is a common industrial process. Energy is imparted to the product surface through the absorption of energy emitted in the near or far infrared spectrum. Nevertheless, the absorption is almost totally dependent on the materials' surface to efficiently absorb as opposed to reflect this energy. Since a great many elastomeric products are black, this methods appears to be ideal. However, the use of infrared heating has been actually quite limited. To a large extent, this is due to the fact it is a "line-of-sight method", wherein energy distribution about the part must be very uniform to be effective. Secondly, environmental contamination has a devastating influence on its efficiency since vulcanization residues tend to contribute to this degradation of performance. If one were to critically observe the majority

of infrared heating installations, one would find a great many were simply infrared air heaters wherein the heated air is the heating media, thus negating the
efficiency of the primary heating method.

Microwave heating is a totally different energy form than that of infrared.
Microwave, being of much higher frequency and shorter wave length than infrared,
is a mass heating method as opposed to a surface heating technique. The material
being heated has a major influence in the efficiency of transformation of electromagnetic energy to heat energy. Microwave heating depends upon the rubber compound's response to the rapidity of the electromagnetic fields oscillation from
positive to negative to positive at the frequency imposed. If the rubber compound
has either polar characteristics or semi-conductive properties, then the product
will heat very efficiently. However, if the rubber compound is deficient in these
properties, the product can act nearly transparent to the microwave field.

There is another method receiving more attention in these days of the "energy
crunch" - the use of ultraviolet (UV) energy. This is not truly a process
method as the compound is designed with materials that react chemically in the
presence of UV and result in vulcanization.

VULCANIZATION METHODS AND EQUIPMENT

The commercially available equipment for vulcanization of elastomeric products
is divided into three classes as follows:

A. Batch Vulcanization

B. Semi-continuous Vulcanization

C. Continuous Vulcanization (C.V.)

Batch Vulcanization Equipment

Batch equipment, as its name implies, is that type of equipment wherein the pre-
shaped product has been placed in trays, coiled on pans, wound on reels, or otherwise carefully prepared and supported so this product can be placed in the batch
vulcanizer.

These vulcanizers are commonly autoclaves, or steam pressure vessels, analogous
to a home pressure cooker. These autoclaves are of a variety of sizes, but typically
may be horizontal cylinders of 25 feet or more in length and 4 feet or more in
diameter. Vertical vulcanizers are generally larger in diameter and shorter in length.
These units are designed to accommodate steam pressures resulting in process temperatures of up to 350°F or more.

Extruded shapes vulcanized in this manner are generally supported on formed trays
to avoid deformation of the cross-section while being heated. This will prevent
the finished part from forming a permanent curvature. Product lengths are confined
to the size of the trays and the length of the vulcanizer available.

Hose products are processed in two ways in the vulcanizer. Many premium low-
pressure hoses and hydraulic hoses are prepared for curing by covering the hose
exterior with a lead casing which forms a continuous mold. This lead covered hose
is wound on a reel and placed in the vulcanizer. After the curing is completed,

the lead sheath is stripped off the hose. Some cables are produced by the lead molded process as well.

More commonly used for the textile-reinforced low-pressure hoses is the open steam curing process. In this process the hose is loosely coiled in pans, usually only one or two layers deep. The pans are stacked with spacers between them, and placed into the vulcanizer for curing. The time required to stay in a vulcanizer and achieve complete vulcanization varies widely, but typical schedules range from 45 minutes to one hour.

The steam vulcanizer or autoclave is the only important batch vulcanization equipment in use today. Hot boxes using heated air are utilized in some specialty applications for a variety of reasons, but are far too slow to support mass production. Typical cure cycles in hot boxes can exceed 24 hours.

Semi-Continuous Vulcanization Equipment

In the semi-continuous equipment for vulcanization, there are two types to be considered:

1. The rotary press
2. Pultrusion methods

The rotary press is essentially a molding operation for a product that is greater in length than the mold. The heated platens of this press work incrementally along the length of the product until it is completely vulcanized from end to end. This process is commonly used for the vulcanization of conveyor belting and similarly large products required to be continuous in long lengths.

Pultrusion or pulse extrusion is a contraction for pulse and extrusion. It is also similar to a molding method. Its use has been confined to fiberglass reinforced plastic-like materials. It is used in Europe and Japan to produce continuous shapes, specialty cables and hoses. In some cases, the technique has been extended into a true continuous molding process, where the product is continuously moving as opposed to being indexed periodically.

In all of these semi-continuous methods, the heat for the process is transmitted to the product from the metal surfaces of the surrounding mold. These mold surfaces are heated by steam coils or electrical resistance heaters.

Continuous Vulcanization (C.V.) Equipment

There is a greater variety of continuous vulcanization (C.V.) methods than either batch or semi-continuous processes. Continuous vulcanization, perhaps surprisingly so, has not supplanted the batch processes to a major degree. One of the main reasons for this, is that C.V. systems are not as versatile as batch methods. C. V. has made major strides in the last few years, particularly in the manufacture of hose products. Nevertheless, a C.V. method is widely utilized in processing of two major products.

Vulcanized wire and cable production has for many years enjoyed the benefits of C.V. This is due to the requirements for long lengths and high volume of production.

The other product using C.V. is that of extruded sponge. C.V. is essential for accommodation of the growth in length due to the "blowing" of the sponge during vulcanization. Many rubber companies today are coming to the realization that to be truly competitive in profit margin specialization, not versatility, is the key. The implementation of this specialization concept will probably result in more proliferation of C.V. systems, both those in use today and some that have not established commerical feasibility as yet.

The commercially significant C.V. equipment are the following:

1. Steam tube vulcanizer

2. Pressurized gas or liquid vulcanizer

3. Hot air vulcanizing tunnel

4. Continuous microwave oven

5. Liquid or pseudo-liquid curing trough

6. Electron beam vulcanizer

Of the six classes of continuous vulcanizers, some are primarily designed to vulcanize under pressure while others are suitable for vulcanization at atmospheric pressure. The pressurized methods are commonly used in the production of electric wire and cable and occasionally used in the production of mandrel-built hose.

1. Steam Tube Vulcanizer –

The steam tube has all of the attributes of the batch autoclave. The major difference is that these tubular vessels, ranging from 150 ft. in length, are operated at higher pressures and resultant temperatures to induce more rapid vulcanization. The more common operating condition for steam tube curing is 250 psi saturated steam with 406°F temperature. The steam tube is sealed at the product entry end by the extrusion head itself being coupled to the tube. Since it is desirable to also cool the product under pressure, the final length of 25% to 40% at the exit end of the tube is filled with water. A flexible seal, shaped to the product, is installed at the exit. Under pressure, the seal will leak water which lubricates the product as it goes through the seal. The system is equipped with a water pumping system to maintain the water level and contain the steam pressure. The great majority of vulcanizable wire and cable is produced by this method. Only a small percentage of hose is produced in this fashion.

2. Pressurized Gas or Liquid Vulcanizer –

A similar method has evolved in recent years in the electric cable industry that uses heated inert gas in lieu of saturated steam. The most common gas used is nitrogen. The advantage of this system is that higher temperatures can be achieved at lower operating pressures, or temperature independent of pressure. In the cable industry, this approach has beneficial quality attributes as well as economic advantages, particularly in the area of energy consumption. Within this method, there are two means of heating the product. One system uses infrared heating, either through infrared (IR) elements or by external heating of the tube to attain IR emission. In this approach, the nitrogen is used as a pressurized blanket. The other method utilizes an external heating system and blower, where the nitrogen is heated and circulated at very high velocity giving efficient heat transfer from the gas to the product.

Another similar method finding favor in production units of smaller capacity, is the use of pressurized eutectic molten salts. This method again uses the continuous tube concept, sealed similarly to the steam tube, where liquefied inorganic salt mixtures are circulated to provide heat to the product for vulcanization. The primary appeal for this method is in the hose and specialty cable industry.

3. Hot Air Vulcanizing Tunnel -

Profile extrusion, both cellular and dense, or in combination, are most commonly vulcanized continuously under atmospheric pressure. The most common method, due to its early origin, simplicity, and versatility is the hot air tunnel. The continuous tunnel is usually fabricated in sections and fitted with a full-length conveyor belt to transport the product through this process. Typical hot air tunnels range in length from 10 feet for some silicone products, up to 150 feet or more.

Hot air methods are attractive for sponge products in particular, where high production speed can readily be achieved. Many dense products are also being produced by the same method, particularly those of smaller cross-sections. The process is simple, and the product emerges with a clean surface. There have been a number of enhancements made available in hot air vulcanization to increase the productivity and efficiency. Such methods are the introduction of high velocity air propulsion, incorporation of infrared direct heating techniques, and the use of microwave energy.

4. Continuous Microwave Oven -

Microwave systems are quite often identified as "stand-alone" systems, but seldom in practice are they employed in that fashion. The microwave vulcanization equipment uniquely fulfills the needs of microwave energy distribution, safety, and general communication requirements. Invariably, microwave is used in concert with another media, such as hot air, to provide the complete vulcanization system. This is necessitated by the fact that microwave energy can provide very rapid heating of a properly compounded elastomeric material. In high speed operations, even though the extrudate has been heated, it may not have reached the full state of cure. To complete the curing process, the product temperature must be retained for additional time in a controlled temperature environment. In these cases, means other than microwave energy are utilized.

Microwave energy has also found use in boosting the capacity of other vulcanization systems by pre-heating the product. Other uses of microwave are those associated with multi-use systems where there may or may not be compounds suitable for microwave heating.

5. Liquid or Pseudo-liquid Curing Trough -

There is a class of C.V. systems that are typified by fabricated troughs containing liquids or pseudo-liquids. In these methods, the product is either pulled or conveyed through a heated liquid. These troughs are much shorter in length than non-enhanced hot air tunnels due to the higher effect of heat transfer. This method does require the cleaning of the product once it has been vulcanized. Products such as hose can be readily cleaned. However, the more intricate profiles that are used in seals and gaskets can pose major cleaning difficulties. The two most common methods are the molten salt bath (also known as L.C.M. or liquid curing media) and the fluidized bed. The L.C.M. used molten eutectic salts while the fluidized bed uses small glass spheres that are fluidized by heated air.

6. Electron Beam Vulcanizer -

Electron Beam vulcanizers, although having made some major strides in both technology and market position, have not made a significant penetration into the field of rubber processing. This method is more commonly referred to as radiation vulcanization.

The reasons that the electron beam vulcanizer has not proliferated are related to cost and throughput requirements for economical operation. Installations cost in the six figures. First, the electron beam accelerator is very expensive and secondly, the heavily shielded facility required to comply with radiation safety is an additional cost.

Radiation vulcanization depends on the voltage and power of the accelerator. The acceleration voltage determines the depth of beam penetration into the product, while the electrical power relates to the amount of material that can be processed per hour.

In most typical applications, a beam scanning approach is utilized to achieve total product coverage and uniform radiation. Scanning can be accomplished either by beam motion or by moving the product with respect to the fixed beam. Both techniques are utilized. In many products with circular cross-sections, the product is festooned within the chamber, which accomplishes multiple passes through the beam, while at the same time being rotated to expose the total circumference to the energy.

The economical application of electron beam vulcanizers to date is limited to certain specialty products of exceptional properties demanded by the military and the aircraft industry, such as special wire, cable and shrink tubing. Because of the high capital expenditure involved in equipment, electron beam vulcanizers are usually not utilized unless the product demand is high in both quality and quantity.

SUMMARY

The discovery of vulcanization was the foundation of the rubber industry. Through vulcanization, an elastomeric material is converted from a thermoplastic to a thermoset with greatly improved elastic properties. Thus, rubber became an engineering material suitable for numerous important industrial and commercial applications. Today, the batch process is no longer the only vulcanization process used in the rubber industry. The continuous vulcanization (C.V.) process and the semi-C.V. process have been gaining popularity, especially for high-volume production of rubber goods.

A wide variety of vulcanization equipment utilizing different methods of transferring thermal energy is currently available. Each has its own advantage an limitations. Therefore, selection of process and equipment must be made carefully, based on the properties and the processability of the elastomeric compound, the size and shape of the article, the quality requirement of the finished product, the production output demand, and the price and operating cost of the equipment itself.

GENERAL REFERENCES

1. Alliger, G. and Sjothum, I.J., eds, "Vulcanization of Elastomers", Chapman & Hall, London, England (1964)

2. Blow, C. M., ed., "Rubber Technology and Manufacture", Butterworth & Company, London, England (1971)

3. Chabinsky, I. J., "Practical Applications of Microwave Energy in the Rubber Industry", Elastomerics, 115 (1), 17 (1983)

4. Evans, C. W., "Continuous Vulcanization in Europe - Present and Future", Rubber Age, 103 (5), 53 (1971)

5. Gohlisch, H. J., "Salt Bath and UHF Methods", Rubber Age, 103 (4), 49 (1971)

6. Newell, W. G., Soden, A. L., and Watson, W. F., "Recent Developments in Fluidized Bed Continuous Vulcanization" (Research Report #185), Rubber and Plastics Research Association, Shawbury, England (1970)

7. Proceedings of Educational Symposium No. 1, "Processing of Elastomers", ACS Rubber Division Meeting, May 1977

8. Schindler, U., "Microwaves in the Extruded and Molded Rubber Goods Industry", Elastomerics, 110 (5), 42 (1978)

9. Schoenbeck, M. A., "Compounding Elastomers for Continuous Curing", Rubber World, 188 (1), 24 (1983)

10. Tadmor, Z., and Gogos, C. G., "Principles of Polymer Processing", Wiley-Interscience, New York (1979)

11. Wiseman, W. A., "Continuous Hot Air Curing", Rubber Age, 103 (5), 65 (1971)

WORK ASSIGNMENT NO. 7

CHAPTER 7.   VULCANIZATION METHODS AND EQUIPMENT

INSTRUCTIONS: Read each question carefully, select one, and only one, appropriate answer to complete each statement.

1.   All vulcanizable polymers have one thing in common, that of

____ (a)   a degree of unsaturation within the polymer structure
____ (b)   the need of sulfur for crosslinking
____ (c)   possessing no plastic-like properties
____ (d)   none of above

2.   The vulcanization process is faster to complete if

____ (a)   the degree of unsaturation of the polymer structure is lower
____ (b)   the vulcanization temperature is higher
____ (c)   the carbon-to-carbon double bonds in the polymer structure are not attacked and not broken
____ (d)   none of above

3.   The most common form of thermal energy used in the vulcanization process is

____ (a)   heated air
____ (b)   saturated steam
____ (c)   heat transfer fluids
____ (d)   none of above

4.   Sulfur is the most widely used vulcanizing agent. The second most popular vulcanizing agent is

____ (a)   organic amines
____ (b)   organic peroxides
____ (c)   phenolic resins
____ (d)   metallic oxides

5.   One disadvantage of saturated steam as a source of thermal energy for vulcanization is that

____ (a)   it is not readily generated and available in a plant
____ (b)   it has low energy content and a low heat transfer coefficient
____ (c)   its temperature is directly related to the pressure in the process and is not very high
____ (d)   none of above

6.   In comparision to saturated steam as a source of thermal energy, heated air has the disadvantage of being

____ (a)   incapable of reaching higher temperatures
____ (b)   inefficient in heat transfer
____ (c)   not easily contained and reused
____ (d)   unable to provide an elevated vulcanization pressure

7. The major advantage of heated nitrogen over heated air as a source of thermal energy for vulcanization is

____ (a) it cannot be easily compressed
____ (b) it has no oxidizing effect on sensitive polymer composite being vulcanized
____ (c) it is much more efficient in heat transfer
____ (d) none of above

8. Heat transfer fluids and pseudo-fluids are very suitable source of thermal energy for

____ (a) high pressure vulcanization process
____ (b) non-pressurized continuous vulcanization process
____ (c) high speed vulcanization process requiring rapid temperature rise
____ (d) vulcanization process to produce product highly susceptible to contamination

9. Microwave heating is not effective as a direct energy transfer method of vulcanization if

____ (a) the rubber compound to be vulcanized has neither polar characteristics nor semi-conductive properties
____ (b) the rubber compound involved is black
____ (c) the surface of the product being vulcanized is very shiny
____ (d) the specific gravity of the elastomeric material involved is high

10. All batch vulcanization equipment requires careful preparation and placement of product before curing. The most widely used equipment of this type is

____ (a) hot air ovens
____ (b) hot water tanks
____ (c) autoclaves or steam pressure vessels
____ (d) none of above

11. The semi-continuous vulcanization method is similar to the continuous molding method. A typical equipment used in this method is the rotary press. The common feature of all semi-continuous vulcanization equipment is that

____ (a) there is no need for application of pressure to the product
____ (b) the heat is trasmitted to the product from the metal surface of the surrounding mold
____ (c) the heat for vulcanization is provided by electrical heaters
____ (d) none of above

12. One of the major reasons continuous vulcanization (C.V.) equipment is still not very widely used is that

____ (a) it is too new and its technologies are not well known
____ (b) it is not as versatile as the batch vulcanization equipment
____ (c) it is not yet capable of high volume production
____ (d none of above

13. The steam tube vulcanizer is usually operated at pressure and temperature higher than that of the autoclave. It is mainly used by the

_____ (a) tire industry
_____ (b) hose industry
_____ (c) electrical wire and cable industry
_____ (d) none of above

14. Hot air vulcanizing tunnel often needs assistance from other equipment such as air propulsion, direct infrared heating, and microwave energy in order to

_____ (a) increase efficiency and productivity
_____ (b) improve cleanliness of vulcanized products
_____ (c) be capable of curing sponge products
_____ (d) none of above

15. In comparison to hot air vulcanizing tunnel, liquid or pseudo-liquid curing trough has the advantage of high heat transfer coefficient. Two of the more commonly used C.V. trough systems are

_____ (a) molten salt bath and fluidized bed
_____ (b) Helicure and Rotocure
_____ (c) steam bath and hot water tank
_____ (d) none of above

CHAPTER 8

TESTING OF RUBBER

Robert D. Stiehler

National Bureau of Standards
Washington, D. C.

INTRODUCTION

Rubber is a unique engineering material. It is the only material that is
easily and extensively deformed by comparatively small forces and recovers
rapidly from large deformations when the force is removed. Consequently, the
tests used to evaluate rubber differ considerably from those used to evaluate
rigid materials, such as metals, refractory and masonry products, and rigid
polymeric materials. For example, tensile tests are commonly used to evaluate
most materials. Rigid materials break at low elongations and have high breaking strengths. Hence, emphasis is placed on tensile strength. On the other
hand, rubber breaks at high extensions and at relatively low rupture forces.
Ultimate elongation is a better measure of quality of rubber vulcanizates.
The extent of elastic recovery from large deformations is generally measured
by set. These and other rubber tests are discussed later.

The properties and performance of a rubber product depend on many factors
including the chemical nature of the rubber, the amount and kinds of ingredients
incorporated into the rubber compound, processing and vulcanizing conditions,
design of the product and service conditions. The first step in developing a
rubber product is research and development. Tests are required of various
rubber vulcanizates so that one may be selected which will perform satisfactorily. The product must be designed and specifications must be prescribed for
manufacture. These specifications must include requirements for the raw materials, the processing and vulcanizing conditions, and the properties of the
product. Testing is required at each step of the manufacturing process.

SPECIFICATIONS AND STANDARDS

Most specifications for products are developed by the manufacturer, but they
are likely to incorporate requirements specified by the user and to include reference standards developed by industry or national standardizing organizations.
For some rubber products, specifications published by the Rubber Manufacturers
Association (RMA) or one of the following national standardizing organizations
are used:

        American Society for Testing and Materials (ASTM)
        1916 Race Street, Philadelphia, Pennsylvania 19103

        American National Standards Institute (ANSI)
        1430 Broadway, New York, New York 10018

        Society of Automotive Engineers (SAE)
        400 Commonwealth Drive, Warrendale, Pennsylvania 15096

        Underwriters Laboratories, Inc. (UL)
        207 East Ohio Street, Chicago, Illinois 60611

Compliance with Federal or Military Specifications is required for products purchased by the Federal Government. Federal Specifications are issued by the General Serivces Administration (GSA), Federal Supply Service, Washington, D.C. 20406. Military Specifications are issued by the Department of Defense (DOD), Defense Material Specifications and Standards Board, Washington, D.C. 20301. Some products must comply with regulations issued by the Department of Transportation (DOT), Washington, D.C. 20590 (e.g., tires for motor vehicles); the Food and Drug Administration (FDA), Rockville, Maryland 20852 (e.g., rubber products in contact with food or drugs); and the Consumer Product Safety Commission (CPSC), Washington, D.C. 20207 (e.g., small toys and bicycle tires).

Other organizations, Federal and State Agencies also issue specifications, but those listed above predominate in number of standards and specifications issued for rubber products. Rubber products in international trade may have to conform with standards issued by the International Organization for Standardization (ISO), the International Electrotechnical Commission (IEC), or the national standards of the country importing the product. These specifications can be obtained from the American National Standards Institute (ANSI). NBS Special Publication No. 352, World Index of Plastics Standards, includes the titles of more than 900 standards for rubber issued by 124 national and international organizations. However, this Index does not include Federal and Military Specifications. NBS Special Publication No. 352 can be obtained from the Superintendent of Documents, U. S. Government Printing Office, Washington, D.C. 20402 (SD Catalog No. C 1310:352).

In order to determine compliance with any specification, testing is necessary. ASTM has issued nearly 200 standards on methods for evaluating raw materials for rubber manufacture, assessing the processability of rubber compounds, and determining properties and performance of rubber vulcanizates. These methods are published in the Annual Book of ASTM Standards. Federal Test Method Standard 601 on Rubber Sampling and Testing has many tests for rubber vulcanizates, but these tests are being superceded by corresponding ASTM Standards. ISO has issued nearly 150 standards for testing rubber and carbon black; most of them are essentially identical to the corresponding ASTM Standards. The Annual Book of ASTM Standards list the titles of ISO Standards pertaining to rubber.

Testing is expensive so only tests required for determining compliance with a specification are usually done. Ideally, the tests should be limited to determining significant characteristics related to performance in service. In practice, many tests being performed have little or no relation to performance. The extra testing results generally from poorly written specifications or the inclusion of unnecessary tests in the specification.

UNITS OF MEASUREMENT

The rubber industry is changing gradually from the use of the English inch-pound system to the use of International System of Units (SI) in standards, testing and products. SI is used in ISO Standards. SI is also used in ASTM Standards either alone or side by side with inch-pound units. SI is an expansion of the MKSA (metre-kilogram-second-ampere) system, one of the many metric systems in use prior to 1960 when SI was adopted by the Eleventh General Conference on Weights and Measures (CGPM), an international treaty organization established by the International Metric Convention in 1875. SI consists of the following seven base units and two supplementary units from which all other units are derived using always the factor one:

quantity	unit	symbol
length	metre	m
mass	kilogram	kg
time	second	s
electric current	ampere	A
temperature	kelvin	K
amount of substance	mole	mol
luminous intensity	candela	cd
plane angle	radian	rad
solid angle	steradian	sr

Nineteen of the derived units have special names. The following eight units with special names are most frequently used in testing rubber:

quantity	unit	symbol	equivalent
frequency	hertz	Hz	$1/s$
force	newton	N	$kg \cdot m/s^2$
pressure, stress	pascal	Pa	N/m^2
energy	joule	J	$N \cdot m$
power	watt	W	J/s
electrical potential	volt	V	W/A
electrical resistance	ohm	Ω	V/A
electric conductances	siemens	S	A/V

To obtain larger or smaller units, sixteen decimal prefixes ranging from 10^{18} to 10^{-18} can be used. The following prefixes are most commonly used in testing rubber:

factor	prefix	symbol
10^6	mega	M
10^3	kilo	k
10^{-1}	deci	d
10^{-2}	centi	c
10^{-3}	milli	m
10^{-6}	micro	μ
10^{-9}	nano	n

ASTM E 380, Standard for Metric Practice, gives further information on SI, including a complete list of derived units with special names and all sixteen prefixes. It also describes the preferred practice for expressing derived units without special names, other units in use with SI, editorial style, rounding values converted from other systems of units, and a list of conversion factors. The following list gives a few factors for conversion of inch-pound units to SI.:

To convert from	to	multiply by
inch	millimetre (mm)	25.4
square inch	square centimetre (cm)	6.4516
inch per minute	millimetre per second (mm/s)	0.4233
foot	metre (m)	0.3048
pound, avoirdupois	kilogram (kg)	0.4536
pound per cubic foot	kilogram per cubic metre (kg/m^3)	1.6018
pound-force	newton (N)	4.4482
lbf/in^2	kilopascal (kPa)	6.8948
inch of mercury (32°F)	kilopascal (kPa)	3.3864
foot pound-force	joule (J)	1.3558
ft·lbf/s	watt (W)	1.3558
horsepower (electric)	watt (W)	746

SAMPLE VS. SPECIMEN

Two terms that are often confused in rubber testing are "sample" and "specimen". ASTM D1566 defines these terms as follows:

sample - the portion or unit(s) selected to represent the lot
specimen - a piece of material appropriately shaped and prepared so
        that it is ready to use for test

In other words, the sample is the material (or number of items) taken from a lot in a manner such that the properties or characteristics of the sample are essentially the same as those of the entire lot. On the other hand, a specimen is a small part of the sample that is actually tested after being suitably prepared for a test. Generally, several specimens are prepared and tested from a single sample.

VALIDITY OF TEST RESULTS

Replicate specimens prepared from a single sheet of rubber vulcanizate often give different results. The source of this variation may be lack of uniformity in the sheet of rubber, changing conditions during testing, operator fatigue, imperfections in the prepared specimen, etc. When tests of a material are made in several laboratories using various types of apparatus and several operators, additional variations in resuls are usually observed.

The degree of agreement in test results obtained by one experienced operator with a single set of instruments under essentially uniform laboratory conditions is called "repeatability", and it represents the best precision that can be expected from the test method. Since "repeatability" does not reflect biases that result from differences in facilities, techniques, and conditions in several laboratories, this precision is not useful in establishing specification requirements. The larger viation observed among laboratories testing the same material is used to determine the precision called "reproducibility" and the validity of a test result. The main factors affecting "reproducibility" are as follows:

1. Differences in design or construction of testing apparatus
2. Differences in calibration of testing apparatus
3. Changes in testing apparatus such as friction, drift of zero point, etc.
4. Differences in operator techniques

5. Operator fatigue
6. Inaccurate measurement of temperature, dimensions, etc.
7. Inhomogeneity of material tested
8. Variations in prepared specimens (dimensions or imperfections)
9. Differences in laboratory conditions (temperature, humidity, pressure, pollutants, etc.)

The reproducibility of testing raw materials can usually be improved through the use of standard materials. The National Bureau of Standards (NBS) issues over 600 standard reference materials (SRM) for testing metals, inorganic materials, and organic materials including rubber. Those for rubber testing include natural rubber (NR), styrene-butadiene rubber (SBR), acrylonitrile-butadiene rubber (NBR), isobutene-isoprene (butyl) rubber (IIR), sulfur, zinc oxide, stearic acid, accelerators, and carbon blacks. These materials serve to verify test systems including apparatus, preparation of standard vulcanizates from the materials, and testing techniques.

The reproducibility of some tests for processability and of testing vulcanizates can be improved through interlaboratory tests such as the Interlaboratory Program for Rubber operated by the Collaborative Testing Service in conjunction with NBS. These programs include tests for tensile properties (ASTM D 412), hardness (ASTM D 1415 and D 2240), Mooney viscosity (ASTM D 1646), and vulcanization characteristics (ASTM D 2084). Interlaboratory tests are made four times per year for each program. For these methods, a laboratory can ascertain the performance of testing apparatus and personnel. For most tests of vulcanizates, programs for verifying laboratory performance do not exist.

A test result may be valid, but the test may not be valid for measuring performance. For example, tensile strength is not a valid indicator of tire tread wear. Tear tests are generally not indicative of service behavior. Hence, it is important that valid tests be selected for evaluating a material or process and that the reproducibility of the method gives a high degree of confidence in the results. Many ASTM methods include the repeatability and reproducibility estimates of precision determined in accordance with ASTM D 3040. They also indicate in their scopes the applicability of the methods.

TESTS OF RAW MATERIALS

An important test for raw materials is the determination of volatile matter, which in most instances is mainly moisture. The processing of rubber compounds is adversely affected by moisture contents above one to two percent. The methods used to determine volatile matter are described in ASTM D 1278 for natural rubber, ASTM D 1416 for synthetic rubber, and ASTM D 1504 for carbon black.

The performance of rubber products is affected by large particles in raw materials that do not disperse. Particles which do not pass through 45 μm openings (U.S. Sieve No. 325) are considered objectionable. ASTM D 1278 includes a method for dirt in natural rubber, and ASTM D 1514 is a method for sieve residue in carbon blacks.

ASTM D 1278 and D 1416 include other chemical tests for natural and synthetic rubbers, respectively. Other chemical tests in the Annual Book of ASTM Standards include 15 tests for carbon blacks and 5 tests for rubber chemicals.

In order to evaluate the vulcanization characteristics of a raw material, it is necessary to mix the material with other compounding ingredients using a standard formulation and mixing procedure, and to vulcanize standard sheets from the standard rubber compound. The Standard Reference Materials (SRM) issued by the NBS are generally specified to be mixed with the raw material being tested. The following ASTM methods are used to evaluate rubbers and carbon blacks:

D 3184 NR (natural rubber)
D 3185 SBR (styrene-butadiene rubber) and SBR mixed with oil
D 3186 SBR mixed with carbon black or carbon and oil
D 3187 NBR (acrylonitrile-butadiene rubber)
D 3188 IIR (isobutene-isoprene rubber)
D 3189 BR (polybutadiene rubber)
D 3190 CR (chloroprene rubber)
D 3191 Carbon black in SBR
D 3192 Carbon black in NR
D 3403 IR (isoprene rubber)
D 3484 BR mixed with oil
D 3568 EPDM (ethylene-propylene-diene terpolymer) and EPDM
  mixed with oil
D 3848 NBR mixed with carbon black
D 3958 BIIR and CIIR (brominated and chlorinated IIR)

The results are affected by the apparatus used to mix and vulcanize the rubber compounds, the temperature of the rubber during mixing and vulcanization, and the testing variables previously mentioned.

TESTS FOR PROCESSABILITY

There are few standard tests for determining the processability of rubbers and rubber compounds. The tests most frequently used are ASTM D 1646 for determining Mooney viscosity and ASTM D 2084 for determining vulcanization characteristics. Figure 1 and Figure 2 show instruments for testing Mooney viscosity and vulcanization characteristics respectively. Viscosity is one factor governing the processability of a rubber compound. The Mooney viscosity scale is arbitrary and based on one rate of shear. Processing is more difficult and energy requirements are greater as the Mooney viscosity increases.

The following parameters can be evaluated by ASTM D 2084:

Viscosity of the rubber compound (related to minimum torque, M_L)
Time of incipient vulcanization (related to time required for torque to increase one unit above the minimum)
Stiffness of vulcanizate (related to maximum torque, M_H)
Time required for vulcanization (related to $t_c(90)$, time required to reach 90 percent of full torque development)
Rate of vulcanization (related to maximum rate of increase in torque)

Figure 3 shows a typical cure curve obtained by ASTM D 2084 method.

Fig. 1 Mooney Viscometer (Courtesy of Monsanto Company)

Fig. 2   Oscillating Disk Cure Meter (Courtesy of Monsanto Company)

178

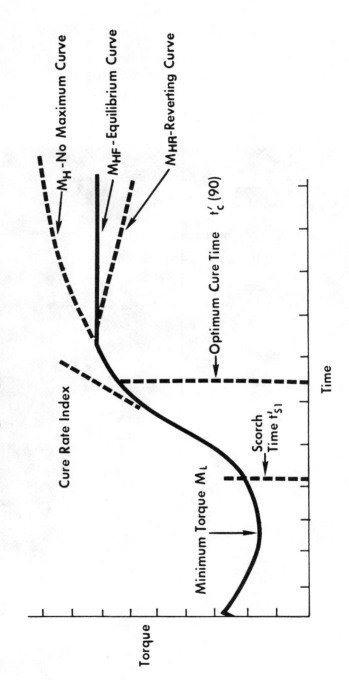

Fig. 3

Rheograph Curve

Viscosity and time of incipient vulcanization (scorch time) can be determined by either ASTM 1646 or D 2084, but the results are not the same numerically. ASTM D 1646 is more sensitive than ASTM D 2084 for measuring these characteristics, but ASTM D 1646 is not suitable for measuring the stiffness of the vulcanizate or the time required for vulcanization. Both ASTM D 1646 and D 2084 methods are sensitive to the mechanical condition of the test apparatus, the temperature of the rubber during test, and slippage at the rubber-metal interface. Clearances between the lower die and the stem of the rotor or disk are critical from the aspect of both the temperature of the rubber specimen and frictional forces. More detailed information on the standardization of the Mooney viscometer and the oscillating-disk cure meter is given in ASTM Special Technical Publication 533, p 19 to 30 (1974).

Other tests that are used to determine processability include:

D 926 Plasticity and recovery of rubber and rubber compounds
D 1917 Rubber shrinkage after milling
D 2230 Extrudability of rubber compounds

TESTS OF RUBBER VULCANIZATES

Most methods for testing rubber apply to vulcanizates. Qualitative and quantitative analyses of rubber products are described in ASTM D 297. Methods for identification of types of rubber in a compound or product are described in ASTM D 3677 using infrared spectrophotometry and ASTM D 3452 using pyrolysis and gas chromotography.

Physical tests of rubber vulcanizates comprise over 70 percent of ASTM methods for testing rubber and rubber products. The physical tests most frequently done are tensile tests, particularly the measurement of tensile strength and ultimate elongation, and hardness. The quality of a rubber vulcanizate of a given stiffness (hardness) is best reflected in the ultimate elongation (strain at failure). The change in this property is useful for determining the stability or instability of rubber vulcanizates in deteriorative environments.

Tensile Tests

A tensile tester is basically a simple device consisting of a pair of grips for stretching the rubber specimen, a force measuring device called dynamometer connected to one grip, and a power actuated device connected to the other grip to separate the grips and extend the specimen. Many designs of tensile testers are in use. Older designs generally have a pendulum, spring or hydraulic capsule for the dynamometer. Newer designs usually have inertia-less dynamometers with electronic sensors. Other features that may be included in a tensile tester are: (1) a compensating mechanism for the dynamometer to compensate for specimen width and thickness and permit measurement of stress directly, (2) an extensometer for measuring extension or strain autographically, and (3) digital devices connected to computers for processing the results automatically. The simpler testers are manually operated. The most elaborate testers are essentially automatic. While the elaborate testers eliminate most manual errors, they are not free from error. Drift in the zero point and in the calibration are the principal sources of error.

Many types of specimens are used to determine tensile properties. ASTM D 412 describes six standard dumbbell-shaped specimens and four standard ring specimens. Other specimens frequently used are: straight specimens, ring specimens cut from tubular products, and products in the form of rings (e.g., O-rings). The type of specimen affects the results obtained for tensile strength and ultimate elongation; smaller specimens tend to give higher values. Dumbbell and straight specimens cut in the "grain" direction (that is the direction of calendering, extruding, or milling during final processing before vulcanization) tend to give higher tensile strength and ultimate elongation than those cut perpendicular to the grain. Ring specimens average properties over both directions. Therefore, specification requirements for tensile properties should be based on a specified specimen, and if straight or dumbbell specimens are used, the direction of the grain should be specified.

For ring specimens, freely-rotating rollers are generally used for grips. The elongation or strain is determined from the grip separation. For dumbbell or straight specimens, grips which tighten as tension increases or pneumatically-actuated grips with constant pressure are used. Breakage of specimens in the grips is particularly troublesome with thin specimens. Bench marks are placed in the region of uniform cross-sectional area of dumbbell or straight specimens to determine elongation or strain. The separation of the bench marks is followed manually during test with a scale graduated in percent elongation or is recorded autographically by means of an extensometer.

Tensile strength is the stress at failure determined by dividing the force at break by the original cross-section of the specimen. The SI unit for stress is the pascal (Pa). Tensile strength is usually expressed in megapascals (MPa). Ultimate elongation is the strain at failure determined by dividing the increase in length between bench marks on straight or dumbbell specimens, or the increase in inside circumference of ring specimens, by the original length between bench marks or of inside circumference. Results are usually expressed in percent of the original length; for example, an elongation of 450 percent indicates an extension of 4.5 times the original length; that is, the final length is 5.5 times the original length.

Stiffness

The stiffness of a rubber vulcanizate can be measured directly by the method in ASTM D 797 or by properties related to modulus; such as stress at a specified elongation (ASTM D 412), elongation at a specified stress (ASTM D 1456), ball indentation under a specified force (ASTM D 531) or hardness (ASTM D 1415 or D2240). Measurement of hardness is the method most commonly used to indicate stiffness. The relationship between the hardness scale and Young's modulus is given in ASTM D 1415. For a highly elastic vulcanizate, one with good elastic recovery, hardness values determined by ASTM D 1415 and D 2240 are in good agreement. For less elastic materials, the values determined by D 2240 tend to be higher since readings are taken within one second; whereas, D 1415 requires readings to be taken after 30 seconds. During this period appreciable creep may occur. The results obtained with ASTM D 1415 are more reproducible. The ASTM D 1415 method is more flexible permitting thin specimens to be tested. ASTM D 2240 is more convenient to use since tests do not have to be made in the laboratory. For specification purposes, ASTM D 1415 is preferable.

Elastic Recovery

The elasticity of rubber or the extent of recovery from large deformations can be measured by static methods (ASTM D 395 Compression Set, ASTM D 412 Tension Set, or ASTM D 1390 Stress Relaxation) or by dynamic methods (ASTM D 945 Mechanical Oscillograph, ASTM D 1054 Pendulum Rebound, ASTM D 2231 Forced Vibration, or ASTM D 2632 Vertical Rebound). ASTM D 395 is most commonly used since it determines recovery after some aging and hence correlates better with service. Products subjected to continuous vibration in service, such as vibration dampeners, should be tested by a forced vibration method (ASTM D 2231) which also measures several properties important in dynamic applications.

The reproducibility of ASTM D 395 Compression Set is not good, but the repeatability is acceptable. Apparently differences in techniques among laboratories, particularly the temperature during conditioning and recovery, are critical. Studies to improve the standard have not been fruitful.

Durability

1. Age Resistance - The durability of rubber vulcanizates is usually determined by an "accelerated aging" test. Such a test consists of determining some property or properties before and after subjecting specimens of the vulcanizate to high temperature in air or oxygen for a specified period. The following ASTM methods are used:

   D 454   Heating under air pressure
   D 572   Heating under oxygen pressure
   D 573   Heating in an air oven
   D 865   Heating in a test tube
   D 1870   Heating in a tubular oven

ASTM D 573 and D 865 are the methods most commonly used since the results correlate better with service. ASTM D 865 provides for heating each vulcanizate in a separate test tube which prevents contamination of one vulcanizate by the volatile products from another vulcanizate. ASTM D 1870 should be used when the product contains an appreciable quantity of a plasticizer that can slowly vaporize. It is used mainly for plasticized plastics that are used in some applications in place of rubber.

The difference in ultimate elongation before and after heating is the most useful criterion for judging the durability of a vulcanizate. The ultimate elongation of practically all vulcanizates decrease during aging; the rate of decrease depends on the temperature, time, and composition of the vulcanizate. At constant temperature, the rate becomes slower with time; that is, the rate of decrease is fastest during the initial period and it becomes progressively less as the heating is continued. Specifications generally require a heating period of 70 or 166 hours. If more durable vulcanizates are needed, higher temperatures are specified. The requirement is usually expressed in maximum permitted decrease in ultimate elongation as a percent of the value for unheated specimens. In addition to ultimate elongation, specifications frequently include requirements limiting changes in tensile strength and stiffness (hardness).

2. Liquid Resistance – Rubber products exposed to liquids in service can swell and deteriorate in physical properties. Some rubbers are hydrolysed in high humidity environment or in water. The following ASTM methods are used to determine the effect of liquids on rubber:

> D 471   Effect of liquids
> D 1468   Change in length during liquid immersion
> D 3137   Hydrolytic stability

ASTM D 471 is the most comprehensive method and is the one most frequently used. Changes in one or more of the following properties are measured: mass, volume, mass of soluble matter extracted, tensile strength, ultimate elongation, and hardness. For coated fabrics, changes in breaking strength, tear resistance, burst strength, and adhesion of coating to fabric may be measured. Many rubber products are exposed to oil or fuel in service. In order to reduce the amount of testing and facilitate the preparation of specifications, particularly for automotive applications, ASTM D 471 provides ten reference liquids, including four oils, four fuels, and two service fluids. The reference liquid chosen for test depends on the particular application of the rubber product.

3. Ozone Resistance – Pollutants in the environment also cause rubber deterioration. Severe surface cracking can occur when very small concentrations (0.00001%) of **ozone** are in the air unless the vulcanizates are made from rubbers inherently resistant to ozone or are protected with antiozonants. The following ASTM methods are used to determine ozone resistance:

> D 518   Surface cracking (outdoor weathering)
> D 1149   Surface ozone cracking in a chamber (flat specimen)
> D 1171   Surface ozone cracking outdoors or in a chamber (triangular specimen)
> D 3395   Dynamic ozone cracking in a chamber

Factors influencing surface cracking are the ozone concentration, temperature, humidity, and strain in the rubber vulcanizate. ASTM D 1149 is the method most frequently used. Tapered or bent loop specimens are preferred since the strain varies in different parts of the specimen and hence they include the most sensitive strain for ozone attack and surface cracking. Specifications for products used in severe outdoor exposure applications or in electrical applications do not permit any surface cracking during the ozone test.

4. Light resistance – Some vulcanizates, particularly translucent ones, are degraded by ultraviolet light. ASTM D 750 describes a procedure for ascertaining deterioration in a carbon-arc apparatus. Temperature and intensity of radiation at selected wave lengths affect the degradation of sensitive vulcanizates. Visual surface cracking or crazing and change in tensile properties are the criteria used to judge the effect of light. The xenon-arc apparatus is replacing the carbon-arc since the xenon-arc spectrum suitably filtered simulates sunshine more closely. The xenon-arc is used for plastics and other polymeric materials, but to date is not extensively used for rubber. ASTM D 2565 describes the use of the xenon-arc apparatus for exposure of plastics. Ultraviolet light

may also cause rubber products to discolor. ASTM D 925 is a method for determining staining of surfaces. Three types of staining are covered; namely, contact, migration, and diffusion. A stain on a surface in the area directly contacting the rubber is called "contact stain". If the stain extends beyond the area of contact, it is called "migration stain". Staining of a white or light-colored rubber veneer, such as white side walls on tires, by material from an underlying rubber compound is called "diffusion stain". ASTM D 1148 is a method for determining discoloration of light colored surfaces by heat and ultraviolet light.

Fatigue Tests

Dynamic flexing also deteriorates rubber products. Dynamic flexing tests do not correlate with service, but they are useful in development work for compounds to withstand dynamic fatigue. The following ASTM Standards describe dynamic fatigue tests in use for this purpose:

D   430 Dynamic fatigue
D   623 Heat generation and flexing fatigue in compression
D   813 Crack growth
D 1052 Cut growth using the Ross flexing apparatus
D 3629 Cut growth resistance (TEXUS flex tester)

ASTM D 430 describes three methods using the Scott flexing machine, DeMattia flexing machine, and duPont flexing machine. The DeMattia apparatus is also used in ASTM D 813 and is the only flexing apparatus standardized by ISO. ASTM D 623 describes two compression methods using the Goodrich flexometer and the Firestone flexometer. ASTM D 623 is used to develop rubber compounds for automotive applications involving flexing in compression; such as tire treads and motor mounts.

Abrasion Tests

Rubber products that rub against another surface in service deteriorate from wear. There are many laboratory tests for determining abrasion resistance of rubber, but none correlates with service. Only two methods remain in the ASTM Book of Standards; namely ASTM D 1630 based on the NBS abrader and ASTM D 2228 based on the pico abrader. ASTM D 1630 is used to evaluate vulcanizates for shoe soles and heels. Misleading results are obtained when vulcanizates made from different types of rubber are compared. ASTM D 2228 is used to develop tire tread vulcanizates. Since tread wear depends on many factors whose effects are not evaluated by ASTM D 2228, road tests of tires are required to determine the quality of tread vulcanizates.

Temperature Effects

Temperature affects the properties of rubber vulcanizates more than any other factor does. At high temperatures, the rubber undergoes further vulcanization and if sufficiently high, the rubber molecule is depolymerized. The black skid marks on roadways are depolymerized rubber and carbon black caused by frictional heating of the tread surface to a very high temperature. The rate of oxidation of the rubber vulcanizate is accelerated and the life of rubber products is reduced by increasing the temperature. Even in a non-oxidizing atmosphere, high temperature affects the physical properties; such as tensile strength, ultimate elongation, and stiffness of the vulcanizate. ASTM D 412 describes measurements of the tensile properties at high temperature. Measurements must be made after the specimen is heated to the specified temperature and before appreciable deterioration has occurred. Because of the difficulty of making reliable measurements at high temperatures, specimens are generally conditioned at specified temperatures and the properties are measured after cooling to room temperature. These tests are described above under 1. Age Resistance.

As the temperature is lowered below room temperature, some rubbers may crystallize (freeze) and become hard and horny. This phenomenon is called a "phase transition". All rubbers at some low temperature, depending on the type of rubber, become rigid and brittle. This temperature is called the "glass transition point". The main difference between a rubber and a rigid plastic is that a rubber has a glass transition point below room temperature and a rigid plastic has a glass transition point above room temperature. The glass transition point is not a fixed temperature for a particular rubber. It depends on the rate of deformation. The glass transition occurs at lower temperatures as the rate of deformation decreases. As a consequence, low temperature tests which deform specimens at different rates do not correlate.

The following ASTM Standards are used for testing rubber at low temperatures:

D 797 Young's modulus at normal and subnormal temperatures
D 832 Rubber conditioning for low temperature testing
D 1053 Stiffening at low temperature using a torsional wire
       apparatus (Gehman Test)
D 1229 Compression set at low temperature
D 1329 Retraction at low temperature (TR Test)
D 2136 Low temperature bend test (coated fabrics)
D 2137 Brittleness point of flexible polymers and coated fabrics
D 3388 Stiffening at low temperature using a torsional wire
       apparatus (Gehman Test for coated fabrics)
D 3847 Directions for achieving subnormal test temperatures

ASTM D 2137 is the method most generally used to determine the lowest temperature for serviceability of a rubber vulcanizate. ASTM D 1053 (or D 3388 for coated fabrics) is generally used to determine the degree of stiffening (increase in Young's modulus) over a range of temperatures. Rubber properties at low temperature can also be determined by the regular methods using apparatus equipped with low-temperature chambers; for example, ASTM D 412 for tensile properties, ASTM D 1415 for hardness, etc. Low temperature tests are usually made in research-and-development studies. In order to reduce the amount of testing at a large number of temperatures, ASTM D 1349 gives 18 recommended test temperatures ranging from -75°C (-103°F) to 250°C (482°F). These temperatures are also recommended by ISO for testing most materials.

The behavior of rubber over a wide range of temperature can be qualitatively determined by differential thermal analysis (DTA). The principle of DTA is simple. The specimen to be tested and a stable reference material of comparable heat capacity and thermal conductivity are placed in the DTA chamber which is equipped with a thermocouple for each material. The thermocouples are connected in a circuit to measure the difference in temperature (ΔT) between them. An autographic plot of ΔT versus the specimen temperature is made as the chamber is cooled or heated. Discontinuities in the plot indicate a phase or glass transition depending on the type of discontinuity. ASTM D 3417 and D3418 describe the DTA procedure for detecting crystallization and glass transition temperatures respectively. At higher temperatures, discontinuities in the DTA curve may be caused by volatilization of compounding ingredients, oxidation, pyrolysis, or other chemical reaction.

Tear Resistance

Some rubber vulcanizates tear easily when nicked or cut, whereas others are tough and tear with difficulty. Various tests are used to measure this characteristic with only fair success. Resistance to tearing depends on several factors such as speed of tearing, crystallization of the rubber on stretching, amount and type of fillers in the rubber compound (particularly reinforcing carbon blacks), type of specimen, depth of nick or cut, etc. Accordingly, results obtained by different methods are not in agreement and no method correlates well with service. ASTM D 624 describes three tear specimens; two of them are crescent shaped in the tearing region. The other specimen has a right angle in the tearing region . Results obtained from specimens in the two shapes are not in agreement either absolutely or relatively. ISO has issued additional tear test methods which have the same deficiencies. Because of the unreliability of tear tests, requirements for tear resistance should be avoided if possible in specifications.

Electrical Tests

The use of rubber for electrical insulation is well known. It is not generally known that some rubber vulcanizates are conductors of electricity and that many vulcanizates conduct sufficiently to prevent the development of static charges on products. The degree of conductance depends on the amount and type of carbon black in the rubber vulcanizate. Typical rubber products requiring low, medium and high electrical resistance are:

low   -   products used in manufacturing plants for explosives
            most products used in hospital operating rooms
            flexible electrical heating tapes
            fuel hose

medium -   tire treads and sidewall vulcanizates
            conveyor belts
            antistatic clothing

high   -   wire and cable electrical insulation
            protective clothing for electrical workers
            boots for spark plugs, distributor, and high tension
            coil wires in motor vehicles

The following ASTM Standards describe methods for determining electrical characteristics of rubber vulcanizates:

D 149   Dielectric breakdown voltage and dielectric strength of electrical insulating materials at commercial power frequencies
D 150   A-C loss characteristics and permittivity (dielectric constant) of solid electrical insulating materials
D 257   D-C resistance or conductance of insulating materials
D 991   Volume resistivity of electrically conductive and antistatic products.

The electrical resistance of rubber increases on flexing. Hence, care must be taken to avoid flexing during handling of the specimens for conditioning or testing. Good electrical contact between the electrodes and the rubber must be established to obtain valid measurements. Surface conductivity must be avoided when testing vulcanizates having a high electrical resistance.

SUMMARY

Over 200 standards issued by national and international organizations are available for testing rubber, rubber products, and raw materials. Only a few of them are used during the manufacture of a particular product. The principal standard methods used for testing raw materials, processability, and vulcanizates are cited. The efficacy of testing depends on how well the tests selected relate to performance and service of the product and on the precision of the tests. Physical tests tend to predominate since they generally relate to performance and service better than chemical tests. The reproducibility of the tests must be good in order that the manufacturer can have confidence in the results and the costs of testing can be kept at a minimum.

Testing of rubber is essential to produce a uniform product and assure satisfactory performance throughout the expected life of the product. Testing starts with the raw materials, whether done by the manufacturer of the rubber product or the suppliers of the raw materials. Testing continues during various stages of the manufacturing process. Finally, the finished product is tested to determine compliance with a specification for the product or to protect the manufacturer from complaints of poor product quality.

GENERAL REFERENCES

1. "Annual Books of ASTM Standards", American Society for Testing and Materials, Philadelphia, PA (1983)

2. Babbit, R.O., ed. "The Vanderbilt Rubber Handbook", R.T. Vanderbilt Co., Inc., Norwalk, CT (1978)

3. Blow, C.M., ed., "Rubber Technology and Manufacture", Butterworth & Co., London, England (1971)

4. Brown, R.P., "Physical Testing of Rubbers", Allied Science Publishers Ltd., London, England (1979)

5. Morton, M., ed., "Rubber Technology", Van Nostrand Reinhold Co., New York (1973)

6. Norman, R. H., and Johnson, P.S., "Processability Testing", Rubber Chem. Technol., 54, 493 (1981)

7. Scott, J.R., "Physical Testing of Rubbers", Maclaren, London, England (1965)

WORK ASSIGNMENT NO. 8

CHAPTER 8. TESTING OF RUBBER

INSTRUCTIONS: Read each question carefully, select one, and only one, appropriate answer to complete each statement

1. The quality of rubber vulcanizates, unlike that of rigid materials,

___(a) cannot be measured solely by tensile strength. Ultimate elongation
is a better measure in many cases.
___(b) is totally dependent on the quality of its major component, the base
elastomer
___(c) is not affected by processing conditions
___(d) need not be tested during processing provided all raw materials were
evaluated and found satisfactory

2. The term "sample" is often misunderstood in rubber testing. ASTM Standard
D 1566 defines "sample" as

___(a) a piece of material appropriately shaped and prepared so that it is
ready to use for test
___(b) the portion or unit(s) selected to represent a lot of material
___(c) a small part of the material that is actually tested after proper
preparation
___(d) none of above

3. In testing, repeatability represents the best precision that can be expected
from a test method. Repeatability is

___(a) the degree of agreement in test results obtained by one experienced
operator with a single set of instruments under essentially uniform
laboratory conditions
___(b) the degree of variation observed among laboratories testing the same
material
___(c) the validity of a test result
___(d) None of above

4. If the test result is valid,

___(a) the test is valid for measuring performance
___(b) the reproducibility of the test method is high
___(c) the repeatability of the test method is high
___(d) none of above

5. There are two frequently used standard tests for determining the processability of rubber and rubber compounds. One of them is ASTM D 1648 for
determining Mooney viscosity by a shearing disk viscometer. The other one
is ASTM D 2084 for measuring vulcanization characteristics with

___(a) a Durometer
___(b) an oscillating disk cure meter
___(c) tensile tester
___(d) none of above

6. M_L, M_H, ts2, and $t_c(90)$ are usually reported from a curve obtained with an
oscillating disk cure meter. M_L is a measurement for evaluation of

___(a) viscosity of the unvulcanized compound
___(b) scorch time of a rubber compound
___(c) time required for vulcanization
___(d) stiffness of the vulcanizate

7. Although viscosity and scorch time (incipient vulcanization) can be determined by either a Mooney viscometer or an oscillating disk cure meter, the former is

____(a) more sensitive to these characteristics
____(b) less sensitive to these characteristics
____(c) also capable of measuring the stiffness of the vulcanizate
____(d) also capable of measuring the time required for vulcanization

8. Infrared spectrophotometry, pyrolysis and gas chromotography are often used in analytical laboratory to determine

____(a) tensile strength of a rubber compound or product
____(b) the identification of the type of rubber in a compound
____(c) processability of a rubber compound
____(d) none of above

9. Dumbbell and straight specimens cut in "grain" direction (that is the direction of calendering, extruding, or milling during final processing before vulcanization) tend to give

____(a) lower tensile strength than those cut perpendicular to the "grain"
____(b) higher tensile strength than those cut perpendicular to the "grain"
____(c) lower ultimate elongation than those cut perpendicular to the "grain"
____(d) none of above

10. Specification requirements for tensile properties should be based on

____(a) dumbbell specimens
____(b) ring specimens
____(c) straight specimens
____(d) a specified specimen

11. The stiffness of a vulcanizate cannot be measured by

____(a) Young's modulus
____(b) stress at a specified elongation
____(c) Durometer
____(d) tensile strength

12. The elasticity of rubber or the extent of recovery from large deformations can be measured by static method or dynamic method. The most commonly used measurement is

____(a) tension set (ASTM D 412)
____(b) compression set (ASTM D 395)
____(c) pendulum rebound (ASTM D 1054)
____(d) vertical rebound (ASTM D 2632)

13. The most useful criterion for judging the durability of a vulcanizate is

____(a) the tensile strength after heat aging
____(b) the difference in ultimate elongation before and after heat aging
____(c) the hardness after heat aging
____(d) the difference in tensile strength before and after heat aging

14. Heat aging tests and low-temperature flexibility tests are important because

___(a) temperature more than any other factor affects the properties of rubber vulcanizates

___(b) every rubber product is required to perform satisfactorily at extremes in temperature

___(c) rubber molecule is most likely depolymerized at either extremely high or extremely low temperature

___(d) none of above

15. In testing electrical characteristics of rubber vulcanizates, care must be taken to avoid flexing during handling of the specimens because

___(a) flexing greatly distorts the shape of the specimen

___(b) electrical resistance of rubber increases on flexing

___(c) flexing increases surface conductivity of the specimen

___(d) none of above

CHAPTER 9

REINFORCING MATERIALS FOR RUBBER PRODUCTS

Ronald J. Dill
Goodyear Tire and Rubber Company
Akron, Ohio 44316

and

Harry Long
Goodall Rubber Company
Trenton, New Jersey 08650

INTRODUCTION

Tires, V-belts, conveyor belts, hose, and expansion joints are basically high performance composites of rubber and reinforcing materials. Textiles and metals are the most commonly used reinforcements in rubber products. They are utilized in the form of yarn, cord, fabric, or wire. The reinforcements fulfill the following basic functions in these composites:

    (a)   Impart load-carrying capacity
    (b)   Serve as the medium for stress transmission
    (c)   Provide dimensional characteristics
    (d)   Determine basic strength and durability

Generally, the functional performance is a reflection of (1) the physical and chemical properties of the rubber compounds and the reinforcing material, (2) the rheology of the matrix, and (3) the geometric structure and configuration of the composite system.

For most applications, vulcanized elastomeric material alone is too elastic and must be reinforced for strength improvement. A wide range of reinforcing materials is currently available to the product design engineers - cotton, rayon, nylon, polyester, fiberglass, steel, and aramid, all of which possess different properties and subsequently different performance characteristics.

Of equal importance is the adhesive treatment used to bond the reinforcing materials to the rubber component in the composites.

Designing a composite system requires full understanding of the application and the environment in which the product(s) will be utilized. For example, in designing a tire, knowledge of vehicle performance and conditions under which the vehicle is required to operate is essential. Details such as load requirements, speed, mileage driven, tire deflection, road surface conditions, etc. must be taken into consideration. In designing a hose, one needs to know the internal pressure or suction, and the extent and frequency of flexing and bending the product is required to withstand.

Certain reinforcing materials such as nylon, which offers very good resistance to heat degradation and flexing fatigue, perform where other materials may fail. Steel, which offers excellent resistance to compressive bending and puncture, is nearly ideal for use as a tire belt material.

In addition to the service condition of the product involved, the method of manufacture for the product also has an impact on the selection of reinforcing materials.

HISTORICAL TRENDS

Chronologically, cotton was the first reinforcing material for rubber products. Rayon largely supplanted cotton in the early 30's because of its improved strength. While it is no longer used for automobile tires, rayon is still used extensively in hose products.

The synthesis of nylon during the 40's led to the development of this material as a tire reinforcement. Initially used in aircraft tires, nylon is still used in large bias tires. Nylon is also very popular for belt carcass.

Polyester was developed as a reinforcement for automobile tires in the early 60's. It is currently a popular material for automobile tires because of its excellent strength and uniformity. Polyester is also used in mechanical rubber goods.

Fiberglass was introduced in the late 60's coincident with the development of belted tires and is currently a very popular tire belt material.

Steel is currently a preferred reinforcing material for radial tires. It is also used extensively for hose products intended for high pressure or high suction service.

Aramid was developed in the early 70's specifically as a tire reinforcement. It is the latest innovation in reinfocing technology and is being utilized in a variety of tire and belting applications.

Figure 1 shows the annual tire cord usage from 1900 to 1980.

REINFORCING MATERIALS

Cotton, rayon, nylon, polyester, aramid, fiberglass as well as steel are the most widely used reinforcing materials in rubber products. Table I shows a comparison of general properties of these materials. The following is a brief discussion on each of them.

Cotton

Cotton is natural cellulose. It is the only natural fiber used to any great extent in the rubber industry. Its strength and elongation are relatively low. It has great affinity for water. This results in an increase in tensile strength and decrease in dimension. Cotton is susceptible to mildew attack. However, it is highly resistant to heat and organic solvents. Cotton yarns are fussy and are easily entrapped by rubber, resulting in excellent adhesions. Cotton has largely been replaced by the stronger synthetic fibers as reinforcing material in products. However, it is still being used to attain high bulk in some applications.

Rayon

Rayon is generated from cellulose (wood pulp), a renewable resource. Unlike cotton, its strength is reduced with increased moisture content. It is similar to cotton in resistance to chemicals and mildew attack.

Rayon has been a rubber reinforcement longer than any others, primarily due to its desirable modulus properties. Because of rayon's relatively low strength and susceptibility to moisture degradation, it is fading in popularity. However, rayon remains a viable reinforcement option in hose products and certain specialty applications.

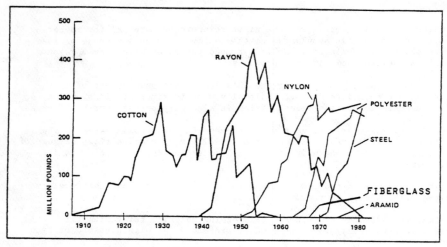

Figure 1 - Tire Cord Usage: 1900 to 1980

TABLE I: General Properties of Reinforcing Materials

	Cotton	Rayon	Nylon	Polyester	Fiberglass	Aramid	Steel
Tenacity (gpd)*	3.4	5.0	8.6	8.0	9.0	18.8	3.4
Elongation @ Break (%)	7.0	9.0	19.0	17.0	4.0	4.0	3.0
Modulus (gpd)*	70	120	50	80	260	500	280
Shrinkage (%)	0.1	0.1	6.0	3.0	0.1	0.1	0.1
Moisture Regain (%)	7.0	11.0	3.5	0.3	0.1	0.1	0.1
Specific Gravity	1.54	1.52	1.14	1.38	2.52	1.44	7.83
Heat Resistance Rating	Fair	Fair	Very Good	Good	Excellent	Excellent	Excellent

*gpd = gram per denier

Nylon

The utility of nylon as a rubber reinforcement relates to its basic chemical structure. Nylon is chemically a polyamide. Two types of nylon are currently in use, nylon 6 and nylon 6,6. Both are synthesized from crude oil. Nylon 6 is derived from an amino acid which contains 6 carbon atoms. Nylon 6,6 is produced by condensation of hexamethylene-diamine and adipic acid, each monomer containing 6 carbon atoms.

The stable aliphatic nature of nylon's molecular structure allows free bond rotation and flexibility which relates directly to excellent heat and fatigue resistance. The amide linkage in nylon's polymer chain provides good adhesive capability. Nylon has excellent strength and very high elongation. It is affected very little by moisture and mildew. Its very high elongation can be reduced to some extent by "heat setting". Nylon 6 has a lower melting point than nylon 6,6 and somewhat poorer heat resistance.

Polyester

Polyester, like nylon, is derived from crude oil. However, unlike nylon, the backbone of the polyester molecule contains aromatic rings. The ring structure imparts improvements over nylon in modulus and dimensional stability. However, the ring structure also tends to block the adhesive bonding sites. Consequently, a more sophisticated adhesive system is required to bond polyester to rubber. Polyester has high strength but not quite as high as nylon. Its properties are not seriously affected by moisture. It is highly resistant to fungal activity.

Fiberglass

Fiberglass is derived from sand (silica) and clay. Other chemicals are added to a molten solution of these two raw materials and the fibers are gravity extruded to form the final yarn.

Because of the excellent strength-to-weight ratio and extremely high modulus, fiberglass has found its way into a variety of rubber-reinforced applications, such as tires, belting, hose, and air ducts. Its resistance to heat and chemicals is excellent. However, its resistance to flexing is poor.

Aramid

Aramid is the newest in the long line of reinforcing materials. It is chemically an aromatic polyamide. It combines the amide linkages prevalent in nylon and the aromatic ring structure of polyester.

This unique chemistry results in a fiber with extremely high strength, modulus and dimensional stability as well as excellent resistance to heat and humidity. On the negative side, its compressive properties are not good. It is vulnerable to shear fatigue.

Steel

Steel has been used as a reinforcing component in all types of composites for many years. It was natural that it was utilized as a rubber reinforcement as well.

Steel cord is manufactured from steel rods which are continuously drawn through dies to smaller cross-sections until the final filament diameters are reached.

Steel cords possess high modulus characteristics as well as excellent strength. They are currently a very popular reinforcement for radial tires. They are also being used in belt carcasses.

Steel wire accounts for a very high percentage of wire consumed by the mechanical rubber goods industry. It is a popular reinforcing material for hose intended for high pressure or high suction service. Grades of steel vary in composition from almost pure iron to material of complex metallurgical constitution. Steel wire provides high strength at a relatively low cost.

Fine steel wire in sizes ranging from 0.008 to 0.028-inch in diameter is the most commonly used reinforcing material in braided or spiralled hose for high pressure or high temperature service. Other round wire of high tensile carbon steel in size ranges of 0.177 to 0.876-inch in diameter is used in the body of larger size hoses for crush resistance and dimensional stability. Wire cables within the range of 0.047 to 0.250-inch diameter are used in hose to provide high bursting strength without compromising flexibility or crush resistance. Wire cable consists of multiple strands of round wire.

Rectangular wire is most commonly used as helically wound reinforcement on the interior of rough bore suction hoses to prevent collapse. It is sometimes used as an external helix embedded in and flush with the rubber cover in order to provide an armor protection against cutting and abrasion.

Half round wire is used primarily as an armor protective spiral wrap around the hose. The wire is wound with the flat side against the hose to provide maximum surface contact with the rubber cover.

Flat wire braid consists of an odd number of wires interwoven to produce a flexible reinforcing member. Use of flat wire braid usually results in better adhesion because of the interstices of the braid.

The most common wire finishes for steel wire used in mechanical rubber goods are copper (drawn finish), galvanized (coated finish), tin (coated finish), and liquor (drawn finish). Round wires usually have a copper or liquor finish. Rectangular wires generally have a galvanized finish.

NOMENCLATURE

Several methods of classifying yarn or cord size are currently in use in the rubber industry.

Cotton is classified by the English system in which the yarn size number is based on the weight of a hank. A hank is 840 yards of material. Thus, a No. 10 cotton yarn has 10 times 840 (8400 yards) of yarn per pound.

Most organic materials such as nylon, polyester, rayon and aramid are described in terms of denier. Denier is the weight in grams of material per 9000 meters of length. Thus, if 9000 meters of a yarn weigh 840 grams, it is a 840 denier yarn. Typical examples of denier are 1000 and 1300 for polyester, 840 and 1260 for nylon, 1100 and 1650 for rayon, and 1000, 1500 and 3000 for aramid.

Fiberglass cord used a different system known as Tex. The Tex System is a universal system in which both staple and filament yarns are rated on the same basis. Yarns are designated by a tex number, which is the weight in grams of material per 1000 meters. Typical fiberglass cord sizes are 330/1, 660/1 and 990/1 tex.

Steel cord has an entirely different method of description designed to call out each filament diameter and the number of filaments per bundle. For example, a 4 x .25 cord is comprised of 4 filaments each 25 millimeters in diameter. A more complex structure 3 x .20 + 6 x .38 consists of 3 filaments in each core, each .20 millimeters in diameter, surrounded by 6 filaments each .38 millimeters in diameter (see Figure 2).

YARNS

Yarn is a linear assembly of fibers or filaments formed into a continuous strand. Textile yarns are widely used in hose carcass to provide strength or collapse resistance or both. The type of yarns chosen are usually based on specific strength, elongation, moisture absorption, and resistance to fatigue, abrasion, heat, chemicals and fungal activity.

The most simple type of yarn is called "singles" yarn. "Singles" yarn consists of a number of very small fibers bound together and usually twisted somewhat to make the yarn behave as a unit. When two or more of these "singles" yarns are twisted together, the result is called "plied" yarn or cord ply. If two or more "plied" yarns are twisted together the result is a cord. If the twist direction is alternated between "singles", "plied" yarns, and cord, the resulting cord is a "cable" yarn.

All natural fibers are made into yarn by twisting together relatively short length fibers. Man-made yarns are produced as extruded, continuous-length filaments. When one filament is used, it is referred to as a "monofilament". Usually a number of very small filaments are combined to form a yarn which is known as a "multi-filament" yarn. Another method of making yarn is to use relatively short lengths of fiber twisted together in a random fashion to form a continuous yarn called "staple" yarn. Staple yarn finds very little use in industrial products.

FABRICS

Textile fabrics are the most popular materials for reinforcement in belting. They are also used as reinforcement in hose, gaskets, and expansion joints. The fabric has properties that depend upon the construction, the material from which the yarns are made, and upon the type of weave.

Fabric is a planar structure produced by interlacing yarns. It is made of warp yarns ("ends") which run lengthwise, and fill yarns ("picks") which run crosswise as the fabric is woven. Usually these two yarns are at right angles to each other. There are four principal types of weave, namely plain weave, twill weave, basket weave, and leno weave. Plain weave is the most common pattern. In this construction, the warp and fill yarns cross each other alternately (Figures 3 to 6 show different types of weave). Fabrics may be made from one type of yarn or a combination of different yarns.

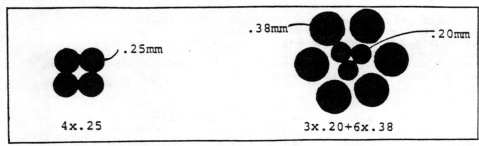

Figure 2 - Steel Tire Cord

Hose Ducks

Most hose ducks are so-called square woven fabrics. The tensile strength of square woven fabric is equal in both directions. Because fabric is applied to hose on the 45° bias, the resultant force of the warp yarn and the fill yarn of equal strength will be on the longitudinal axis of the hose to reduce movement of the hose under internal pressure. Hose ducks are generally of soft open weave. Hose is made from a wide range of square woven fabrics, starting with sheeting up to 33-oz. ducks. The weight in ounces of 3-ft. of a 40-in. wide fabric is the size designation of hose ducks. Thus, a 3-ft. length of a "10-oz. hose duck" in 40-in. width weights 10 oz. Sheetings are designated by the number of yards per pound. Thus a 3.60 yard length of a "3.60 sheeting" weighs one pound.

Belt Ducks

Fabrics are used extensively as an inner load support member in belt constructions. Belt duck is not square woven and its tensile strength is not equal in both directions. Its predominant strength is in the warp in order to withstand the longitudinal stresses encountered by a belt in service. The warp strength of a belt duck is often twice as much as the fill strength. Belt ducks are generally stronger and more elastic than hose ducks. Some of them are made of tighter twisted yarn. Usually, they are of hard and tighter weave. Size designation of belt duck is based on the weight in ounces of 3-ft. of a 42-in. wide fabric.

Woven Cord Fabrics

Woven cord fabrics were originally developed for tires and therefore are also known as tire cord fabric. They are designed to give only warp strength. The warp yarns of cord fabrics are very strong while the fill yarns are weak and spaced far apart. The fill yarns are merely used to hold the warp yarns in position so that the fabrics can be impregnated with rubber (see Figure 7). They are not intended to impart any lateral strength to the finished product. Besides being used extensively in tire carcass, woven cord fabrics are also utilized as reinforcing material in belts and expansion joints. The manufacture of tire cords will be discussed later in this chapter.

Leno Fabrics

Leno or breaker fabrics are loosely woven fabrics of tightly twisted yarns. They are woven with a locked weave so that the mesh of fabric remains open. Leno or breaker fabrics are used to increase the bond between cover and the load support member of conveyor belts or the reinforcing member of hose.

Solid Woven Fabrics

Solid woven fabrics consist of multiple layers of warp and fill yarns held together with binder yarns (see Figure 8). They are generally composed of cotton yarns and nylon yarns. Solid woven fabrics are used mainly in belt construction.

Fig. 3

PLAIN WEAVE

Fig. 4

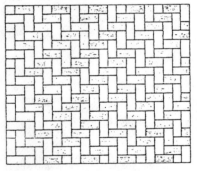

TWILL WEAVE

Fig. 5

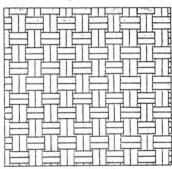

BASKET WEAVE

Fig. 6

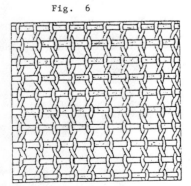

LENO WEAVE

Fig. 7

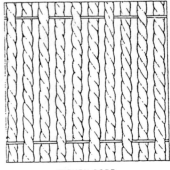

WOVEN CORD

Straight Warp Fabrics

The straight warp fabric consists of the straight warp yarns, with fill yarns laid above and under the warp yarns, and both of them hold together with a binder yarn (see Figure 9). The warp yarns are essentially without crimp. Either nylon or polyester yarns are generally used as straight warps while cotton or man-made yarns are used as the fills and the binders. Straight warp fabrics are used mainly in belt constructions.

TIRE CORD MANUFACTURING

Tire cords of organic materials are generally a series of fine filaments designed to work as a cord unit. Nylon, polyester, rayon and aramid yarns are converted from individual bundles of fine filaments into multiple-ply cords at textile mills.

The incoming yarn is twisted on a ply twister to a specified number of turns per inch. This twisted yarn is called a cord ply. Two or more cord plies are combined and twisted in the reverse direction, to the same number of turns per inch, to form the final cord construction. A typical cord construction is 1000/3 polyester which consists of 3 plies of 1000 denier polyester twisted in the cord bundle.

Cords are woven on looms into cord fabric with a specified number of ends per inch dependent upon the ultimate end use.

Woven cord fabric is then coated with an adhesive system and properly ten-silized to attain the desired properties prior to being shipped to a plant for further processing.

Figure 10 shows a schematic of the cord manufacturing process.

Fiberglass cord is manufactured in a manner similar to the organic materials ...with some important differences. The adhesive (or impregnant) is applied by the fiberglass manufacturer prior to twisting. This insures total encapsulation of each filament by rubber. The dipped fiberglass is twisted and then shipped to the rubber manufacturer for further processing.

Fiberglass cord when received by the rubber manufactuers simply requires weaving prior to calendering or is creel calendered essentially elminating the weaving step.

In the case of steel cord, a brass coating performs as the adhesive system. Unlike fibrous reinforcement, steel is normally creel calendered instead of woven and calendered.

ADHESIVE TREATMENT OF TEXTILE REINFORCEMENT

Textile reinforcement made from organic materials, be it in yarn, cord, or fabric form, requires the application of an adhesive treatment to bond the re-inforcement to rubber. Although the adhesive represents only a small percent of the reinforcement's total weight, it performs an important function; that of stress transfer between the relatively low modulus rubber and the high modulus reinforcing material.

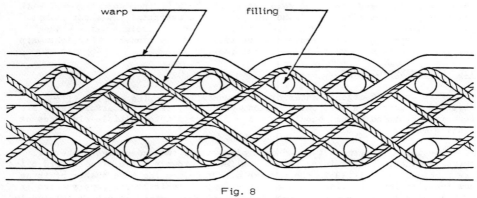

Fig. 8

SOLID WOVEN FABRIC

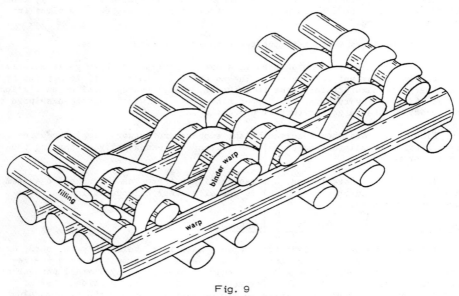

Fig. 9

STRAIGHT WARP FABRIC

The chemical components of the adhesive are specific for the material being treated and the rubber matrix employed. Generally, adhesive consists of highly reactive chemicals, such as resorcinol-formaldehyde resins and iso-cyanates, dispersed in a rubber latex medium which co-cures with the rubber during vulcanization.

The method of applying the adhesive to the reinforcement is as selective as the adhesive itself. The application of the adhesive is performed under controlled conditions of time, temperature, and tension. These conditions are determined to produce adhesive treated textile reinforcements with those properties necessary to meet the ultimate end use requirements...tensile strength, dimensional stability, fatigue resistance and durability.

SUMMARY

The rubber industry consumes a very large quantity of reinforcing material in the manufacture of its products. Yarns, cords, fabrics, and wires are among the most commonly used reinforcing materials in tires, hose, belts, gaskets, and expansion joints. They are just as important as the elastomers in affecting the properties of a finished product. Through successful development of man-made fibers and technical advancements of metallurgy, a wide variety of reinforcing materials is available to today's product engineers. Like other engineering materials, yarns, cords, fabrics, and wires need to be understood and used correctly. Knowledge of their basic properties and dynamic behavior is essential to proper selection of reinforcing materials for each type of service. More importantly, this knowledge is indispensible in any attempt to develop the lowest cost product suitable for each application.

202

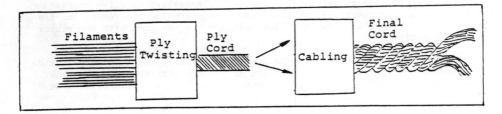

Figure 10 - Cord Manufacturing Process

GENERAL REFERENCES

1. Dickinson, R. H. and Leslie, L. L, "Wire for Reinforcing Rubber"
   Philadelphia Rubber Group Meeting, September 1979

2. "Conveyor and Elevator Belt Handbook" (IP-1), the Rubber Manufacturers
   Association, Washington, D.C. (1980)

3. "Fiber Glass Yarn Products Handbook", PPG Industries, Inc.

4. Goswami, B.C., Martindale, J.G., and Scardino, F.L., "Textile Yarns -
   Technology, Structure, and Applications", Wiley-Interscience,
   New York (1977)

5. Kaswell, E.R., "Wellington Sears Handbook of Industrial Textiles",
   Wellington Sears Co., Inc. New York (1963)

6. "Kevlar", E.I. duPont deNemours & Co.

7. Loeble, W.D., "Fabric and Rubber - Partners for Performance",
   Philadelphia Rubber Group Meeting, 1979

8. Moncrieff, R.W., "Man-made Fibres", Heywood & Co. Ltd.,
   London, England (1962)

9. Ross, J.D., "Fiber Reinforcement for Mechanical Rubber Goods",
   Philadelphia Rubber Group Meeting, September 1979

10. Stanhope, H.W., "Polyester Fabric Reinforcement for Conveyor Belts",
    ACS Rubber Division Meeting, May 1975

11. Wake, W.C. and Wootton, D.B., eds., "Textile Reinforcement of
    Elastomers", Allied Science Publishers Ltd., Englewood, NJ. (1982)

WORK ASSIGNMENT NO. 9
CHAPTER 9. REINFORCING MATERIALS FOR RUBBER PRODUCTS

INSTRUCTIONS: Read each question carefully, select one, and only one, appropriate
answer to complete each statement.

1. Reinforcing materials fulfill many basic functions in rubber products, be it
tire, belt, or others. Their inclusion improves the performance of the
rubber composites. However, reinforcing materials usually do not

___(a) impact load-carrying capacity
___(b) provide dimensional characteristics
___(c) determine basic composite strength and durability
___(d) improve chemical resistance of the composite

2. Of equal importance to the physical and chemical nature of the reinforcing
material itself in a rubber composite is

___(a) the adhesive system used to bond the reinforcing material to rubber
components
___(b) the specific gravity of the rubber components in contact with the rein-
forcing material
___(c) the color of the rubber components involved
___(d) none of above

3. Proper selection of reinforcing materials for a rubber product requires

___(a) precise awareness of the application and environment in which the
product will be utilized
___(b) knowledge of the manufacturing process through which the reinforcing
material is produced
___(c) familiarity with the raw materials used to produce the reinforcing
material
___(d) none of above

4. Cotton is a natural fiber. It was the first reinforcing material used for
rubber products. Although its popularity has declined considerably, it is
still being used effectively to attain high bulk in some applications.
Cotton is well-known for

___(a) high strength and elongation
___(b) not being affected by moisture and mildew
___(c) excellent adhesion to rubber
___(d) none of above

5. Rayon is regenerated cellulose. Despite of its long period of popularity,
it has a major limitation; that of

___(a) low modulus
___(b) very good resistance to chemicals and mildew attack
___(c) susceptibility to moisture degradation
___(d) high shrinkage

6. Some of the most desirable properties of nylon as a reinforcing material in
rubber products are

___(a) low elongation and low shrinkage
___(b) high strengh and good resistance to flex fatigue
___(c) high modulus and good dimensional stability
___(d) none of above

7. Like nylon, polyester is derived from crude oil. The major difference between them are related to the backbone of their molecular structure. In comparison to nylon, polyester is superior in

___(a) strength
___(b) adhesion to rubber
___(c) modulus and dimensional stability
___(d) none of above

8. One of the outstanding properties of fiberglass is

___(a) very high elongation at break
___(b) extremely low modulus
___(c) very low specific gravity
___(d) excellent resistance to heat and chemicals

9. In addition to excellent resistance to heat and humidity, aramid is well-known for its

___(a) superior strength and modulus
___(b) very good compressive properties
___(c) outstanding resistance to shear fatigue
___(d) none of above

10. Steel is often selected as a preferred tire belt material because

___(a) its specific gravity is high
___(b) it is strong, flexible, and elastic
___(c) it bonds easily to other components of a tire
___(d) it offers excellent resistance to compression bending and puncture

11. Round wire of high tensile carbon steel in size ranges of 0.177 to 0.876-inch in diameter is widely used

___(a) in the body of large size hoses for crush resistance and dimensional stability
___(b) in braided or spiralled hose for high pressure service
___(c) as helically wound reinforcement on the interior of rough bore suction hoses to prevent collapse
___(d) as an armor protective spiral wrap around the hose

12. Denier is

___(a) length in numbers of 840-yards of material per pound
___(b) length in numbers of 100-yards of material per pound
___(c) weight in grams of material per 1000 meters
___(d) weight in grams of material per 9000 meters

13. Fabric is

___(a) a linear assembly of fibers or filaments formed into a continuous strand
___(b) a planar structure produced by interlacing yarns
___(c) plied yarns twisted together
___(d) none of above

14. The number of "picks" denote the number of fill yarns in a fabric. The fill yarns

___(a) run lengthwise
___(b) run crosswise as the fabric is woven
___(c) run at a 45° angle to the warp yarns of a square woven fabric
___(d) none of above

15. Most hose ducks as well as belt ducks are plain weave. However, unlike belt ducks, the hose ducks are square woven fabric with the tensile strength

___(a) higher in the warp yarn direction
___(b) higher in the fill yarn direction
___(c) equal in both directions
___(d) extremely weak in the fill direction because the fill yarns are very fine and spaced far apart

CHAPTER 10

RUBBER PRODUCTS FOR COMMERCIAL APPLICATIONS

Thomas J. Leo

Wyrough and Loser, Inc.
Trenton, New Jersey 08638

INTRODUCTION

Rubber is defined as a material that is capable of recovering from large deformations quickly and forcibly, and can be, or already is, modified to a state in which
it is essentially insoluble (but can swell) in boiling solvent, such as benzene,
methyl ethyl ketone, and ethanoltoluene azeotrope.

The specific engineering property which all of the various synthetic and natural
rubbers have is the ability to elongate under stress at room temperature, to at
least twice the original dimension and then recover to no more than 1.5 times original dimension in one minute when the stress is removed. The use of a specific rubber optimizes the achievement of this property under specific environmental conditions.
Generally the rubber requires vulcanization and incorporation with other engineering
material to make useful products.

In the following pages a brief description of commercial products using rubber
and called "Rubber Products" will be given. Obviously these will be broad categories
and each individual product, in fact, encompasses a class of products. Each class
may utilize a specific type of rubber to accomplish a specific application.

The manufacture of rubber products involves various operations. Many of these
operations are common to all rubber products, but some are very specific. In dis-
cussing the products in this chapter, an effort is made to highlight some of the
special operations required and, where applicable, some of the specific types of
rubber used.

PNEUMATIC TIRES

The pneumatic tire, as a product category, leads all other rubber products in
production volume. The making of a tire, though considered by some an art, is in
reality no small achievement in the progress of mankind. A refinement of the ancient
"invention" of the wheel, the modern pneumatic tire is a remarkable combination of
rubber, metal and textile. Amond the major components of a pneumatic tire are
treads, side wall, inner liner, breakers, carcass plies, and bead wires (see Figure 1).
Breakers or breaker belts are tread bracing components on belted-bias tires and radial
tires. Woven cord fabrics of nylon or fiberglass are widely used in breaker belts.
Carcass plies are the strength components of a tire. Cords of polyester, aramid,
and steel are popular materials for tire carcass. Bead wire provides rigidity and
retains an inflated tire on the rim. High tensile steel is usually preferred for
this function.

Rubber Components

Numerous rubber compounds are used in a tire, taking advantage of special properties of various elastomers, and by the use of various compounding ingredients

Fig. 1   Major components of a pneumatic tire

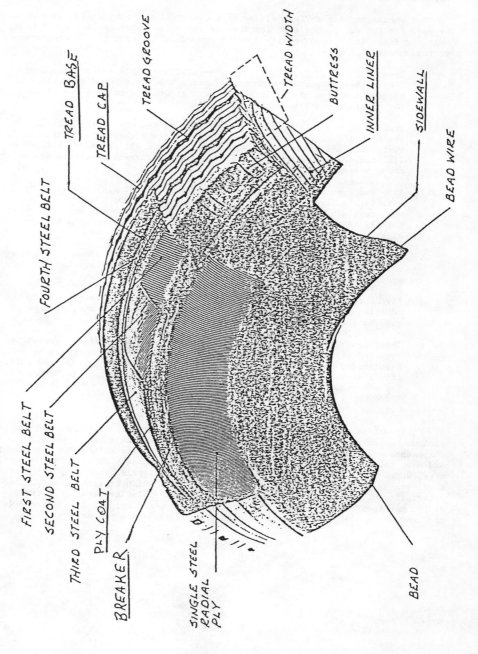

FIRST STEEL BELT

SECOND STEEL BELT

THIRD STEEL BELT

PLY COAT

BREAKER

SINGLE STEEL RADIAL PLY

FOURTH STEEL BELT

TREAD BASE

TREAD CAP

TREAD GROOVE

TREAD WIDTH

BUTTRESS

INNER LINER

SIDEWALL

BEAD WIRE

BEAD

optimizing certain properties to function in specific portions of the tire.

The pneumatic tire may use six or more different compounds. Two compounds may be used for the tread, one each for the cap and base. Side wall, breaker coat, ply coat and inner liner also require special compounds in order to function properly as components of a tire.

1. Tread Cap - Natural (NR), styrene-butadiene (SBR) and/or butadiene (BR) rubber compounded with fine furnace blacks are used to achieve maximum traction and minimum wear, cut growth and rolling resistance for the road contact portion of the tire.

2. Tread Base - This portion, which connects the cap to the rest of the body of the tire, is compounded for maximum thermal and oxidative resistance and minimum heat build-up. It uses NR, SBR and/or Isoprene (IR) rubber compounded with a little coarser furnace blacks to achieve these properties.

3. Side Wall - This portion is compounded to resist flex cracking, weather cracking, and curb scuffing while keeping a nice appearance. The side-wall must adhere well to the inner areas of the tire and may be made from NR, BR, SBR, ethylene-propylene terpolymer (EPDM), and/or a halogenated elastomer such as neoprene (CR) or chlorobutyl.

4. Wire Breaker Coat - Maximum adhesion to metal and maximum resistance to heat buildup are the prime properties required for "breakers". They generally are NR or IR.

5. Ply Coat - This is similar to the breaker in that it must achieve good adhesion to cord and resist heat buildup. However, it must also have good oxidative and thermal stability.

6. Inner Liner - Resistance to air permeation is the critical property required of the inner liner and the elastomer most often chosen is a halogenated butyl rubber. The compound also requires thermal and oxidative resistance and adhesion to the rest of the tire. NR is also used for the inner liners.

Equipment

Equipment used for the production of pneumatic tires is numerous. To mix the various compounds, Banburys and mixing mills are used. Extruders spew out the tread components and rubber calenders apply the compounds to the reinforcing components and make the breaker strips to adhere all the parts to each other. The pneumatic tire, which varies in size from the small, slender bicycle tires to the gigantic multi-ton earth mover tires, is vulcanized in molds which have the general characteristics of an inflatable smooth inner component (bladder) and metal tread design machined outer casting. Individual "watch case" molds and the "Bag-O-Matic" are common examples of equipment used in the vulcanization process.

FLAT BELTING

The trade term "flat belting" is almost synonymous with the act of conveying materials. The applications vary from moving food packages at the supermarket check-out counter to the multi-mile conveying of coal and ore from the mines to the processing center. Flat belting may also be used in power transmission. Though flat belts may be a little simpler in construction design than tires for a small application, they can be every bit as complicated for the larger application. Like tires, flat belting uses rubber in conjunction with textiles and/or metal (usually steel) in its construction. The major components of a flat belt are cover, breaker, carcass reinforcement and skim coating (Figure 2). The carcass is the load-bearing component which is usually made up of plies of textile fabric or a single layer of steel cable. As a general rule, textile fabric must be coated with a rubber compound by a "frictioning" operation and/or a "skim coat" operation at a calender. The breaker is used between the carcass and the top cover to improve impact resistance and adhesion.

Rubber Cover

The rubber cover may be compounded with NR, SBR, nitrile-butadiene rubber (NBR), neoprene (CR) and/or EPDM. It must resist wear, cracking, gouging, oxidation and have traction. The "pulley" side of the flat belt is often different from "top" side of the flat belt. The pulley cover is usually thinner than the top cover, which is also known as the carry cover.

Breaker

In order to improve adhesion between the carcass and the top cover, the fabric construction of the breakers is usually either leno weave or woven cord.

Skim Coating

Skim coating is used to promote adhesion and hold the load-bearing plies together. It must keep fibers from rubbing against each other and cutting each other. Properties such as good tack, pliability, low heat buildup and resistance to thermal degradation are necessary.

Equipment

The calender is the basic flat belt building machinery. The flat press and the rotary press (Rotocure) are two pieces of equipment especially designed for vulcanizing flat belting.

TRANSMISSION BELTING

Though a very small portion of flat belting is used to transmit power, V-belts are considered to be synonymous with transmission belting. Generally flat conveyor belting is sold in lengths that are "spliced" or linked into their "endless" configuration at location of actual application. V-belts are generally vulcanized in their endless configuration.

V-belts transmit power between V-shaped sheaves. They are preferred in applications with limited space. V-belts are made in an enormous number of sizes and

Figure 2
MULTIPLE-PLY BELT SHOWN WITH
FOUR PLIES, A BREAKER, AND RUBBER-CAPPED EDGES

Figure 3
Typical Expansion Joint Construction

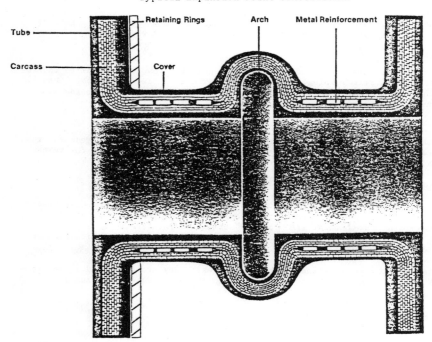

lengths. Common components are cords, top cushion, bottom cushion, and fabric jacket. The cord section is the load-bearing component supported by rubber cushion. It is enveloped by the fabric jacket. The cords are generally a synthetic fiber. The jacket is usually made of one or more plies of woven fabric. Vulcanization of V-belts is accomplished on collapsible mandrels and interlocking rings.

HOSE

Hose can be described as a flexible pipe or conduit. By definition, hose must contain a reinforcing component, as a simple hollow rubber cylinder is called a "tube". The two basic elements of a hose are therefore, tube and reinforcement. Most hose, however, also has an outer cover. The purpose of hose is to move material from one place to another even though the relative position of the two places may keep changing. Figures 4 to 8 show typical hose constructions.

Since the variety of fluids needed to be conducted and the variety of environments to which hose must be subjected is so great, nearly every type of commercially available elastomer is used in the manufacture of hose.

Tube

The tube is the component which comes in contact with and therefore, must be resistant to the effects of the fluid to be transmitted. A mixture of air and sand as in a sandblast hose would require an especially abrasion resistant NR tube. A fuel oil delivery hose may require an oil resistant NBR tube. A paint spray hose conducting lacquer with its strong solvent content would require a polysulfide rubber tube.

Cover

The cover protects the reinforcement and the tube from the outer environment encountered. Hose under the hood of a car must be protected by a cover resistant to heat, oil and gasoline fumes. CR is serviceable up to about 250°F., chlorosulfonated polyethylene rubber (CSM) may be required at 300°F, ethylene/acrylic rubber may be the choice for 325°F service.

Reinforcement

There are so many types of hose that one of the means of classifying them is by the method of applying and type of reinforcement used in making the hose. The seven most common classes are as follows:

1. Knitted Hose - Knitting is an open loop construction that makes a very flexible hose. It is used mainly for garden hose and hose subjected to low pressures only.

2. Vertical Braided Hose - This type of hose is generally subjected to higher pressures of the fluid being transmitted. Textile yarn such as rayon, nylon, or polyester are braided over the tube at very high speeds by the vertical braider. More than one braid ply may be applied. Layers of rubber are used between such reinforcing plies. They must have adhesive properties to bond these plies together.

3. Horizontal Braided Hose - This construction is used for hose of even higher pressure and for hose requiring an exact inside diameter.

212

TYPICAL HOSE CONSTRUCTIONS
(Courtesy of Rubber Manufacturers Association, Inc.)

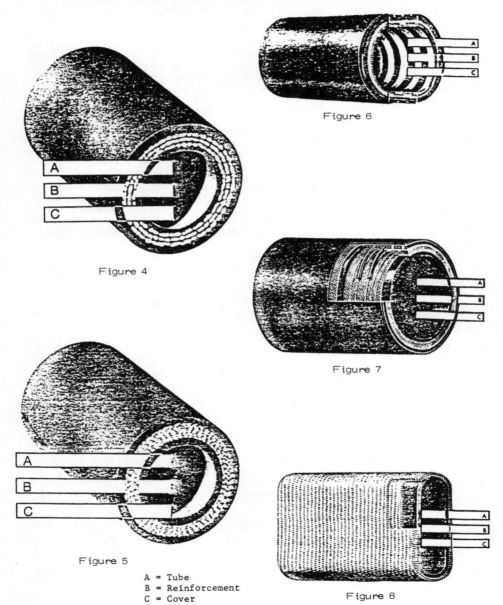

Figure 6

Figure 4

Figure 7

Figure 5

A = Tube
B = Reinforcement
C = Cover

Figure 8

Mandrels are used in the manufacture of this type of hose. Steel wire is often used as reinforcement.

4. Wrapped Fabric Hose - This type of hose is reinforced with impregnated woven fabric rather than yarn. The woven fabric is generally cut on the bias and can be applied by hand or machine. Because of its bulk and stiffness, this type of reinforcement is often used in application involving suction or vacuum.

5. Wire Spiralled Hose - This type of reinforcement is widely used for hose subjected to very high impulse pressures, such as hydraulic hose. Wire spirals are generally applied in pairs in opposite directions. This balances the twisting effect of applying the spiral wire.

6. Woven Jacket Hose - This type of construction is widely used for fire hose. Its design is such that it can lie flat, when not in use, taking up far less space than when conducting water. Looms are used for circular weaving of the jackets.

7. Hand-built Hose - This type of construction is usually utilized to provide very large size hose with great strength and excellent crush and collapse resistance. It is made by hand-building various components on a steel mandrel. The reinforcement is often a combination of helix wire and plies of wrapped fabric. Depending on the service requirements, the helix may be applied over, underneath, or in-between plies of wrapped fabric. Rotary drill hose and oil suction and discharge hose are generally hand-built.

Equipment

One special class of equipment used in making hose in addition to the equipment applying the reinforcement is the lead press or lead extruder. Lead sheathing is often used as the mold for vulcanizing hose. The lead sheathing is extruded over the cover of the hose with the lead press (hydraulic forming of lead billet into the sheath) or lead extruder (continuous forming of the sheath from controlled refreezing of molten lead). Hose is also vulcanized in open steam, unwrapped or in a fabric wrap, in hot air ovens or by continuous fluid bed vulcanizers.

EXPANSION JOINTS

Rubber expansion joint is a flexible connector designed primarily to relieve stress caused by thermal changes in a rigid piping system. It also insulates against vibration and sound generated by pulsating equipment, such as reciprocating pumps and compressors, which may be transmitted through the rigid piping system.

Major components of an expansion joint are tube, carcass reinforcement, and cover. The carcass is the flexible and supporting component. It usually consists of rubber impregnated fabric plies with metallic wire or rings imbedded. Figure 3 shows a typical expansion joint construction.

Expansion joints are generally hand-built or molded. The hand-built method is very similar to that utilized in production of hand-built hose.

RUBBER COVERED ROLLS

Rubber covered rolls find application in paper making, plastic film production, printing, graphic arts, steel fabricating, textile manufacturing, metal coating, and leather processing. The use of printing rollers in the graphic arts industry probably accounts for the largest volume of this product sold.

Elastomers used in rubber covered roll manufacture vary accoridng to application, with NR and SBR being used for paper mill press rolls and hard rubber rolls; NBR for printing, textile mill and metal coating rollers using an aromatic system; EPDM for metal coating rollers using a ketone system; and CR used for steel mill rolls.

The construction of rubber covered rolls generally consists of a metal core, a coat of rubber bonding adhesive and the rubber cover. Adhesion to the core is an extremely important requirement on this product. Large rolls are generally built up with calendered sheeting, ground to size, wrapped with tape and vulcanized in open steam or a water filled autoclave. After curing, the roll is unwrapped and re-finished with a grinding operation. The surface must be properly smooth and there-fore all operations must be carried out with great care.

Small rolls are normally produced by molding. Medium sized rolls are sometimes produced by extrusion.

RUBBER FOOTWEAR

Rubber footwear products have been moving more and more into the thermoplastic elastomer area because of the economic pressures of reducing the labor cost of manufacturing. For high quality canvas sport and casual shoes, natural rubber is still used along with some IR and SBR. Rubber components of footwear are "Boot uppers", "outsoles", "insole sponge", "foxing" and "lining gums".

Rubber based heels and soles have also been encroached upon by the thermoplastic elastomers. Oil resistant soles and heels are made with CR or NBR. Rubber soles and heels are vulcanized in molds separately from the shoes and then attached.

WIRE AND CABLE

Rubber compounds used for wire and cable fall into two classes, namely, insula-tion and jackets. Insulation must have a very high order of electrical resistance and the ability to retain that electrical resistance under the adverse conditions of aging, moisture and elevated temperature. Jackets provide wear resistance and resistance to the elements. Jackets are generally compounded with CR, CSM or NBR/PVC blends.

Insulation compounds may be made with NR, SBR, Butyl (IIR) or EPDM. EPDM is becoming more and more the choice, especially for high voltage applications because of its naturally low level of soluble salt content. The vulcanization of wire and cable is somewhat similar to hose in that lead sheathing can be used as the mold in some cases. Most often a steam tube vulcanizer is used for continuous vulcanization (C.V.). Tight cures must be attained in very short times with the CV method. Steam pressures in excess of 200 psi and temperatures of over 200°C (392°F) are common for curing wire and cable.

SPONGE RUBBER PRODUCTS

Sponge is an elastic porous mass. Sponge rubber with open-cell structure obtained its name from the natural occurring sponge. Man has also devised a way to make a nonporous sponge, however, by making a closed-cell (non-interconnected cells) structure. Open-cell sponge can be made from rubber latex. It is compounded with fillers, plasticizers and vulcanizing agents and then whipped with air to a froth and vulcanized in molds. The trapped moisture and air make the open celled structure.

Similar compounding of dry rubber with carbonates and fatty acids also provides an open-cell sponge during vulcanization due to the release of CO_2 by the reaction of the carbonate (generally sodium bicarbonate) and the fatty acid.

Closed-cell sponge is produced by incorporation of relatively small amounts of "blowing agents" in fine particle size. Sponge rubber is used in the following products:

1. Carpet underlay (often open-cell from latex)

2. Mattress filling (open or closed-cell)

3. Upholstery filling (open or closed-cell)

4. Insulation (closed-cell)

5. Door and window seals (closed-cell)

Elastomers used to make sponge rubber products are NR, SBR, CR and EPDM. Sponge may be vulcanized in molds or continuously vulcanized after extrusion. In order to produce a uniform extruded sponge product, a very delicate balance between rate of cure and rate of blow must be maintained, both in the chemical composition of the compound and throughout its entire manufacturing process.

HARD RUBBER

Hard rubber is one of the exceptions to the definition of rubber. It is compounded so it will not elongate to at least twice its original dimension when stress is applied and will not return to essentially its original dimensions when the stress is removed. Hard rubber, however, still retains some of the useful rubber properties. Hard rubber can only be extended or compressed very slightly, but it has a very high percentage of retraction upon removal of the stress. It is insoluble in the solvents mentioned in the beginning of this chapter.

Hard rubber is compounded with a large amount of sulfur (12 to 35 parts per 100 parts of rubber). NR and SBR are the primary elastomers used to make hard rubber.

Products made with hard rubber include steering wheels, caster wheels, electrical insulation, battery boxes, and bowling balls. Tank linings are also made with hard rubber compounds.

SPORTING GOODS

Bowling balls were mentioned as a hard rubber product, but rubber is used in many other sporting goods. Such goods include golf balls, tennis balls, basketballs, footballs, soccer ball bladders, handballs, racketballs, squash balls, hockey pucks, golf club grips, tennis racket grips, protective equipment, padding, wet suits, swim fins and inflatable rafts.

The elastomers used in making sporting goods include SBR, CR and EPDM.

Most of the products mentioned are molded.

MOLDED GOODS

"Molded goods" is a kind of catchall term covering a wide variety of products whose ultimate shapes are created by the molds in which they are vulcanized. Some are simple products such as auto floor mats, truck mud flaps, sink drain mats, and bathtub mats. Most of these products are made by compression molding method. Other products like spark plug caps and connectors are made by transfer molding method.

Other types of molded goods include diaphrams, seals, O-rings, grommets, motor mounts, stoppers, gaskets, seals, bumpers, wiper blades and sleeves. Products with irregular shape and complex configuration are usually made by transfer molding or injection molding methods.

Virtually every type of elastomer is used in molded goods.

MISCELLANEOUS RUBBER PRODUCTS

With all the products listed under molded goods, one might think there could not be any miscellaneous products, however, there are still a great number of products that have not been named.

There are rubber coated fabrics such as raincoats, rubber boots, and rubber gloves that are made by spreading solvated rubber compounds over cloth and evaporating the solvents. There is friction tape made by "frictioning" rubber onto a cloth with a calender. There are other calendered sheet goods that are used for roofing and for pond liners. Fuel cells are made from fabric reinforced rubber sheeting.

It is evident there are many commercial applications for rubber products and the list can get longer and longer.

SUMMARY

Rubber products have commercial applications virtually everywhere. They are being used in transportation, industry, agriculture, recreation, national defense as well as our own home. Rubber technology is still expanding. New elastomers, new rubber chemicals, new reinforcing materials, and new processing equipment are continuously being developed by scientists and engineers here as well as abroad. It has not been an easy task to account for all the major rubber products widely used today. It is even more difficult, if not impossible, to predict how many more rubber products will be available in the future for the benefit of mankind.

The demand for better products is always present. The challenge of product development for new commercial applications today is as great as ever.

GENERAL REFERENCES

1. Babbit, R. O., ed., "The Vanderbilt Rubber Handbook", R. T. Vanderbilt Co., Inc. Norwalk, CT (1978)

2. Blow, C. M., ed., "Rubber Technology and Manufacture", Butterworth & Company, London, England (1971)

3. Carmichael, C., "The Seals Book", Penton, Cleveland, Ohio (1964)

4. "Conveyor and Elevator Belt Handbook" (IP-1), the Rubber Manufacturers Assoc., Washington, DC (1980)

5. Eirich, F. R., ed., "Science and Technology of Rubber", Academic Press, New York, (1978)

6. "Hose Handbook" (IP-2), the Rubber Manufacturers Association, Washington, DC (1979)

7. McPherson, A. T., and Klemin, A., eds., "Engineering Uses of Rubber", Rhinhold Publishing Corporation, New York (1956)

8. "The Rubber Industry in the U.S.A.", the Rubber Manufacturers Association, Washington, DC

9. "Sheet Rubber Handbook" (IP-40), the Rubber Manufacturers Association, Washington, DC (1980)

10. "Technical Handbook - Rubber Expansion Joints and Flexible Pipe Connectors", Fluid Sealing Association, Philadelphia, PA (1979)

11. Wood, E. C., "Pneumatic Tyre Design", Heffer, Cambridge, England (1955)

WORK ASSIGNMENT NO. 10

CHAPTER 10. RUBBER PRODUCTS FOR COMMERCIAL APPLICATIONS

INSTRUCTIONS: Read each question carefully, select one, and only one. appropriate
answer to complete each statement.

1.   The tread, sidewall, inner liner, breakers, carcass plies and bead wires are
major components of a pneumatic tire. The rubber tread cap is the road contact
portion of a tire. It must be

_____ (a) highly resistant to weather, ozone and flex cracking
_____ (b) impermeable to gases and vapor
_____ (c) highly resistant to abrasion and cut growth
_____ (d) easily bonded to the breakers and the carcass plies

2.   The major function of the carcass plies in a pneumatic tire is to

_____ (a) impart strength and contain growth
_____ (b) provide rigidity and retain an inflated tire on the rim
_____ (c) brace the tread and maintain tread profile of an inflated tire
_____ (d) none of above

3.   Conveyor belt, like most flat belts, generally consists of top cover, carcass
reinforcement with skim coating, bottom cover, and breakers. The belt carcass

_____ (a) is usually made up of plies of open weave fabric for good adhesion
_____ (b) is the load-bearing component which is usually made up of plies of strong
textile fabric or a layer of steel cable
_____ (c) is usually made up of plies of square woven fabric
_____ (d) none of above

4.   V-belts transmit power between V-shaped sheaves. They are preferred over flat
belts especially in applications with limited space. The load-bearing component
of a V-belt is

_____ (a) fabric jacket
_____ (b) cord section
_____ (c) rubber cushion
_____ (d) none of above

5.   Hose can be described as

_____ (a) a flexible pipe or conduit for moving materials from one place to another
_____ (b) a flexible hollow cylinder
_____ (c) a flexible connector for relieving stress caused by thermal changes in a
rigid piping system
_____ (d) none of above

6. The major components of most hoses are inner tube, reinforcement, and outer cover. Numerous types of reinforcing materials are used in hose products. Hose is classified by the method of applying the reinforcement. Most hose in very large inside diameter is

____ (a) knitted hose
____ (b) braided hose
____ (c) woven jacket hose
____ (d) hand-built hose

7. Most medium size (2 to 4 inch in ID) hose subjected to high pressure are most likely to be

____ (a) vertical braided hose
____ (b) horizontal braided hose
____ (c) knitted hose
____ (d) wrapped fabric hose

8. Woven jacket hose construction is normally used for

____ (a) fire hose
____ (b) hydraulic hose
____ (c) garden hose
____ (d) oil suction and discharge hose

9. An expansion joint is used mainly for relieving stress and insulating vibration and sound in a rigid piping system. Its carcass reinforcement usually consists of

____ (a) textile braid with helix wire
____ (b) spiralled wire and open weave breakers
____ (c) fabric plies with metallic wire or imbedded rings
____ (d) none of above

10. The largest user of rubber covered rolls is the graphic arts industry. The construction of rubber covered rolls generally consists of metal core, a bonding adhesive coating, and the rubber cover. The single most important property requirement of this product is

____ (a) hardness of the rubber
____ (b) diameter of the core
____ (c) adhesion to the core
____ (d) thickness of the cover

11. Rubber compounds used for wire and cable fall into two classes, namely jackets and insulation. Jackets provide wear resistance and resistance to the elements, while insulation possesses

____ (a) high tensile strength and ultimate elongation
____ (b) proper dielectric strength and resistance to heat and oxidation
____ (c) resistance to moisture and steam
____ (d) none of above

12. Open-cell structure of sponge rubber is produced by using the trapped moisture and air in the rubber latex. Manufacture of sponge rubber with closed-cell structure requires the use of

____ (a) a very soft compound with a slow cure rate
____ (b) a nitrogen releasing blowing agent in a dry rubber compound
____ (c) a compound with low Mooney viscosity at 212°F
____ (d) none of above

13. Some of the well-known hard rubber products are steering wheels, caster wheels, and battery boxes. Hard rubber compounds usually contain

____ (a) no plasticizer
____ (b) large amount of carbon black or silica
____ (c) large amount of sulfur
____ (d) none of above

14. Most of the rubber sporting goods are produced by

____ (a) extrusion
____ (b) calendering
____ (c) molding
____ (d) hand-built

15. Molded goods with irregular shape and complex configuration are most likely made by

____ (a) compression molding
____ (b) transfer molding or injection molding
____ (c) bladder molding
____ (d) none of above

CHAPTER 11

GLOSSARY OF COMMON TERMS USED BY THE RUBBER INDUSTRY

Harry Long

Goodall Rubber Company
Trenton, New Jersey 08650

The compilation of common rubber terms in this chapter is intended to help the readers to better understand the language of the rubber industry. The definitions given here are neither fully detailed nor highly technical. Many of them have been simplified for general understanding by those with little or no technical background. Therefore, they should not be relied upon as the sole or precise meaning under all circumstances.

The emphasis of this chapter is placed on terms widely used throughout the rubber industry. No attempt is made to include terms pertinent to only certain types of products. Definitions of some terms not included may be found in the text of the chapters involving them. To those who desire either a more detailed definition of each term or a larger glossary, reading of the following references is recommended:

(1) "Glossary of Terms Relating to Rubber and Rubber Technology" (STP184A), published by the American Society for Testing and Materials

(2) "Hose Handbook" (IP-2), published by the Rubber Manufacturers Assoc.

(3) "Conveyor and Elevator Belt Handbook" (IP-1), published by the Rubber Manufacturers Association

(4) "Glossary of Technical Rubber Terms", published by B. F. Goodrich Co.

(5) "Dictionary of Rubber Technology", by A. S. Craig, published by Philosophical Library, Inc., New York (1969)

(6) "Dictionary of Rubber", by K. F. Heinisch, published by John Wiley & Sons, Inc., New York (1974)

(7) "Elsevier's Rubber Dictionary", by R. Stitching, published by Elsevier Publishing Co., New York (1959)

abrasion - the surface loss of a material due to frictional forces.

abrasion resistance - the resistance of a material to loss of surface particle due to frictional forces.

accelerated aging - a method in which an attempt is made to produce and measure the effects of natural aging in a shorter period.

acid resistance - the ability to resist the action of identified acids within specified limits of concentration and temperature.

adhesion - the state in which two surfaces are held together by interfacial forces which may consist of molecular forces or interlocking action, or both.

adhesion failure - the separation of two materials at the surface interface rather than within one of the materials itself.

adhesive - a substance capable of holding materials together by surface attachment.

age resistance - the resistance to deterioration by oxygen, heat, light, and ozone or combination thereof during storage or use.

aging - (1) the irreversible change of material properties after exposure to an environment for an interval of time; (2) exposing materials to an environment for an interval of time.

air bag - an inflatable rubber container placed inside a rubber product during vulcanization in a mold to provide molding pressure.

air checks - the surface markings or depressions due to trapping air between the material being cured and the mold or press surface.

air pocket - voids, due to ply separation or entrapped gas.

air trap - see air checks.

ambient temperature - the temperature of the atmosphere or medium surrounding the object under consideration.

backing - (1) a layer or liner of material on the underside of a sheeted product for mechanical reinforcement; (2) a soft rubber layer between tube and/or cover and carcass to provide adhesion.

back rind - distortion of the mold parting line, usually in the form of a ragged or torn indentation.

bagging - a condition during mill mixing when a rubber stock exhibits no adhesion to the rolls, sags off the rolls and fails to form a bank at the nip of the rolls.

bank - the reservoir of material at the opening between rolls of a mill or calender or at the spreader bar.

bare back - (1) the textile face of an article that is free of any rubber coating; (2) the surface of rubber bales that are shipped without being packaged.

batch - product of one mixing operation in an intermittent process.

bias angle - (1) acute angle between the direction of the cut and the direction of the wrap in the production of wrapping for hose; (2) acute angle between the direction of the cut and the direction of the cords in the production of tire cord fabric plies.

bite - see nip.

bleeding - surface exudation.

blister - a cavity or sac deforming the surface of a material usually due to expansion of an entrapped gas.

bloom - a change in the surface appearance of a product caused by the migration of a liquid or solid material to the surface due to incompatibility.

blow - the volume expansion during the forming of sponge rubber expressed either in percent or a ratio.

boardy - (1) in coated fabrics, stiff or tinny effect, or a too close texture stock; (2) in vulcanized compound, very stiff material, usually due to high filler content or resin modification.

bond - the union of materials by use of adhesives, usually used in relation to parts vulcanized after attaching.

breakdown - (1) in cellular rubber, defect due to local collapse of cell structure; (2) preliminary mastication and milling of raw rubber or a rubber mix to render it more suitable for further processing.

breaker ply - an open-mesh fabric used (1) to increase the adhesion between the cover and the carcass of a belt and to spread impact or (2) to anchor a hose tube or cover to its carcass and to spread impact.

brittle point - the hightest temperature at which a rubber specimen will fracture under sudden impact.

buckled ply - wrinkling, folding, or buckling where one layer is not adhering smoothly to another.

buffing - the grinding of a surface producing a roughened or a velvety texture.

bulk density — the density of loose material (powder, cubes, etc.) expressed as a ratio of weight to volume.

butt seam — a seam made by placing the two pieces to be joined edge to edge.

— C —

calender blister — the small air bubbles often found in sheeted rubber when running on the calender.

calender crown — the curvature of the rolls of a calender to compensate for the deflection of rolls because of the pressure of the rubber between them.

calender stop — a mark left on the surface of a rubber sheet or sheeting due to interruption of calender roll motion.

carbon black — elemental carbon in finely divided form used to reinforce elastomeric compounds.

carcass — the fabric, cord, or metal reinforced section, or all three, of a rubber product as distinguished from the rubber tube, cover, or tread.

catalyst — a chemical that in small quantities accelerates a chemical reaction without itself necessarily becoming part of the final product.

cement, rubber — a dispersion or solution of an elastomer or compound in a volatile solvent for use as an adhesive or coating.

chalking — the formation of a powdery residue on the surface of a material resulting from degradation.

chatter marks — defects on calendered sheeting consisting of transverse narrow bands of alternately thicker and thinner material.

checking — the short, shallow cracks on the surface of a rubber product, resulting from damaging action by environmental conditions.

churn — a vessel used for making rubber cement, in which rubber compounds are stirred into solvents.

C I — the abbreviation for cloth-inserted, indicating a sheet of rubber containing one or more plies of fabric covered with rubber.

coat peeling — during coating at a calender, a portion of rubber coat being picked off from fabric and sticking to calender roll.

cold check — a split, crack, fissure, or roughness in calendered sheets caused by improper warming of the stock or the temperature of rolls.

cold flow - continued deformation under gravitational force, at or below room temperature.

cold rubber - SBR polymerized at a temperature of 5°C (41°F) or below.

compatibility - property of different materials to blend together and form a homogeneous system.

compression set - the residual deformation of a material after removal of the compressive stress.

contact stain - discoloration of a product by another material or by a rubber article in the area directly touching it.

corrugated cover - a longitudinally ribbed or grooved exterior.

count - in woven fabric, the number of warp ends, or number of filling threads, or both, in fabric, of unit area, generally 1 inch^2 (645 mm^2).

cracking - (1) a sharp break or fissure in the surface of rubber articles that develops on exposure to the atmosphere, light, heat, or repeated bending or stretching; (2) the treatment of raw rubber by passing it through moving corrugated rolls.

cracker mill - a mill in which the two rolls are deeply corrugated or cut with angular grooves used for breaking down rubber.

crawl - the shrinkage of milled rubber and calendered stocks after removal from the rolls. It may sometimes create a curl effect.

crazing - a surface effect on rubber articles characterized by many minute cracks.

creep - the deformation, in either cured or uncured rubber under stress, which occurs with lapse of time after the immediate deformation.

crimp - in fabric, (1) the sinusoidal curvature impressed in the warp or filling during weaving; (2) the difference in distance between two points on a yarn as it lies in a fabric and the same two points when the yarn has been removed from the fabric and straightened under tension.

crown - the difference between the diameter at the center and at the edge of a cylindrical roll.

crow's feet - small flow marks of V shape on calendered sheeting.

crude rubber - a raw material of the rubber industry. The preferred term is raw rubber.

crystallinity - orientation of the disordered long chain molecules of a polymer into repeating patterns. Degree of crystallinity effects stiffness, hardness, low temperature flexibility and heat resistance.

cure - the act of vulcanization.

- D -

damping - the dissipation of energy with time or distance, ability to absorb energy to reduce vibration.

delamination - separation or splitting, either between plies in laminated goods or occasionally within the homogeneous part itself.

die - detachable part of an extruder to produce the profile of an extrudate.

dielectric strength - the measure of a product's ability to resist passage of a disruptive discharge produced by an electric stress; the voltage that an insultating material can withstand before breakdown occurs.

dipped fabric - a cloth coated by passing through a solution or a dispersion, and drying.

doughs - masticated rubber in concentrations of 20 to 30 percent in a solvent resulting in a product having elastic after effects as well as plastic flow.

drift - see creep.

duck - a compact, firm, heavy, plain weave fabric made from cotton or synthetic fibers, or a combination of both. Duck is also known as canvas, army duck, belt duck harvester duck, hose duck and shoe duck.

dumbbell - a standard, flat strip specimen shaped like a dumbbell that is used in many physical tests.

durometer - an instrument for measuring the hardness of vulcanized rubber and plastic.

durometer hardness - an arbitrary numbering scale that indicates the resistance to indentation of the indentor point of the durometer. High values indicate harder materials.

dynamic properties - mechanical properties exhibited under repeated cyclic deformations.

- E -

ebonite - a hard rubber made by vulcanization of rubber with high levels (greater 30 parts) of sulfur, where the high hardness is due to the action of the sulfur.

elongation - extension produced by a tensile stress.

ends - (1) a wrap yarn of a fabric. They run lengthwise in the fabric. The ends per inch are the number of warp yarns per inch of width; (2) the number of cords per inch of width in cord fabric.

extraction - the process of removing one or more components of a homogeneous mixture with a liquid (solvent) in which the components to be removed are soluble but not the mixture as a whole.

exudation - delayed phase separation of incompatible material, also called bleeding, blooming, spewing or sweating.

even motion - a 1:1 ratio of surface speed of two adjacent rolls (mill or calender).

- F -

fabric picks per inch - the number of filling (weft) yarns, (filaments or fibers) per inch.

fatigue, dynamic - the deterioration of a material by repeated deformation.

filling - the weft strands in fabric that run at right angles to the warp.

flash - the excess material protruding from the surface of a molded article at the mold parting line. Mold overflow.

flex cracking - a cracking condition of the surface of rubber articles such as tires and footwear, resulting from constantly repeated bending or flexing in service.

flexing - bending of a flexible material and allowing it to return to its original dimensions.

flow marks, lines or cracks - variants by degree, with "cracks" the most severe of surface imperfections caused by imperfect flow of the raw compound during forming.

fluxing - a process in which two or more materials are blended to form a homogeneous mass in the melted or highly plastic state.

formulation - kinds and proportion of ingredients for a mix, together with the method of incorporation. Also called recipe.

friction pick-off - rubber compound sticking to the fast roll during frictioning at a calender.

friction ratio - ratio of surface speeds of two adjacent rolls (mill, calender or refiner), also called friction motion or odd motion.

frictioning - a process of impregnating a woven fabric with rubber using a calender whose rolls rotate at different surface speeds.

frosting - fine surface greying or a whitening usually due to environmental degradation of a rubber vulcanizate, also called chalking.

furnace black - a carbon black obtained by burning natural gas or petroleum oil, or both, in a large furnace with a low percentage of the theoretical amount of air required for complete combustion.

- G -

gel - a semi-solid system consisting of a network of solid aggregates in which liquid is held.

gelling - formation of a uniform solid coagulum from which the aqueous phase has not separated.

glass transition point - temperature at which a material loses its glass-like properties and becomes a semi-liquid.

grain - the unidirectional orientation of rubber or filler particles occurring during processing (extrusion, milling, calendering) resulting in anisotropy of a rubber vulcanizate.

green strength - (1) the resistance to deformation of a rubber stock in the uncured state; (2) uncured adhesion between plied or spliced surfaces.

gum stock, gum compound - a rubber compound containing only those ingredients necessary for vulcanization and small amounts of other ingredients for processing, coloring, and for improving the resistance to aging.

- H -

hard rubber - see ebonite.

hazing - a dulling of the finish. See also bloom, chalking, and frosting.

heat build-up - the generation of heat due to hysteresis when rubber is rapidly or continually deformed.

heat history - the accumulated amount of heat a rubber stock has been subjected to during processing operations, usually after incorporation of the vulcanizing agents. Incipient cure or scorch can take place if heat history has been excessive.

Holland cloth - a completely filled woven fabric with a smooth glass finish on both sides, used as a separating medium for rubber gum stock.

hydrolysis - chemical decomposition of a substance involving the addition of water.

hysteresis - the heat generated by rapid deformation of a vulcanized rubber part. It is the difference between the energy of the deforming stress and the energy of the recovery cycle.

- I -

impact strength - measure of the toughness of a material, as the energy required to break a specimen with a single blow.

incompatibility - inability of materials to form a homogeneous system.

- K -

kinking - a temporary or permanent distortion of a product, induced by winding or doubling upon itself.

knitted fabric - a flat or tubular structure made from one or more yarns or filaments whose direction is generally transverse to the fabric axis, but whose successive passes are united by a series of interlocking loops.

knit mark - where raw stock did not unite into a homogeneous mass during the vulcanization. This is also called poor knitting.

knitted ply - the interlaced loops of yarn forming a continuous tubular structure.

- L -

lamination - the making of products from sheets of materials united by heat and pressure.

layer - a single thickness of rubber or fabric between adjacent parts.

legs - tension filaments that appear between two adhering frictioned fabric plies as they are pulled apart.

liner - a separator, usually cloth, plastic film, or paper, used to prevent adjacent layers of material from sticking together.

loading - the kind and quantity (volume basis) of fillers mixed with rubber.

logy - sluggish, slow recovery.

low temperature flexibility - the ability of a rubber product to be flexed, bend, or bowed at specified low temperature without loss of serviceability.

- M -

masterbatch - a preliminary mixture of rubber and one or more compound ingredients for such purposes as more thorough dispersion or better processing, and which will later become part of the final compound in a subsequent mixing operation.

matrix - (1) mold or form in which anything is cast or shaped; (2) continuous medium in which discrete particles are dispersed, as chopped fiberglass in polyester resin.

mill - a machine with two horizontal rolls revolving in opposite directions used for the mastication or mixing of rubber.

modulus - the ratio of stress to strain. In the physical testing of rubber, the load necessary to produce stated percentage of elongation, compression or shear.

Mooney scorch - a measure of the incipient curing characteristics of a rubber compound using the Mooney viscometer.

Mooney viscosity - a measure of the viscosity of a rubber or rubber compound determined in a Mooney shearing disc viscometer.

- N -

necking down - a localized decrease in the cross-sectional area of a rubber product resulting from tension.

nerve - the elastic resistance of unvulcanized rubber or rubber compounds to permanent deformation during processing.

nip - the radial clearance between rolls of a mill or calender on a line of centers.

- O -

off gage - not conforming to thickness specified.

open seam - a seam whose edges do not meet, creating a void.

optimum cure - the state of vulcanization at which a desire combination of properties is attained.

oxygen bomb - a pressure-resisting apparatus used in an aging test in which rubber is deteriorated in hot compressed oxygen.

ozone cracking - the surface cracks, checks, or crazing caused by exposure to an atmosphere containing ozone.

- P -

pale crepe - the highest grade of unsmoked plantation natural rubber.

permanent set - the amount by which an elastic material fails to return to its original form after deformation.

permeability - the quality or condition of allowing passage of liquid or gases through a layer.

p h r - abbreviation for parts per hundred of rubber, used for indicating the proportions of ingredients in a rubber compound.

pigment - (1) a dry colored powder used for coloring paint, rubber or other mediums; (2) sometimes incorrectly used to include all fillers and reinforcing agents as well as colors.

plasticity - (1) a measure of the resistance to shear of an unvulcanized elastomer; (2) a tendency of a material to remain deformed after reduction of the deforming stress to or below its yield stress.

plied yarn - a yarn made by twisting together in one operation two or more single yarns, also called cord ply.

ply - one layer in a laminated structure.

ply separation - a loss of adhesion between plies.

pock marks - uneven blister-like elevations, depressions, or pimpled appearance.

porosity - the presence of numerous small holes or voids.

post cure - heat or radiation treatment, or both, to which a cured or partially cured thermosetting plastic or rubber composition is subjected to enhance the level of one or more properties.

press cold ends - the area of reduced temperature at the press platen ends resulting in a partially cured product at that point.

press lap - the mark of the area of overlap of one press cure length on the next.

press mark - an irregularity in the surface of a vulcanized product caused by the press ends or by corresponding irregularities in the press surface.

pricker marks - (1) a perforation of the cover of a hose or belt performed before vulcanization; (2) a hold caused by a hand prick in removing article from mold.

processability - the relative ease which raw or compounded rubber can be handled in rubber machinery.

pure gum - see gum stock.

- R -

raw rubber - unprocessed, vulcanizable elastomer, normally implying the natural product.

rebound test - method of determining the resilient properties of vulcanized rubber, by measuring the rebound of a steel ball or pendulum falling from a definite height onto a rubber sample

recipe - see formulation.

reclaim or reclaim rubber - the product resulting from the treatment of scrap vulcanized rubber in various operations. It is generally used as an extender or processing aid in natural rubber and SBR compounds rather than by itself.

resilience - the property of a material that enables it to return to its original size and shape after removal of the stress which causes the deformation.

reversion - (1) a deterioration of physical properties that may occur upon excessive vulcanization of some elastomers, evidenced by a decrease in hardness and tensile strength, and an increase in elongation; (2) a similar change in properties after air aging at elevated temperatures. Natural rubber, butyl, polysulfides and epichlorohydrin polymers exhibit this effect (extreme reversion may result in tackiness). Most other polymers will harden and suffer loss of elongation on hot air aging.

rheometer (Monsanto) - an oscillating disk cure meter used for determining vulcanization characteristics of a rubber compound.

rind - see flash.

Rotocure - a rotory press.

R P M - the abbreviation of revolutions per minute.

- S -

scorch - premature vulcanization of a rubber compound, generally due to excessive heat history. Also see Mooney scorch.

screwdown - motorized device for nip adjustment of a calender to control sheet thickness.

selvage or selvedge - the lengthwise woven edge of a fabric, usually has an increased number of ends per inch.

semi-cure - a preliminary incomplete vulcanization applied to an article in the manufacturing process to cause the rubber to acquire a degree of stiffness or to maintain some disired shape.

set - strain remaining after complete release of the load producing the deformation.

set up - scorched. When an unvulcanized rubber stock is considered to be "set up", it can no longer be processed smoothly.

shelf aging - the natural deterioration of rubber articles kept in storage or "on the shelf" under atmospheric conditions.

shelf life - the time an unvulcanized rubber stock can be stored without losing any of its processing or curing properties.

shell - a hollow, light, metal cylinder on which rubber sheet, or rubberized fabric from calendering is wrapped.

Shore hardness - see durometer hardness.

sink - a collapsed blister or bubble leaving a depression in the product.

skim coat - a layer of rubber material laid on a fabric but not forced into the weave. Normally laid on a frictioned fabric. Sometimes called skim.

slab - a thick sheet, generally laminated.

sley - the number of warp yarns or ends per inch in woven fabric.

sloughing - surface deterioration of rubber after solvent immersion.

smoke sheets - plantation natural rubber sheets that, after passing through a mill that puts the conventional ribbing design on them, are washed and hung on racks in a smoke house where they undergo a combined smoking and drying process.

specific gravity - the ratio of the mass of a unit volume of a material to that of the same volume of water at a specified temperature.

spew - (1) surplus material forced from a mold on closure under pressure; (2) cement runback at splice.

spider - a part with three or more spokes supporting the mandrel in an extruder die.

spider mark - (1) a weak spot or fault caused by failure of the extruded compound to re-unite after passing around a spoke of the spider; (2) the grain produced at point of joining of stock after passing spoke of the spider.

splice - a joint or junction made by lapping or butting edges, straight or on a bias, and held together through vulcanization or mechanical means.

sprue - (1) the primary feed channel that runs from the outer face of an injection or transfer mold to mold gate in a single cavity mold or to runners in a multiple cavity mold; (2) the piece of material formed or partially cured in the primary feed channel.

sprue mark - a mark, usually elevated, left on the surface of an injection or transfer molded part, after removal of the sprue.

state of cure - the cure condition of a vulcanizate relative to that at which optimum physical properties are obtained.

static wire - a wire incorporated in a rubber part to conduct static electricity.

stiffness - rigidity, tendency to resist deformation under a stress.

stitching - a method of butting or joining two pieces of uncured rubber together by means of a stitching roller, a hand held tool comprised of a wheel with a narrow serrated edge.

stock - unvulcanized, mixed rubber compound of a definite composition.

stock guides - fitted plates near the roll ends which keep the stock in the bank of a mill or calender.

strain - deformation resulting from a stress.

stress - forces per unit of original cross sectional area that is applied to a part or specimen.

stress relaxation - the decrease in stress after a given time of constant strain.

strike through - (1) in coated or frictioned fabric, a penetration of rubber compound through the fabric; (2) in woven fire hose, the penetration of the rubber backing through the jacket.

substrate - a material upon the surface of which an ahesive promoter is applied for any purpose such as bonding or coating.

sun checking or sunlight checking - surface deterioration in the form of cracks, checks, or crazing caused by exposure to direct or indirect sunlight.

swelling - the increase in volume of a specimen immersed in a liquid or exposed to a vapor.

- T -

tack - the ability to adhere to itself; a sticky or adhesive quality or condition.

tear strength - the maximum force required to tear a specified specimen, the force acting substantially parallel to the major axis of the test specimen.

tensile strength - the maximum tensile stress applied during stretching a specimen to rupture.

thermal black - a soft carbon black formed by the thermal decomposition of natural gas. It has relatively little stiffening effect on rubber, but imparts toughness, resilience, good resistance to tearing, and fair abrasion resistance.

thin spot - undergage area.

tie gum - an intermediate adhesive layer employed to promote bonding of two surfaces.

- U -

ultimate elongation - the maximum elongation prior to rupture.

undercure - state of vulcanization less than optimum. It may be evidenced by tackiness or inferior physical properties.

- V -

veneer - a thin protective film placed on a rubber substrate for protection against ozone cracking. It is also a thin film or sheet applied over a substance to prevent or reduce oxygen or ozone attack, to act as a migration barrier, or to beautify the finished article, or all.

viscosity - the resistance of a material to flow under stress.

volume swell - see swelling.

vulcanizate - preferably used to denote the product of vulcanization, without reference to its shape or form.

- W -

warm-up mill - an ordinary mixing mill used for breaking down or plasticizing uncured rubber compounds before forming them on a calender or extruder, in the process of manufacture.

warp - (1) the lengthwise yarns in a woven fabric or in a jacket; (2) the deviation from a straight line of a hose while subjected to internal pressure.

warping - twisting out of shape, deminsional distortion.

water marking - a discoloration of the surface of an open steam cured article caused by condensation during or immediately after vulcanization.

water resistance - the ability to withstand swelling by water for a specified time and temperature.

wavy plies - in multiple-ply construction, a nonparallelism of the layers, when one or more plies are out of line.

weak spot - usually, an area where material is missing or undergage.

weathering - the surface deterioration of a rubber article during outdoor exposure, such as checking, cracking, crazing or chalking.

weft - an English term for "filling" in fabrics.

weftless fabric - a cord fabric without filling yarns.

wetting - completeness of contact between particles dispersed in a medium, such as carbon black in rubber.

wetting agent - a substance that reduces the surface tension of a liquid, thereby causing it to spread more readily on a solid surface.

woven fabric - a flat or tubular structure composed of two series of interlacing yarns or filaments, one parallel to the axis of the fabric and the other transverse.

woven jacket - a textile product woven into seamless tubular or sleeve form, generally used as reinforcement and/or cover in fire hose.

wrinkled ply - see buckled ply.

- Y -

yield point - the first stress in a material less than a maximum attainable stress at which an increase in strain occurs without an increase in stress.

Young's modulus - the ratio of normal stress to corresponding strain for tensile or compressive stresses below the proportional limit of the material.